ELEVEN SECONDS

Best wishes

Travis

Roy

ELEVEN

A Story of Tragedy, Courage,
and Triumph

SECONDS

TRAVIS ROY

with

E. M. SWIFT

WARNER BOOKS

NEW YORK   BOSTON

Warner Books
Hachette Book Group USA
237 Park Avenue
New York, NY 10169

Visit our Web site at www.HachetteBookGroupUSA.com.

First Edition: January 1998
20 19 18 17 16 15 14 13 12 11

Warner Books and the "W" logo are trademarks of Time Warner Inc. or an affiliated company.
Used under license by Hachette Book Group USA, which is not affiliated with Time Warner Inc.

Library of Congress Cataloging-in-Publication Data
Roy, Travis.
   Eleven seconds : a story of tragedy, courage & triumph / Travis
Roy with E.M. Swift.
      p.   cm.
   ISBN 978-0-446-52188-8
   1. Roy, Travis.   2. Hockey players—United States—Biography.
I. Swift, E. M. (Edward McKelvy)   II. Title.
GV848.5.R69E54   1998
796.962'092—dc21
   [B]   97-25213
                                                        CIP

To Mom, Dad, Tobi, and Keith

You have given me my strength to get me through the toughest times of my life. Because of you I am able to look forward to my future and hope for many more times of happiness together. My pride and love for you are immeasurable.

To Maija

I knew you were special from the first time I kissed you. You have given me the happiest times of my life, and you have held my hand and pulled me through the worst times. We have been through a lifetime of emotions together, and nobody can take that away. No matter what happens in our futures, you will always have a piece of my heart. I love you.

To Coach Parker

Your words and support have been as valuable to me as anything I will ever have. I look forward to each and every moment I spend with you. Thank you for being there.

Acknowledgments

I would like to give my most sincere thank-you to the thousands of people who have helped me, my family, and Maija through the past year and a half. Individually I would like to thank Ed Carpenter, Ed Swift, Alan Mooney, Ed Anderson, Century Bank, Freedom Capital, Palmer and Dodge, Woolf Associates, and the Friends of Travis Roy. We would never have been able to get through this without you.

Prologue

Sometimes, while seated in my chair high above the ice at the south end of the arena, I find myself staring down at the corner to the left of the visitor's goal, knowing that's where it all ended, and where it all started. Just staring.

And sometimes, before a game, I sit in the middle of the locker room and ask myself, "Is this real? Is this really happening?"

I am in one of my favorite places in the world, watching my teammates get ready to go on the ice, in a wheelchair. My locker stall is there, fourth from the right, with my nameplate above it. My stuff is still hanging in the stall: gloves, shin pads, pants, helmet. No one is dressing there. I hate looking at an empty stall. Anyone's empty stall.

The music is blaring from the sound system, pumping my teammates up for the game. The VCR and television, the ones on which we study videotapes of the other team, are behind me, but I can see them if I turn my head. The big red carpet covering the locker-room floor still looks new, and my teammates are stretching while sprawled upon it. Chris Drury. Mike Sylvia. Dan Ronan. I watch them instead of limbering up with them. There is a nervous tension in the room, but I am not part of it. It's like I'm stuck in a dream.

Strangest of all for me is the large photograph hanging beside the door, a picture of me in my Boston University uniform lining up for a face-off at center ice, the only face-off of my college career—eleven seconds before the accident. You can't miss it as you

walk out that door on your way to the ice. You are not supposed
to miss it.

None of it seems real. It's all so dear and so familiar, and yet it's
exactly like a bad dream. Most of my life now seems like a dream,
while most of my dreams seem like real life: the life I knew and
still hope for. I am always walking in my dreams, or running, or
riding my bike. Or I'm skating, and my life is going on as I'd always planned. Even when I dream I'm in a wheelchair, I'm always
getting better, moving my hands and arms around. Picking things
up. Moving my fingers. I am about to rise up and walk free. I
never dream of myself getting worse, or existing the way I am
now. They're enjoyable dreams, and I love going to bed. I'm always hoping to dream when I go to sleep. The more real the
dreams the better. Sometimes I want to dream the rest of my life
away, and not wake up and have to get back into this chair.

What has happened to me doesn't really happen to people.
That's what I'm thinking as I watch my teammates prepare for a
game. To reach your lifelong dream, then eleven seconds later
have a freak accident, a one-in-a-million accident, that leaves you
in a wheelchair for the rest of your life. That only happens in
dreams. And I think, How could it have happened? Not *why* did
it happen, which is what a different sort of person might ask. *How*
could it happen? To me, who was always such a fine, well-
balanced skater?

I wonder that every time I go into the BU locker room. I go
through that exact thought process.

ELEVEN SECONDS

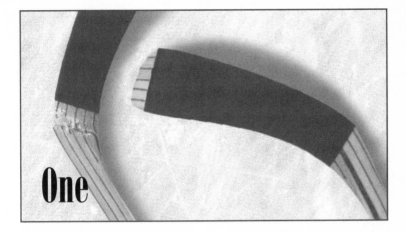

One

I still love hockey. I'm not angry at the sport. I'm not angry at anything, or anyone. What I am is sad. Sad that it all ended so soon. Sad that, without a medical breakthrough, I won't be able to teach my children what my father taught me. Sad that I won't be able to play the game that brought me such joy anymore, a game I played better than I did anything else. I'm not so disconsolate that I won't get through this. I don't need, or even like, sympathy. But I miss excelling at something. I miss being part of a team—part of the jokes, part of the joy and the pain, part of the locker-room camaraderie. I miss the pure physical act of skating, of flying over the ice.

My earliest memories of skating are of the power-skating clinics taught by my dad, Lee Roy, and a man named Carl Walker at North Yarmouth Academy in Maine. That was the rink my father managed when I was growing up. My father was Mr. Youth Hockey in southern Maine, founding the Portland Youth Hockey Association in 1972, when basketball was the winter sport of choice throughout the state. Over the years he managed four different rinks in Maine, including the Cumberland County Civic

Center, coaching kids from Mites to college age. He ran summer hockey camps, sharpened skates, drove the Zambonis. In 1972, when he started, there were six high school teams in the state. Today there are 43.

You can't play hockey if you can't skate, my father would tell me. We did nothing at those clinics but work on our edges, learning to shift our weight to the inside edge, to glide, to push off, to stop. I was five, six, seven years old. These clinics were not fun. You never saw a puck. The only fun drills were when you did barrel rolls, falling, tumbling, and getting back up. But I loved being out on the ice. Dad didn't have to tell me twice to grab my skates.

My dad is a big man, about six foot two and 230 pounds, and firm. He always wore the same sweat suit, a black one, with straight legs and red and white stripes up the side. A practical outfit for a practical man. He had three or four whistles, and a bag full of pucks. He'd gather the stuff together, then we'd head off to practice, twice a week, from 6 to 7 P.M. I was four years old when I started playing organized hockey, and I spent five years with my father's Mites team, which included kids up to eight years old. Other youngsters would come and go, but I stayed, a Mite for life. For years I was the youngest and the smallest, but because of all those tedious power-skating schools, I could skate as well as anyone else. Not necessarily faster. But I was better balanced. More agile. One season Dad would have me play forward, the next year defense. I learned both aspects of the game.

Year after year we always did the same drills on the ice: basics and fundamentals. Passing and skating and stickhandling. My father was always showing kids how they could improve their skating, but he made practices fun, too. He was excellent with kids, knowing not just when to yell at a kid, but also *how* to yell at him. He never drove anyone to tears. He was brought up in Swampscott, Massachusetts, and spoke with a lilting New England accent, more of a Maine accent than a Boston one. He often wore a wry smile on his face on the rink, one that put a twinkle in his eye.

Kids amused him. When one of his players fell down at the first sting of pain—a shot off the ankle, a slash on the wrist, a bump into the boards—and then lay theatrically on the ice as if struck by a splitting maul, Dad would always yell the same thing: "Get up, you're not hurt! Get up!"—with that wry smile gently in place.

He treated me the same as everyone else. A little harder, if anything. During one game, I skated past the bench and yanked off my glove to show him the blood dripping down my hand. I'd been slashed, and part of my fingernail had been torn off. "What do I do?" I asked.

"What do you mean?" he said, surprised I was out of position. "There's a shift going on."

I was still breathing, so I wasn't hurt. You can't treat other people's kids the way you treat your own son. At home he was a little more of a disciplinarian. If, as a boy, I wanted to do something or go somewhere, I could ask Mom, and if she said no, I could continue to work on her, to reason with her to try to get her to change her mind. Dad, you only asked once.

Yet my father's a very calm man, without a temper. He doesn't get mad; he gets disappointed. My sophomore year in high school, he had a Porsche 944. He's very mechanically minded, a do-it-yourself-type guy. He could fix the plumbing. Paint the house. Do all the maintenance on the cars. "Jack of all trades, master of none" is how he liked to describe himself.

I'd driven the Porsche before, but only with his permission. Once when he was away, I drove the Porsche to school without asking. It wasn't far. Usually I walked. I parked the Porsche beside the rink, but I left it in neutral and forgot to set the parking brake. It was on a very slight incline, and the car rolled about 50 feet, across a road and down a gully, nose-diving 25 feet. A tow truck had to haul it out. When the estimates were done, it had caused over $5,000 in damages.

That car was my dad's pride and joy, and I was devastated. My mom made me call him in Syracuse, and when I told him I'd taken the Porsche to school, he sensed what was coming next from my tone. "Oh, Trav. What'd you do?" he asked.

I told him the story. He listened, and he didn't yell at me. He asked where the car had been towed and told me whom to call to have the estimates done. He knew how badly I felt. Even when he came home, he didn't yell at me. I wouldn't have felt as bad if he had. That was when I learned that it hurts much more to disappoint your parents than to be yelled at or grounded. I wanted never to disappoint him again.

I had no idea that he'd been a hockey star at the University of Vermont. He never talked about it. But he'd played for the Catamounts in the mid-'60s, when they were just starting their hockey program, and was the team's MVP. He'd been elected into the UVM Hall of Fame. From our practices, I could see he was good, that he could shoot the puck hard and accurately. He could stick-handle through 15 kids who were buzzing around his feet for three or four minutes at a time—just standing there without moving his feet, stickhandling.

I knew he was a great skater. Every time he'd stop, the snow would spray up in a perfect arc. When you're a kid, that's what you're concerned about: making the snow spray up in an arc. You can't do it without stopping quickly. And my father's quick starts always left a groove in the ice, a perfect little slash from the sharpened edge of his blade. He knew more about the game than any coach I ever had, at least until I got to high school. But I never knew he was a star.

In some ways my mother, Brenda Goodsell Roy, is the opposite of my father. She's small, five feet two, and not at all athletic or mechanically minded. She has the hardest time with common-sense stuff, like how to strap down my wheelchair when I ride in the car, or how to take it out of gear. Over the years she's probably been to 90% of my hockey games, but she still knows very little about the sport. It's hard for me to understand how she couldn't have picked up more. She used to come to the games and afterward ask simple questions about it that she should easily have known for herself. I used to feel like asking her, Where have you been the last 15 years? We tease her, my dad and I.

Yet in things that matter, she's a very strong, capable, energetic lady. She's like the all-American mom, whatever that means these days: raising my older sister, Tobi, and me while holding down a full-time, highly responsible job. She taught math for twelve years at Deering High School in Portland. Six years ago she switched to administration, and became assistant principal. Last year, 1996, she planned and organized my sister's wedding, dealt with my injury and rehabilitation, and took over as interim principal at Deering, one of the largest high schools in Maine. Every one of those things was a success.

Mom's very organized. She likes everything to be planned out and written down, to the last detail. If there are loose ends, she gets nervous and worries about them. Tries to tie them up, immediately. My father lets things work themselves out. He doesn't need all the answers right away, which is the way I am.

Throughout the whole ordeal, Mom's been the glue that's held everything together. She may be small, but she's a lot tougher than she looks. She has a very soft and sincere voice, and her confidence comes across in her words. She's tender, too. Mom's sensitive to other people's feelings. I think I get my gentleness from her. If someone is sad, or frustrated, or embarrassed, I pick up on it pretty quickly, and I've always been able to talk to them about it.

After my first few days back at Boston University last year, after my accident, I remember my mother, almost panicky, wanting to know everything that was going on. Who were my caretakers? When had they arrived? How was the food? How was I eating? How were my classes? Was I getting around all right? How was the elevator working in the dorm? Were the other students nice? It was driving me nuts. She was in tears by the end of the conversation. Finally I told her, "Mom, if it makes it any easier for you, you're having a harder time with this than I am."

I come from an emotional family. All of us cry a lot, only my parents cry at different things. My mom cries at movies and at happy things, anything cheesy and corny. It's kind of a family joke. The sad part of a movie comes, and it's "Bring out the Kleenex, there goes Mom." My dad only cries at family-related things. It was from him that I learned early on it was okay to cry. He's a big man, a strong man, and if it's all right for him to show his emotions, it's all right for anyone. It feels so much better. When my dad was inducted into the University of Vermont Hall of Fame, three-quarters of the way through his speech, he started to cry. I'll never forget that. He's a very good public speaker. I think I inherited that from him.

I look like my father. There's a picture of Dad in his UVM uniform, and a picture of me in my Tabor Academy uniform that you would swear was the same kid. The only difference was he shot right, and I shot left. But everything else—the blond hair, the blue eyes, the jaw, the slope of the shoulder—it's him. Even our numbers, 14, were the same.

Growing up in Yarmouth, I played other sports besides hockey. I was pretty good at soccer and lacrosse and tennis. I could ski. I was a good runner, especially distance running. But hockey was my love. None of the other sports were even close.

It's the most exciting sport: fast—the fastest team sport—with the finesse of basketball and the physical contact of football. Because I was always the smallest kid out there, at first I hated the hitting. I was scared to death of the big kids bodychecking me. But before long I discovered that if you go into the corner worrying about getting hurt, you're going to get hurt. If you go in with an aggressive attitude, everything changes. If you brace for the hit, the bodychecker's not expecting it. If you move just a little, at the last instant, he'll miss. That's why it's so hard to hit Wayne Gretzky. He has great vision, and when he sees you coming, he steps aside at the last instant, just enough to make you miss and look bad.

You're always part of the action in hockey. In soccer, the ball can get into one end of the field, and if you're playing defense, you can wait forever for the game to return to you. In baseball, you can go the entire game without touching the ball. You're trapped by your position. But hockey is fluid. It's like water in a bottle: Tip the bottle and everything moves. You're able to touch the puck each time you get on the ice, because the puck slides all over the ice, and you can skate wherever you want. The flow is continuous, spontaneous, creative. The action is all-inclusive.

The hockey locker room is another part of the game's appeal. No other locker room in sport is quite like it. I loved the smells, stale and damp and musty, like a cellar, but sweaty and rich, too, unlike anywhere else. We arrived a half hour before the game, at a minimum, and while dressing, putting on our equipment piece by piece in a certain order, each player with an order all his own, we talked about grades, about girls, about hockey. There were no adults there—at least not once we were old enough to tie our skates. It was a ritual that helped make the team into a team.

The time to ourselves in the locker room gave a twist to our friendships—a good twist. Once I started playing for travel teams, many of my teammates were from other towns and other schools. I only knew them from the time we had together in the locker room. After the game, it would have been easy to get undressed quickly and leave. But we always lingered at least 45 minutes, only five of which were spent getting undressed. Parents would come in and say, hurry up, hurry up. But no one ever hurried. You made your best friendships in a hockey locker room.

It was part of the fabric of life in Yarmouth, of life all over New England. I suppose it's the same in the Great Lakes, upstate New York, certainly Canada. Hockey season was just that. A *season*, like summer, or fall. When I was young, we played our games Sunday mornings, and afterwards I'd go right from the rink to church. I'd sit in the pew in my hockey gear. Looking back, it seems like I should have felt self-conscious and odd. But it was natural enough at the time. Hockey was such a big part of our lives. From September to April, most of my family's free time, and a great deal of money, were tied up in hockey. For a portion of the summer as well. My mom and dad didn't just drop me off at the rink and come back two hours later to pick me up, like they might have at a gym or a pool. They couldn't tell me to ride my bike to the game. Often they had to get up in the pitch dark in the dead of winter, then drive me to a freezing cold arena before dawn. Sometimes it would be snowing, and we'd have to shovel the driveway first. Almost every weekend my parents would travel long distances, since games were played all over the state. They gave up ski weekends and Christmas vacations.

Two or three times a year we'd travel to a holiday tournament, and that was the best time of all. We'd stay in a hotel with 15 of my best friends. The kids would play street hockey in the halls and banquet rooms, taking half a roll of toilet paper, crumpling it up, and wrapping it with tape to make a puck. Or we'd swim in the hotel pool and play video games until everyone ran out of quarters. The parents would hang out together, making new friends.

It's why, I think, my family received so much support and love and attention following my accident. Hockey's such a big part of the lives of all the families who have kids playing. The hockey community is as tightly knit as any community in sport. You couldn't help but forge a special bond with other families who shared that kind of commitment.

Which is one of the most important things I learned from hockey: commitment. I was committed to being the best player I could be. I was a very focused kid. That and my understanding of the game were probably my biggest assets. I knew, somehow, where my teammates were on the ice. Some of it was vision, but some of it I just *knew*. I can't explain it. You can't teach it. It was like another sense, one developed from having watched so much hockey growing up. As a result, I was a better playmaker than a scorer. But I could do both. And, because of soccer, I was good with my feet—as good with the puck in my feet as when it was on my stick. And, because of all those boring power-skating clinics, I had good balance. I almost never fell to the ice. That sounds ironic, because of my accident, but it's true.

The summer before I entered seventh grade, I went to hockey camp, and one of the counselors suggested we make a list of our hockey goals. So that's what I did. It's the only list I've ever made. I wrote down where I was, and where I wanted to get to in hockey. Then when the camp was over I showed the list to my parents.

I wanted to make the Casco Bay travel team. I wanted to make the Maine all-star team. I wrote down how many points I wanted to score that season, how many points I wanted to score the next season, that I wanted to make the top three in scoring my freshman year in high school. There were 10 or 15 steps in the list. At the bottom I wrote that I wanted to play for a Division I college, then in the American Hockey League, then for the U.S. Olympic team, then in the National Hockey League.

I don't know how far I would have gone. To some extent, my size was working against me, at least as far as an NHL future was concerned. But when I look back at that list, it amazes me how much of it came true.

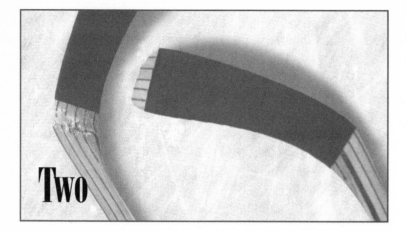

Two

For a period of about seven years when I was young, my father worked at the Cumberland County Civic Center as assistant director of operations. The Civic Center was the home of the Maine Mariners, a minor league hockey team originally affiliated with the Philadelphia Flyers, then the New Jersey Devils and, later, the Boston Bruins. The Mariners were members of the American Hockey League—one step down from the NHL.

I grew up in that building. Dad used to get me to sell raffle tickets to the players to help finance my hockey season with the Casco Bay Youth Hockey Association. I was five years old, with hair so blond it was almost white. Dad would send me into the locker room with a full book of tickets, and I'd come out with nothing but stubs. They couldn't say no. The players would rag on my dad: "Come on, Lee, give us a break." But at the same time they'd be reaching for their wallets.

Every Saturday night, about three hours before game time, my father would take me with him when he went to work and let me run on the ice with my shoes before anyone else was in the building. I'd take my stick and a puck, and score any number of heroic goals. When I was seven or eight, one of the Mariners' trainers asked me to help him set up cups of Gatorade and Pepsi in the locker room between periods. From that time on, I became an unpaid gofer. I didn't miss a Saturday night game until I was 17 years old.

I'd go into the locker room to see if I could help out, delivering tape, gathering towels, fetching gum. I was only in there on Saturdays, so most of the players didn't know my name. One day, when the locker room was completely quiet, one of them called out, "Hey Clifford. White tape." I waited for someone to move. Then I realized everyone was looking at me. So I went and got him white tape. Clifford became my nickname for the year—the only nickname I've ever had.

Eventually I became a full-fledged stickboy, with my own trainer's outfit, bought for me by Ed Anderson, the owner of the Mariners, so I'd feel I was part of the team. I learned to sharpen skates. I carried out the sticks to the lucky fans who played Score-O between periods—those patrons who tried to win a prize by shooting a puck through a hole in a billboard hung from the net. Three or four times a year, after the end of a Mariners practice, I'd put on my stuff and would shoot on the goalies. I remember Chris Terreri, Bill Ranford, Kirk McLean, Bob Froese, Pelle Lindbergh. I shot on them all before they played in the NHL. They'd allow some to get past on purpose, letting me think I had scored.

Tom McVie was the Mariners coach the first three years I was stickboy. He'd already had a couple of stints as a head coach in the NHL, and he took me under his wing. The first thing you noticed about him was his voice: a great, booming, gravelly foghorn that was unmistakable, the absolute opposite of Kerri Strug's. It wasn't just deep. It was two or three times deeper than the deepest voice I'd ever heard, like it was coming from the bottom of a well. It took me a long time to believe it was his real voice, and not some trick device through which he was speaking.

He was animated, personable, always upbeat. McVie was a

health and fitness expert—a step ahead of the rest of the league in terms of off-ice conditioning. Everyone's focused on that now, but this was in the early 1980s. Most of the other coaches told the players to stretch on their own, but McVie had the entire team do it together, so he could make sure they were stretching properly. He led the workouts himself. He passed out a health handbook to all his players, which talked about the problems brought on by drinking and smoking. It discussed keeping your personal life under control. He gave me one of those handbooks, and I read it and never forgot it.

He always stressed the right things when he talked to me. How's school, Clifford? he'd ask. How's the family? How's your mom? If he asked about hockey, it was always, "Are you getting any assists?" All the coaches for the Mariners were like that.

I learned. My father likes to say there probably aren't a half dozen kids in the United States who had the exposure to hockey I did. After McVie left the Mariners, I worked under Mike Milbury, Rick Bowness, E. J. McGuire, and John Paddock, all of whom went on to coach in the NHL. I worked the visitor's dressing room, too, so I tapped into an endless wealth of hockey knowledge. It was like getting a master's degree in the sport. The coaches would let me listen in between periods, before and after the game, to the strategy changes and the pep talks. I saw how hard the players worked. How hard they skated and hit. I learned which stories stayed in the locker room, and which I could bring home.

I never saw a coach rip into his players like Milbury. He had a huge temper, really scary, and I knew enough to get out of the room when he was angry. Once he became enraged at a call by a referee and, in protest, threw a water bottle onto the ice. The ref gave him a bench penalty, and Milbury went ballistic. He went up and down the bench firing out water bottles, one after another. Then he grabbed all the spare sticks—a big number, since there were 20 players and each one had at least two spares—and hurled them onto the ice. All the rolls of tape followed. I was watching from the penalty box, which is where I sat during the games, and took the initiative to help the trainer and equipment manager clean up the mess. I was about ten years old, and got a standing ovation afterwards. The next day the *Portland Press Herald* published a picture of me in the sports section, this tiny blond-haired kid walking through a sea of debris, carrying an armful of sticks. I thought I was pretty hot stuff.

I took that job very, very seriously. All my friends thought I was lucky. And I *was* lucky. The job didn't pay anything, but I was always being given old pairs of shoulder pads, shin pads, and, when I got older, helmets to take home. I never had to buy any tape or sticks. Hockey equipment isn't cheap, so it meant a lot to us financially. And there were other benefits. Autographs, of course. Learning hockey by osmosis. Plus I saw some things that, for a young boy, were hard to believe. I watched players get stitched up in the middle of a game, then go right out and play like nothing had happened. Bruce Shoebottom, a tough fighter, got cut up nearly every game. I was in the training room one time as he was getting a shot of Novocain before his stitches. The doctor picked up the needle and thread, but Shoebottom stopped him. "Let Travis do it," he said.

I almost threw up. He had this big gash on his lip. "No way," I said. But he talked me into cutting the thread after the doctor had stitched him.

Even after my dad left the Civic Center and returned to North Yarmouth Academy, I continued working as stickboy. My parents knew how much I enjoyed it, and they'd drop me off at 5 P.M., then would come back about midnight to take me home. It was just one more sacrifice they were willing to make. During Christmas and spring vacations I'd show up every day at the Mariners practice, as long as I had a ride in and out.

I was under no illusions about what kind of life those players led in the minor league. It was a meat market. Every few weeks new players would come and old players would go. There was very little stability. So I learned early on that hockey was a business. It wasn't as glamorous a life as most kids my age thought it to be. Professional hockey was definitely my goal back then, and, deep down, I believed I would make it. At what level, I couldn't say. But if I'd been stuck in the minors, I wouldn't have stayed very long. Five years, at the outside. That's one of the reasons I was intent on getting my education.

My father used to tell me I couldn't play Division I unless I was accepted at a college, and I wouldn't be accepted at a college, regardless of how good a player I was, unless I kept the grades up. I went to three different schools in my five-year high-school career, each one more difficult than the last, both athletically and academically. But hockey was always the engine. It drove every decision we made about my education.

It's why I left Yarmouth High School after freshman year. Yarmouth High had a terrific hockey program under the coaching of Jack O'Brien, a retired pharmaceutical executive for Johnson & Johnson. His teams had won the Maine Class B championship four years in a row when I got there, and he became my first real mentor in the sport. Coach O'Brien was huge on discipline and, having been a Marine, very militaristic. His own son, Mike, who was the assistant coach, called him Sir. Never Dad, which is what I'd called my father on the ice.

Things started coming together for me as a hockey player under Coach O'Brien. As a freshman, I played first line with two seniors. We lost in the state finals. But Coach O'Brien knew, and my father knew, that if I were going to reach my goal of playing Division I, I needed to play against better competition. Coach O'Brien has contacts throughout the hockey community. Using his associations with prep-school and college coaches, and professional scouts, he's helped many Maine players move on to higher levels of the game. And it was Coach O'Brien who, more than anyone else, helped steer me on my path to Division I, which was the place I wanted to go.

So sophomore year I transferred to North Yarmouth Academy, which was the private school where my father managed the rink. The hockey team was coached by Kevin Potter, a former Division II all-American at Bowdoin. NYA, a Class A school, played a more difficult schedule than Yarmouth High, and in addition to the Class A opponents we faced from Maine, we had a number of games against prep schools out of state. That's when I discovered there was still a higher level of high-school hockey being played.

Since my father ran the rink, I had certain responsibilities, and liberties, that other players my age didn't have. I sharpened skates for my dad, and sometimes drove the Zamboni. I picked up some extra money cleaning the locker rooms. Whenever the school was closed for a snow day, I would call a friend and the two of us would spend the day playing on the ice by ourselves. In the evenings, if my homework was done and I felt in the mood, I'd take the keys to the rink and a bucket of pucks, and would shoot for a couple of hours on the Shooter Tutor—a plywood board I'd hang from the goal that had four holes cut out of the corners.

I loved skating by myself, the feeling of exhaustion before bed that came from a good hard workout. I loved the sounds one person could make on a rink: the crunching of the ice beneath your blades; the clang of a puck hitting the post; the echoing of a shot off the boards; the crisp slap of a slap shot, as the blade of the stick smacks the ice, then, a millisecond later, makes contact with the puck. I loved the swishing sound of the puck hitting into the net. That's what I remember best when I think of those nights alone on the rink: the sounds. Hockey sounds.

Afterwards, damp with sweat, I'd lock up and flip off the lights, then step out and look up at the night sky. You couldn't help it. There's nothing like the Maine sky on a winter night, the air so cold the snow crunches and squeaks beneath your boots, the steam rising off your neck, the skeletons of maple trees silhouetted by more stars than one can count, or even believe. I loved it. I think of those nights often, and would give anything to be able to relive them.

I played in the summertime, too. After my junior year, my last year at North Yarmouth Academy, I tried out for a summer league called Hockey Night in Boston, which attracted the top high-school talent from all over the country. Organizers held a four-day tryout in Concord, New Hampshire, 1 hour and 45 minutes from Yarmouth, which cost $250 just to attend. It was some racket. I was one of 160 kids vying for only 20 spots on the northern New England team. The year before, I'd been cut. But if you made it, a round-robin tournament went on for another six weeks. All the college and professional scouts attended so they could watch the best against the best. That was the main purpose of Hockey Night in Boston.

For me, it was a big step. An important step in my development. I'd been all-state in Maine that season, but no one knew who I was. None of the scouts came up to Yarmouth to recruit. There were 12 teams in the Hockey Night in Boston competition: four representing Massachusetts, and one each from New York, Connecticut, Rhode Island, New Brunswick, the Midwest, mid-Atlantic, and northern New England. There was also an at-large team. I was the last forward selected by northern New England. Dead last. Maybe it was because I was one of the smallest forwards out there. I didn't know, but it lit a fire under me. I wanted to prove everyone wrong, to prove I belonged out there with the top kids my age.

I skated hard throughout the Hockey Night in Boston tournament and ended up being voted the biggest surprise of the competition. Northern New England finished second overall, which no one had expected. We lost in the finals to New York. I had two goals in that game, and a hat trick in the semifinals, which we'd won 4–3—in overtime. My final stats for the summer were 12 goals and 22 assists, for 34 points in 13 games. It was the first time I'd shown people I could play against the top high-school players in the country.

I'd already decided that I was going to repeat my junior year and transfer to Tabor Academy, a boarding school in Marion, Massachusetts. I didn't know a soul there, but Tabor was a hockey powerhouse, as good as any prep school in the East. I wasn't sure if I was a good enough player to excel at that level, but I didn't want to be the best player on my team anymore. I decided I'd rather be a third- or fourth-line player at Tabor than a star at NYA. I figured it was the only way I'd ever make Division I.

When I explained all that to Coach Potter, he didn't try to talk me out of it. Much as he wanted me to stay at NYA, what he said was, "Trav, follow your dreams."

Sometime in August, I found out that Tabor's coach, Peter Hermes, wasn't returning. I didn't really care about that. I had chosen Tabor because of the hockey program and academics, not the coach. Tabor had been 27–2 the previous year. But as a result of Hermes's departure, nearly the entire Tabor hockey team was transferring elsewhere. Once the word got out that a couple of kids were leaving, the rest began to follow. Out of 18 returning lettermen and six recruits, only two ended up coming back.

I was asked by other players at Hockey Night in Boston what I was going to do. I had no idea what was going on. But by that time there wasn't any financial aid available at other prep schools. So my decision came down to whether to stay in Maine, at NYA, or go to Tabor, where the program had been decimated.

I was ready to move on, to try some new things. I'd never lived away from home before, and I was looking forward to that. But the main thing was I had to find out if I could play at the next level. Whether there'd be anyone playing with me, I didn't know. Like my dad, I tended to let things work themselves out when I didn't have all the answers. So I stuck with the plan.

It was the best decision I ever made.

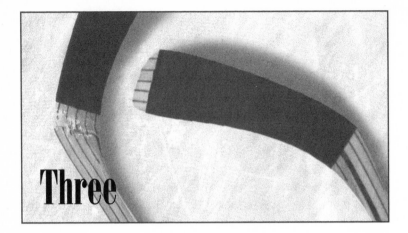

Three

Tabor Academy is built on Sippican harbor, on the west side of Buzzards Bay. Some 300 yachts and sailboats are moored in the harbor, lending an air of opulence to the oceanside campus that is somewhat, but not altogether, misleading. Tabor's performing arts center is also on the waterfront, and two sports fields—plush and green—run down to the sea. There are no brick buildings on campus. Rather, the dormitories are Tudor-style or simply sided with gray cedar shingles, so that they almost look like homes. Altogether, it's a strikingly beautiful school.

The two years I was there, the student body had about 450 kids, 100 of whom were day students. My dorm had 17 other guys, many of them repeat juniors like myself. My roommate was Angus Leary. He was a football player, and football season started earlier than any other sport. So when my parents drove me down early for soccer tryouts in the fall of 1993, Angus had already moved in and selected a bed.

You could tell it had been slept in by the blanket and pillow. But his bed didn't have any sheets. When I opened the closet, all I saw were two pairs of khakis, one blazer, one tie, and one pair of black sneakers, like coaches wear, which were the closest thing he owned to dress shoes. There was also a pair of football cleats with three different lengths of spikes scattered on the floor beside them. Tabor's got a dress code, and here was a guy with two outfits for the whole year—if he didn't change his coat or his tie.

North Yarmouth Academy had also had a dress code, and I prided myself on being a natty dresser. I had three blazers, ten pairs of slacks, twenty dress shirts, and about forty ties. I also had a nice pair of cowboy boots and some dress shoes. I didn't know if I'd brought too much stuff, or if he'd brought too little. I guess something in between would have been sufficient. My father started reading one of the book reports that Angus had left lying around and commented, "You're not going to get much help from your roommate, Trav."

"Why?"

"You spell better than he does."

That was a scary thought. When I finally met Angus, I couldn't believe my eyes. He was five ten and 220 pounds of muscle. Dauntingly, he had a buzz cut that gave him the appearance of having a perfectly square head. A total cube. A football head, we called it. Angus was from Carver, Massachusetts. I'd heard of mill towns, logging towns, and fishing villages. But Carver was a cranberry-bog town. He had nine brothers and sisters, and they were a closely knit, hardworking family. It turned out that Angus and I were perfect for each other. We roomed together for two years and became like brothers. Even now, if we haven't been in touch for months, when we see each other we pick up right where we left off.

My best friend was Matt Perrin, from Cape Cod. He was olive-skinned, short and stocky, a good-looking kid. He was an only child, and we hit it off right away. It was just him and his mom at home, which must have been lonely at times. But he never complained. Matt was a very honest and true person, true to his friends and true to his abilities. We played both soccer and hockey together.

When we talked, we talked about anything but athletics. We'd talk about fishing, water sports, girlfriends, family, life. Having never had a brother, I loved spending time with Matt. He became like a brother to me, too. Often we'd go down to the waterfront—there was a dock outside our dorm—and at night we could sit, listening to the waves and watching the reflections in the water while we pondered our futures, or whatever happened to be on our minds.

After my accident, Matt often used to return there by himself. His father had died of a heart attack when he was in grade school. I'd known that. What I hadn't known, because Matt never talked about it, was that his father's heart attack occurred while he was watching Matt play hockey in Walter Brown Arena—the same arena where I broke my neck. Matt told me that on the anniversary of my accident. That was tough, and he was still trying to work it out. He must have recoiled every time he thought of the place.

Everyone at Tabor seemed to come from a different background. Some students were from other countries. Others were from the inner city, the South, the Midwest. Having spent my whole life in Maine, I loved the diversity of the school. I'd met one African American in all my years of schooling before Tabor. I wanted to learn more about the world, more about different kinds of people. Tabor gave me my first taste of that.

And, most important, Tabor was where I met Maija Langeland. Maija (pronounced My-ah) was also a junior. She lived in Duxbury, on the northern shore of Plymouth Bay, and had been going to Tabor since her freshman year. She was dating one of the other guys in my dorm, so Maija and I were just friends at first. She was bright and funny and outgoing, and I found her attractive. She had light brown hair, which she wore straight and long, and was slender and fit. But I never thought of her in a romantic way. In fact, she was trying to set me up with her roommate, who, like me, was from Maine and very blond. Maija thought we'd be the perfect couple.

Maija and I would talk. She used to tell me about the hockey players from the year before, when the team went 27–2. They'd been called the Dream Team, and the entire school would come to their games. Every player on the squad had been recruited, so they weren't just confident, they were cocky. Arrogant. She said they acted as if they were already playing Division I college hockey. A lot of them did, eventually. But at Tabor they acted like they had the run of the campus.

I hated that stuff. That's how hockey players are often stereotyped: cocky, big-headed, even crude. I did everything I could to avoid being thought of that way. I used to lie sometimes when someone I didn't know asked if I played hockey. I wanted to be judged for who I was, rather than stereotyped, and there was a real stigma to being a hockey player at Tabor because of that previous group. Our team wasn't nearly as successful on the ice—I think we were 8–14–2 that first, rebuilding year—but we weren't as bad as everyone predicted we'd be.

Our coach was Tim Pratt, who'd been the assistant coach of the team the year before. He'd never been a head coach before, but he did an amazing job. We won games we should never have won. We won the Avon Christmas tournament, for instance, and Avon Old Farms was the team that had beaten the so-called Dream Team the year before in the semifinals of the New England prep-school championships. That was the highlight of our year.

Coach Pratt didn't pretend to have all the answers. That was the best thing about him. He knew the game really well, but he was also open to suggestions and was willing to listen and learn. He especially listened to what I had to say, and would sometimes come and ask me after practice or class what I thought about certain lines, or with whom I wanted to play. He wouldn't always follow my suggestions, but he'd always listen. We didn't have a whole lot of talent on that team, but my teammates were good kids who worked hard and were fun to play with. I'd much rather play with those kinds of teammates than ones who thought they were heroes.

The following summer Maija and her boyfriend broke up. I'd heard about it through the grapevine, so when she called me in August to see how I was doing, I told her I was sorry about her boyfriend. Maija and I were good enough friends that I didn't really think anything about her calling. Having a relationship with her still hadn't crossed my mind.

We were both proctors our senior year, and at Tabor proctors have to come back to school a few days early for a leadership training course. We were taken to a YMCA camp on the Cape, where we participated in something like a proctor retreat. The dorm parents were there, too, and they went over what was expected of us in our role as proctors. They told us what to do if we found any kids on our floor doing drugs, or drinking alcohol, or stealing. They discussed how to handle rape. Plus there were lots of activities planned: a rope course, a scaling wall, waterskiing in the ocean, swimming in a freshwater pond. The session lasted three days and two nights, and I hung out with Maija more than anyone else. But I didn't see anything coming. It was all very natural and relaxed.

Afterwards I went to stay with Matt Perrin, who lived nearby, and Maija went back to Duxbury. She called us the next day with another girl from Tabor. They were just hanging out, and Maija asked us to come down to her friend's house for a party. She said her friend had a hot tub and a swimming pool, and a third girl—a gorgeous model—was also visiting. That clinched it. Matt and I were on our way as soon as we'd hung up the phone.

She'd pulled one over on us. When we got there, no hot tub and no gorgeous model. I was pretty naive, but I was beginning to pick up on things, and began wondering if there might not be something there. Later that night, after the others had gone inside, Maija and I had our first kiss by the pool. It was some kiss, the best one I'd ever had. For her, too. It sent shivers right down my spine. That sounds like a cliché, but it's exactly what happened. It was electric, a kiss that changed the way I looked at the world. We still talk about that kiss sometimes.

Once we got back to school, though, things became more complicated. We had kind of a rocky start. First I had to extract myself from a fledgling relationship with a girlfriend who was four years younger than I was. That was definitely a good move. Then Maija started having reservations about having a new boyfriend so soon after her former one, who'd been the first love of her life. It was tough for her. And it was tough for me, too, since her other boyfriend had been a friend of mine. I had some twinges of disloyalty. We both had to get past all that.

I think we knew, though, that the potential was there for something pretty wonderful. We'd been such good friends. So we worked at it. We weren't taking any classes together, and we weren't in the same dorm, so we had to make an effort just to see each other. To spend time together. I was playing soccer—I was co-captain of the team with another of my best friends at Tabor, Ian Conway—and was traveling most weekends on hockey recruiting trips. You were allowed five visits, and I went to Boston University, Vermont, New Hampshire, Maine, and Harvard.

I suppose Harvard sells itself to most kids, but I never felt comfortable there. I sensed an arrogance about the place, like I was supposed to be on my hands and knees asking what I could do to get in. Academics had never come easily to me. I'm not the smartest kid, but I'd always compensated for it with my work ethic. I knew that if I went to Harvard, I wouldn't have been able to enjoy my college career. I'd never have been able to come out of my room. I'd have gone from the classroom to the rink, then back to my room to study. Either that or I'd have flunked out. So, even though coach Ron Tomassoni told me my board scores and grades were within reach, I never applied. I forget how many essays there were on the application, but it was too many.

Maine had been the first school to offer me a full ride and a four-year scholarship, but there was a cloud over the program, which was under NCAA investigation. So sometime late in the fall, after a lot of thought, I signed my letter of intent with BU. I liked the players who were already there, the coaching staff, and for consistency there was no better program in the country. Just as important, I liked the idea of living in Boston. For a kid from Yarmouth, it was a pretty exciting place, offering more cultural diversity than Vermont, New Hampshire, and Maine, the other schools I was still looking at.

Because of hockey, though, the city would never feel too big. It would never overwhelm me. My older sister, Tobi, explained that to me. The hockey program at Boston University would give me a center and a focus I could always return to if I ever felt I was getting lost.

Tobi was three years older than I was and she, too, was going to be living in Boston the next year, when I'd be a freshman. She'd been accepted at a nursing position in neonatal care at Beth Israel Hospital, and she was moving up from South Carolina with her fiancé, Keith Van Orden. The prospect of living in the same city together excited us both.

Tobi and I had been close growing up, but then we'd sort of drifted apart during high school and college. I guess it was all kind of natural. Not many high-school girls want to be hanging out with their little brothers. When she was in college, we never really saw much of each other. She was in Syracuse, and I was in Marion. During summers we both worked.

Still, she influenced me more than she knew. Tobi wrote me a letter from college—she'd gone to Syracuse University, which is where she met Keith—telling me to watch out for alcohol and drugs in high school, and to take my time before getting into a relationship involving sex. All the big topics, the important topics young people face, I learned about from Tobi. It meant the world to me that, after missing most of my high-school career, she'd be able to see me play in college. It meant the world to her, too. Keith and Tobi, who'd hoped for a winter wedding, had postponed their wedding date until April 27, so it wouldn't conflict with BU's hockey season.

I spent my last few months at Tabor enjoying my friends and the boarding school experience. Ian Conway was a day student whose family, who lived right there in Marion, kept a motorboat in the harbor. Three times that spring he got me and another kid up at 4 A.M. to go bluefishing. It would be pitch black outside when we staggered down to the harbor, watching the reflection of the dock lights in the water, and we'd be out in the ocean in time to see the first red streaks of the dawn. We never caught a darn thing, but it was wonderful. On the way in, once Ian had decided that the fish weren't biting today, we'd waterski. It was a pretty great way to start a school day.

As often as possible I went on weekends with Maija to her home in Duxbury. By January, we'd fallen in love. I got to know her mother, Linda Langeland, who was divorced, and Maija's 13-year-old sister, Wesleigh. They were a warm, loving family who made me feel at home, and I enjoyed making Wesleigh laugh. She decided I was beyond all hope the time we went shopping at the Gap. I was feeling pretty good about life, and I tried on a woman's hat. Then I turned to a nearby lady. "Madam, do you think this hat's me?" I asked.

She looked at me in alarm. "I don't know you," the lady said, scurrying off. Wesleigh got a big kick out of that sort of thing. So did Maija, I guess.

In the spring, I played on the golf team, took up ceramics, which I discovered I had a knack for, and spent many long and pleasurable hours working at the wheel, molding the clay into small gifts for teachers and friends—coffee mugs and colorful fish. To my surprise, I won the school prize for excellence in ceramics, an accomplishment I took special pride in because it had nothing to do with sports. It was important to me that people saw me as more than one-dimensional.

Which may have been one of the reasons I gave my speech. Tabor has a tradition of having seniors address the school at morning assembly. It's optional, but I volunteered to give a talk on April 17, my twentieth birthday, a landmark that made me the oldest student in school. To highlight that point, I started by asking the student body to stand en masse, then to sit back down as I called out their birth years: 1980 . . . 1979 . . . 1978 . . . 1977 . . . 1976 . . . When I got to 1975, I was the last person standing.

I told a couple of funny stories about flunking kindergarten, being the first kid in my class to get my driver's license, the first to be able to buy cigarettes, all the while having a baby face that made me look like the youngest boy in the class. Looks deceive, I suppose, was the message. Then I read them something called Travis Roy's 10 Rules of Life:

"In no particular order, my first rule of life is to be yourself. I learned this lesson early in my high-school career. My freshman year my purpose was to fit in, but also be recognized—by the upperclassmen. So I did things I thought would be cool. In my town the Grateful Dead is quite popular, so I decided that an easy way to be accepted was to portray myself as a Deadhead. Over the first couple of months I bought five Grateful Dead T-shirts, and every Grateful Dead album I could find. I finished the image with a pair of Birkenstocks. I tried very hard to become a Deadhead, but the harder I tried, the worse I looked, and the worse I felt. This may come as a surprise to you, but I'm not a Deadhead. Instead of being accepted, I was being laughed at. The upperclassmen could see right through me. My friends also tried the same approach, but it took them longer to realize their acts weren't working either. Some of them still haven't figured it out.

"My second rule of life is to never take things for granted. I learned this lesson during my first few months at Tabor. My parents worked very hard to give me the opportunity of a private school education. They are proud to be able to send me away to boarding school, and I'm proud to be here. I couldn't believe, and still can't believe, how anybody can not feel fortunate to be here. There aren't many places that have the people and the facilities we do. But some people still continue to complain. I don't know what else anyone could ask for in a high school.

"My third rule of life is to set goals. In the seventh grade I sat down at my desk one night and wrote two pages of goals. The list only pertained to hockey. At the time, all I wanted to do was succeed in athletics. A few years later, it occurred to me that the only way I was going to accomplish my hockey objectives was to have strong grades, so I could go to college and play sports. I wanted to play hockey my whole life, but I also recognized this wasn't possible, and I'd need something to fall back on. My safety net is my academics. I know now that it is my academics that will take me the farthest.

"Rule number four: Resist peer pressure. This particular subject I hesitate to talk about. I find the only way to discuss it is to preach about it. Most of the upperclassmen here already have dealt with peer pressure, and have made their decisions, so this rule is directed at the underclassmen. When I was a freshman, I really didn't feel there was much peer pressure out there, but today, I realize I was wrong. There was a lot of peer pressure, but it rarely involved me. After learning my lesson about being who you are and not trying to be someone else, I learned to associate with people who liked me for who I was, and not for what I was or wasn't doing.

"Rule number five: Respect. I've learned that the more you respect others, the more they respect you. Some people believe that you earn respect. I disagree. I believe that everyone should start out with the same amount of respect, and it is theirs to lose— young or old.

"Rule number six: Your friends are one of the most important aspects of your life. Having gone to three different high schools, I've met a lot of good people and made a lot of friends. However, it isn't until you're away from your friends for a period of time that you realize just how much they mean to you. Many of the friends you make in life will seem to disappear over time, but your true friends will always remain in your life. . . . I know they will always be there for me. Maybe I will not always have a great house, or great sums of money. But I will always have great friends.

"Rule number seven has to do with what I've learned about love. I've learned there are many different types of love: love for sports, love for friends, love for my girlfriend, and love for my family. I also feel that everybody has their own definition of love, and there is no right or wrong way to love. I do know that love comes from deep within, and nobody can tell you who to love and who not to love. The last thing I've learned about love is it's a continuous lesson, and I will always keep learning from it and about it.

"Rule number eight is the only lesson I didn't have to learn. Family is the one thing I've always known about. I considered writing this speech about my family, but because I've inherited strong emotions from both my parents, I felt I could never make it through the speech without crying. This is because I have so much love and pride for my family. I've been very lucky to have a family that loves me and supports me 100 percent. Today my parents have made the three-hour trip from Maine to listen to this 15-minute speech. There's no way I could ever thank them for everything they've done for me, except to tell them I love them.

"My ninth rule of life is pride. I believe that pride in yourself, pride in your family, and pride in your friends should always be remembered and acknowledged. Tell your friends that you're proud of them, tell your parents that you're proud of them and of what they've done. When I put the name Travis Roy on a piece of paper, or the back of my shirt, I'm showing my pride for myself, my family, my friends, my school, and my teammates.

"Rule number 10. I'm a wise 20-year-old high-school senior,

wise enough to know that my life is just beginning and there will always be more lessons to be learned. Thank you for listening."

The speech was well received. Sometimes I'm a little amazed that it was delivered before my accident, and not after it, because so much of what I said is more applicable now than it was before. Proud as I was of my family that day at Tabor, I'm prouder of them now, and I still have no way of thanking them except by showing them love. I've never been more grateful for my friends, who indeed have proved they would always be there for me. I continue, even now, to learn there are different kinds of love. I've had to set new goals and throw away old ones. And I'm able to take nothing in life for granted.

Rule number 10? Well, wise as I felt on my twentieth birthday, I had no inkling of the enormity of the lessons waiting beyond the next bend.

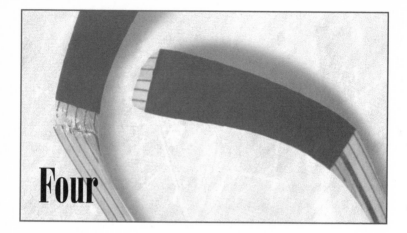

Four

By the end of June 1995, I'd moved to Boston to begin training with Mike Boyle, the BU strength coach. I'd never lifted a weight in my life. I was five ten and 163 pounds when I started—a string bean. Within two months I'd already gained ten pounds.

I lived that summer in Chestnut Hill with Dr. Alan Ashare, a director of USA Hockey. I'd met him in April while playing for Team Massachusetts in the Chicago Showcase Tournament. Dr. Ashare, by an eerie coincidence, was the chairman of USA Hockey's Committee on Safety and Protective Equipment, and the foremost expert on hockey-related spinal-cord injuries in the country.

His wife, Sue, was a partner in a soup-and-salad business in Concord named Bombay Duck. She offered me a job, and from 9 A.M. to 4 P.M. I was usually up to my elbows in pasta, making gargantuan salads. I loved it, to be honest. It was just me and five older women. I'd haul out a huge tub, throw in fifty to a hundred pounds of pasta, dump in a bunch of sliced tomatoes and scallions, maybe some croutons, sliced carrots, some dressing. One of our most popular recipes called for peanuts and ginger. I'd put on long, cellophane gloves and stir the concoction with my arms. Then I'd dole it out in five-, eight-, or 10-pound servings.

By 5 P.M. I was at the BU gym, across the street from the hockey arena. I worked out five days a week for about two hours. Only varsity athletes were allowed to use that particular facility, and mostly it was filled with football players. Every one of them was built like Angus. But when it came to football heads, his cube with eyebrows was still in a class by itself.

Boyle had created a separate weight-training program for hockey players. He was very big on stretching and calisthenics, and we alternated heavy lifting days with light ones. We spent a lot of time at the track, running sprints one day and distances the next. He had us run stadium steps. And sometimes he'd attach an ordinary tire to a harness and have us do fifty-yard sprints while dragging it behind.

After the workout, I'd drive down to Duxbury to have dinner with Maija, her mother, and her sister. Maija was working as a tour guide at the King Caesar House, one of Duxbury's historical landmarks. I often beat her home, and would pass the time playing basketball in the driveway with Wesleigh. It wasn't long before I didn't feel like a house guest. I'd set the table at night for Mrs. Langeland, and help clean up. She didn't have to ask. It was like I was a member of the family. Mrs. Langeland told me that if Maija and I ever broke up, I'd be welcome to visit anytime.

But that wasn't about to happen. Maija and I had a blast that summer: going to movies; to the beach; getting together with Angus and his girlfriend, Shannon; going to Red Sox games. Maija's father and stepmother lived just down the road from her mother, and sometimes we'd borrow Mr. Langeland's Boston Whaler and go for a ride in Buzzards Bay. We spent every free moment together.

We'd talked about marriage in general terms, but Maija was only 18, and we both had four years of college to get through.

There was no rush. Maija used to talk about the need for us to take a break from each other occasionally, so we could have some time on our own. So we could develop independence. She'd been burned in her previous relationship, and her parents had been divorced, so she was a little more cautious and circumspect about our future than I was. She knew that not all loves lasted forever. But she trusted me. She saw I was stable.

Once the school year began, we continued to get together every weekend and talk on the phone every night. Maija was at Holy Cross, which is in Worcester, about an hour outside of Boston. At first we were spending every weekend together, either at her dorm or mine. But when hockey started the first week in October, I began having trouble keeping up with my studies. Plus Maija was spending so much time at BU that she wasn't making friends at Holy Cross as fast as she'd have liked. So we decided to spend just one day and one night together on weekends, either Friday–Saturday or Saturday–Sunday. That way each of us could have a normal college life. That was the plan, anyway.

Maija asked me sometime that fall, "So Trav, how good are you? Are you good enough to play in the NHL?"

I told her I wasn't expecting it, but I'd love it if it were to happen. I figured I had two strikes against me. First, I wasn't Canadian. Second, I wasn't over six feet tall. Still, you get three strikes, right? I told Maija that I'd always believed if you expected something, or predicted it would happen—a gift, a grade, some very important personal goal—something bad would come along to prevent it. That was my theory. So I lived by Travis's Law: Never predict, never expect. I never liked to talk about things until they actually happened.

The fact is, though, that list I'd made back in the seventh grade, little by little, was coming true. Hockey at BU was going well. I was in the best shape of my life. The assistant coach, Pertti Hasanen, who was Finnish, had introduced us to a drill called Russian circuits. We'd hold a 35-pound disk in our hands and do a circuit of 15 different exercises, forty seconds each. We'd jump up and down and spin around with the disk; squat with the weight held over our heads; or stand with arms fully extended out front, turning the lead plate back and forth like a steering wheel. That was the hardest one. But as a result, my upper body was beginning to have some real definition to it. And my legs were in great condition. Running and endurance had always been my strong suit. I'd actually gotten myself into trouble with the upperclassmen the second day of school, when I lapped the entire team on a timed five-mile training run. "That'll cost you, Roy," the seniors grumbled when I passed them.

The upperclassmen didn't cut the freshmen any slack. The Terriers had won the national championship the year before, and we had to prove that we belonged. We were treated like freshmen, not equals. They barely talked to us. A few of the other freshmen knew some of the older guys from summer leagues, but I didn't know anyone, and I felt a little like an outcast.

I just worked hard and kept quiet. Once we started skating, the practices were shorter than I'd expected, but higher in intensity. I wondered at first, Do I fit in out here? The speed of the drills, the velocity of the passing—it was intimidating. And it was far more physical than I was used to. I was shocked at the fighting in practice, the slashing and the stickwork. They liked to test the new guys, so I took my share of it, but I knew better than to retaliate. I wasn't one to slash or punch back. But I kept thinking, What was that for? This is ridiculous. We're teammates.

We had one exhibition game against the University of Toronto, and I played left wing on a line with Chris Drury and Mike Sylvia, two lettermen from the year before. We scored on our first two shifts. It was all Drury—I didn't even get an assist—but I was thinking, It can't be this easy. Toronto wasn't very good, and the final score was something like 14–2.

It was hard to tell where I stood. Right up to the opening game against North Dakota, Coach Parker kept fiddling with the lines.

One day in practice I'd be skating on a line of all freshmen—me, Brendan Walsh, Albie O'Connell, and Scott King—with each of us taking turns sitting out. I figured at least two members of that unit wouldn't dress, maybe more. The next day I'd be back with Drury and Sylvia, two of the stars from the previous year. So I was getting mixed signals. But I knew one thing: I wanted to be in the lineup for the opening game. We all did. That was the game they were raising the 1994–95 NCAA Championship banner. Walter Brown Arena was going to be a madhouse.

That's all people on campus were talking about. Raising the banner. The day before the game, Thursday, October 19, Coach Parker called me into his dressing room before practice. He said he wanted to discuss the rotation for the first three games. Very matter-of-fact. I still couldn't read whether it would be thumbs-up or thumbs-down. There were five full-scholarship freshmen, the coach said, and each of us was going to sit out one of the first three games. He told me I was going to dress the opener against North Dakota, playing with Drury and Sylvia. In the second game, against the University of Vermont, I was going to start on right wing—my off wing—with team captain Jay Pandolfo and Bob LaChance. The third game, against Northeastern, I'd sit out.

It was perfect. Storybook, as my father would later describe it. First, to be playing in the opener at home, when the banner was hoisted to the rafters. And next, just as meaningful—more meaningful, in fact—to be *starting* against the University of Vermont, my father's alma mater. I knew it would mean the world to him.

And Coach Parker knew it, too. I may not have fully appreciated that at the time. Coach Parker understood how much it would mean to my dad. It didn't take much to imagine what my father's reaction would be when he found himself sitting in the stands up at Burlington, surrounded by as many friends and relatives as he could find tickets for, as the starting lineup was introduced. *Playing right wing, for Boston University, Travis Roy . . .* He'd be crying before the announcement was out. I thanked the coach, and left his office so full of excitement and pride I could have lifted a bus.

Maija called that afternoon after practice. We talked every day, and I knew she wanted to find out if I'd made it into the lineup. She knew how important it was to me. I didn't say anything about it at first. Practice was fine, I said vaguely. What's going on with you? I could tell she was afraid to come right out and ask, and I enjoyed hearing her tap-dance around the subject. Finally she couldn't hold back. "So Trav, did you find out anything at practice?"

"About?"

"About whether you're playing tomorrow night."

"Oh. I didn't mention it? I'm dressing. I'm playing with Chris Drury and Mike Sylvia."

She didn't know that much about the sport, but she knew how huge that was and gave a little cry of delight. Then I told her everything, about starting next week against Vermont, and how nervous I'd been, and excited I was. Now that it was actually happening, I didn't mind talking about it. Letting it out. My dream was coming true. I was going to play tomorrow night for the best college team in the country.

Maija told me she was definitely coming to the game, and asked me to get tickets for her and a friend from Tabor who was visiting, Laurel Simonini. "Are you nervous?" she asked.

"A little. Sure. Mostly excited."

"What should we do afterward to celebrate?"

"I don't know. Something." Then I had an idea. "Want to go dancing?"

That surprised her, since I almost never took her dancing. So that's what we decided to do. And maybe Sunday we'd go see a movie. Maija said she'd like to see Brad Pitt's new release, *Seven*. I told her where she could pick up the tickets for the game, and to be sure to get there early, because they were raising the banner that night and Walter Brown was going to be packed. She'd be sitting with my parents, who were driving down from Maine. And Tobi. And Tobi's fiancé, Keith Van Orden.

Maija hadn't spent much time with my family before. In light of what happened later, it's important to mention that now. They'd met at my Tabor graduation, of course. And briefly in April, when I'd made my "10 Rules of Life" speech. They were all in the stands at Walter Brown Arena during Midnight Madness, which was the first official on-ice practice of the hockey season, a date determined by the NCAA. But that was about it. Maija didn't know my family nearly as well as I knew hers. And they certainly didn't know her. She was just, in their eyes, Travis's girlfriend.

I can't remember ever being so excited the day of a game. My roommates were all freshmen hockey players—Scott King, Dan Ronan, and Michel Larocque—and all of us were dressing except Scott. At 12:30 we had a pregame skate, followed at 2 P.M. by a team meal of pasta and chicken at T. Anthony's on Commonwealth Avenue. Then I came back to the room and took a nap. At about four o'clock Matt Perrin woke me with a phone call to wish me luck. He wanted in the worst way to be there, but he said he'd watch the game on television since it was being shown on the New England Sports Network.

At about five o'clock, before heading to the arena, the four of us posed for a photograph. Roommates and teammates, before our first game. A girl named Kathy, who lived down the hall at Shelton, took the picture. I still have it in my drawer somewhere. I looked healthy and fit and attractive, like some sort of model. A kid who could take on the world. I don't much like to look at it, to tell you the truth.

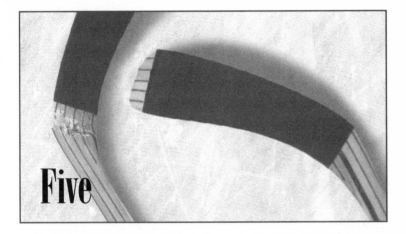

Five

Before every game I liked to freshly tape two sticks. I'd start at the heel, taking a roll of black friction tape, and I'd wrap it smoothly all the way to the toe. Then I'd rub paraffin wax on the tape's tacky surface, which prevented snow from sticking to the blade.

That night there was so much energy in the locker room. Everyone was pumped up for the opening game. I remember watching Jay Pandolfo, the captain, stretch in the middle of the room. And Chris Drury, who was my center that night. I remember thinking, That's the kind of player I want to be.

Drury was a great skater, which was also my strong point. But I couldn't shoot the puck as well as Chris. It was his attitude, though, that really set him apart. He was very quiet and intense. He had an inner thing going, a focus you could almost put your hands on. He knew what he was doing, and nothing could distract him from his business. It was infectious. He was one of those rare players who elevated the play of everyone around him.

Chris knew how to win, that's for sure. In 1989 he'd been the winning pitcher for Trumbull, Connecticut, in the Little League

World Series, baffling an all-star team from Taiwan with something called "the dart." That was his pitch. It did something funny—I don't know what, but they couldn't hit it. Then, his first year at BU, the hockey team won the national championship. That was no coincidence. Drury's presence in the locker room was huge.

I stretched, then got dressed the same way I always did. First I put on my cup, then my garter belt, and pants. I pulled on my uniform socks, left first, then right, attaching them to the garter belt. Then I put on my skates. I liked to be barefoot beneath my skates. I liked to feel the leather against my skin. Then I slipped the shin pads into the red-and-white socks, which were clean and new, taping them firmly in place. Then I put on my shoulder pads, elbow pads, my number 24 jersey (my high-school number, 14, was already taken), my helmet, and gloves. I never wore a T-shirt. Even at Tabor, where the sides of the rink were open and it was often bitterly cold, I never wore a T-shirt. Once you began to sweat, it would feel like a heated coat.

We went out for warm-ups, and right away I did a couple of fast laps, which felt great after the tension of waiting. My adrenaline was pumping, and I quickly broke a light sweat. I felt sleek and strong and fast. I kept glancing up for Mom and Dad and Maija, but couldn't find them. You don't want to be staring up at the stands. Not as a freshman. Not the first game. We took shots to warm up the goalies, and did a few simple passing drills. Then, before we filed off the ice, a small group of players stood in a crescent at the edge of the crease and flipped pucks into the top of the net. I watched. This wasn't the place for a rookie. Mike Grier, who the next year would jump to the NHL, was always the last one off the ice, and he stood by the gate and patted us with his stick on our way back to the room.

Coach Parker followed us in and wrote the lines and defense pairings on the board. Drury, Sylvia, and I were the third line out. It's another BU tradition that the players return to the ice helmet-less for the pregame introductions. So we gave our helmets to the trainers, who lined them up by number on the bench. When, at last, it came time to head back out for the start of the game, we filed out numerically. Having number 24, I was near the end of the line. I liked that. At Tabor I'd always liked to go out last.

The crowd greeted our appearance with a roar, and the band broke into the BU fight song. It gave me chills to be part of all that. The wind felt great flying through my hair—I'd never done that before, skate out for a game without my helmet—and Maija later told me that, blond as I was, I was the easiest guy to identify on the ice. Then the entire Terriers team lined up on the red line, and, with the crowd roaring, they hoisted the championship banner, where it took its place alongside the banners of the 1977–78, 1971–72, and 1970–71 championship teams. It was an emotional moment. I knew that two of my high-school coaches had taken the trouble to be there for my first college game: Coach O'Brien and Mr. Pratt. Watching that banner go up, seeing my teammates in uniform beside me, I finally knew I'd made my goal. I was thinking, You did it, Travis. I was proud of myself, and proud of my family. It was all I could do to hold back my tears of pride.

Those of us who weren't starting took our places on the bench. I couldn't believe how fast the pace was for the first shift. I was thinking, Boy, are these guys good. And for an instant I had another twinge of self-doubt. Did I *really* look like that when I played? Instinctively, I knew I belonged. Once I got out there, I knew I could do it. But the skating was so much faster and harder than in high school, the hitting so intense, and it was weird watching it from so close.

On the second shift of the game, at 1:45, Chris O'Sullivan scored a goal to give us a 1–0 lead. The place, naturally, went wild, and O'Sullivan celebrated the first goal of the season so excessively that Coach Parker gave him a little lecture about it when he came off the ice. Our line was the next one up, and Drury, Sylvia, and I climbed out for the face-off at center ice. The band was playing, and the fans had already started to chant "Sieve! Sieve! Sieve!" at the North Dakota goalie. The place was crackling.

That's when the picture was taken, the one that now hangs beside the BU dressing room door. My one face-off. My last face-off. It's still difficult for me to believe. My world was one of endless possibilities right then.

Drury won it, and dumped the puck in deep. It's a play that happens 100 times a game, a million times every college hockey season. I was the nearest forward, but it was clear that the North Dakota defenseman would easily beat me to the puck. BU has always been known as a physical team—it's one of our trademarks—and not many people knew I could be physical. I wanted to surprise them. I wanted to show I could deliver a good clean solid hit. It's the best way to start a game, anyway, to get your head in the game. It sends a message. We're coming at you all night. Every chance.

The defenseman turned to retrieve the puck from the corner, and I had him lined up with pretty good speed. Controlled speed. I wasn't charging. Just before I got there, though, something happened. I can't say what. I was too excited, perhaps. Too pumped up. Something. I don't remember losing my balance, but I deflected off him. There wasn't the impact there should have been. Then I blacked out for a fraction of a second—no more than that.

I've never really studied the replay. Over the next few months, in the hospital, it was probably shown to me ten times. But I was always in my bed, and the television was some distance away, and I never saw it clearly. What I could see, though, troubled me. I hit the endboards with my helmet, and when I was falling, my body was out of control. It was going whichever way it wanted, like a stuffed scarecrow someone had tossed onto the ice. It wasn't a natural fall at all. I don't like to watch it. I don't watch it. Not now.

When I came to, I was facedown on the ice. I went to get up, and there was nothing. Nothing. You can't describe it. A split second earlier I'd been light and fast and powerful, full of juice, and now there was nothing there. It was as if my head had become disengaged from my body. I was turning the key in the ignition on a cold winter morning, and the battery was completely dead. Not a spark. Just click, and nothing. And right away it passed through my mind I was probably paralyzed. Strange, that. I'd never heard of such an injury in hockey, but it was one of the first things into my head. And just as quickly, I knew it was over. Eleven seconds after my first face-off, college hockey was finished for me.

I was lying with my chin on the ice, and my head tilted slightly to the side. Most of my field of vision was only the ice. Just the clean, white, slightly imperfect sheet of ice. I remember it getting all shiny and smooth again from my breathing in the same place over and over. So it looked like it was newly surfaced just in front of my face. I couldn't move my head either way, and my neck ached.

I could see the fans in the first row, and some of the players. Mostly their skates and their legs. Nobody panicked. Larry, the trainer, got out there pretty quickly, and he was soon joined by the team doctor, Anthony Schepsis. They knew it was a dangerous situation. Two student trainers, both girls, were there, and they were trying to comfort me. Just relax, one was saying, in a very soothing voice. Things are going to be okay. It was a serious moment, but it was nice to hear her voice like that. I needed someone to talk to me, to soothe me. Then Dr. Schepsis asked me, "Travis, can you feel anything in the foot?"

"No."

"Can you move your arm?"

I tried. "No."

Then he asked, "Can you feel this?"

I couldn't. I wondered what he was doing. Then I saw that he was moving my arm. He was picking it up and moving it, and I felt nothing. It was like it was someone else's arm. I was so calm until then, probably because I wasn't in any pain. But that's when I started getting emotional. That's when I asked to see my father.

He'd known it was a bad situation. Almost before anyone else, Dad knew. Because of what he'd always said when I was a kid. "Get up! You're not hurt. Get up." I always had. My whole career, I'd always bounced back up. I'd never once been helped from the ice. I'd never broken a bone. Never had stitches. Never missed a game due to injury. I'd always been ridiculously healthy. So, of all those people in the crowd, Dad knew better than anyone else that I wouldn't have been lying there unless I *couldn't* get up. And without a word to my mom or to Tobi, he'd risen from his seat and walked down to the edge of the rink.

"You Mr. Roy?" someone asked him.

"Yup."

"Travis is asking for you."

He was escorted onto the ice. He tried to sound relaxed, to put the best possible face on things, because . . . well, what else could he say? He was almost as scared as I was. I heard his voice before I saw him. "Hey, boy. Let's get going. There's a hockey game to play." The tone was gentle, though.

"Dad," I said, "I'm in deep shit."

I almost never swore around him. Around anyone. And for a moment my father didn't know what to say. Never in my life had I seen my dad when he didn't know what to say.

I said, "I can't feel anything. And my neck hurts." It was just a small ache, but I could feel that much. I knew it was over. I just knew.

"Dad?"

"Yeah, Trav. Take it easy."

"I made it."

He knew what I meant. That's when the tears started to come, rolling down my cheeks one at a time. Dad, too, started to cry. I don't remember saying anything else. I started to focus on little things. My helmet was in an awkward position, and I wished I could move it. My chin was still on the ice. For some reason it wasn't too cold.

I noticed how quiet everything was in the building. I couldn't believe how 3,500 people could be so quiet. I wished someone would drag me off the ice and work on me in the privacy of the training room, or beneath the stands, so the game could continue. I hated being in the spotlight like that. I could almost feel all those eyes directed at me. It was horrible. The paramedics came out, and they were just drawing more and more attention to me as they worked to get me onto a stretcher.

Coaches don't usually come onto the ice and tend to injured players. They let the doctors do their work. But Coach Parker came out, and I was glad he came out. I wanted to thank him for giving me a chance to realize my goals. So I did that, because I knew I wasn't going to be back on the ice for him again.

"Just lie still," he said.

The paramedics were putting a neck brace on me. I still had my helmet on, and the brace didn't fit well beneath it. It seemed like hours before they'd stabilized me enough to slide a board beneath me. I was aware, mentally, that they were touching my body. But I couldn't feel their hands. I wouldn't have known anyone was touching me if I hadn't been watching. Then they hoisted me onto the stretcher. When they lifted me up, I could feel it in my gut, like the feeling you get when you're falling. They buckled me in and taped my head still. Then, at last, they wheeled me off the ice.

All I could do was look straight up. I saw people hanging down from the balcony as we passed below, straining for a look. Then I saw Maija.

"Stop," I said. "Please stop."

They stopped, and Maija caught up. I looked pretty normal, except that I was strapped onto a stretcher. I wasn't cut or bleeding. I tried to sound calm. "So, I guess I'll see you at the hospital, eh?"

"I guess so."

"Don't worry about me." The last twenty minutes or so must have been scary as hell for her. I didn't like to think about that.

"All right. But I will worry about you."

I saw the bright flickering lights of the ambulance waiting outside the arena. I'd asked if Maija could come along with me, but there was room for only one family member in the ambulance, and my dad sat in the front. Tobi, Keith, and Coach O'Brien rode in a lead cruiser. Maija and my mother followed behind. The equipment manager came out then, and, as I lay in the back of the ambulance, unscrewed the face mask of my helmet. We sat there the longest time trying to figure out which hospital they were taking me to.

Then we were moving. All I could do was stare straight up. I listened to the sirens. I could hear the voices of the paramedics quietly talking. I felt the ambulance bounce slightly as it crossed the subway tracks, and tried to figure out what was going on by the sounds, where we were in the city. I was alert, and not in much pain. Just an ache. It felt like I was in a box all by myself. I could have closed my eyes, but for some reason I kept looking at the bright white lights in the ceiling of the ambulance right above me. I'd never ridden in an ambulance before, and the lights were the only things I could see.

They took me to Boston City Hospital. Things began to happen pretty fast around me—strange faces, strange sounds—and I knew I was in the emergency room. They had put an oxygen mask over my face to help me breathe. After a while my family came in, and Maija. They allowed them in for a few minutes to give me support, then the doctors were going to go to work on me. They had to attach some sort of "halo" to my head to stabilize my entire spinal column. I didn't understand it. I just knew they were going to take me away.

I wanted a kiss from Maija before they did. She was right there at the bedside, and I wanted to kiss her. "Take off the mask," I asked her, my words muffled. It took me a couple of tries before she understood me.

"I can't take off the mask," she said. "I'm not the doctor."

"Take off the mask!" I repeated, more frantically this time. "Maija, please take it off. Just take it off!"

She'd never seen me like that before, and it frightened her to see me frantic and helpless. She just shook her head, near tears, repeating, "I'm not the doctor. I can't."

"Then get the doctor."

Someone, maybe my mother, did. The doctor came into my field of vision. I looked him in the eyes and said, "Please take off the mask. I want to give my girlfriend a kiss."

He understood, and took off the oxygen mask. Maija leaned over and kissed me on the mouth. I told her I loved her. I told her not to worry about me. I hate it when people worry about me. And she said, "I love you, too."

Then the doctor put the oxygen mask back on, and they left.

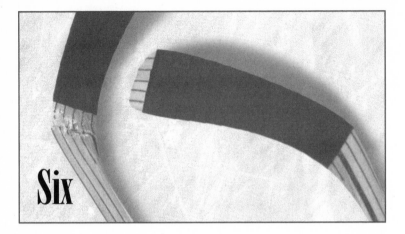

Six

There is a woman from Yarmouth who my family knows named Priscilla Simmons, who teaches English at my mom's high school. Mrs. Simmons has a son named Pat. He, too, is a quadriplegic. He was injured a year before me in a car accident when he was a sophomore in college, and, by coincidence, the accident happened near my family's summer home in Vermont. My mother and sister had been the first friends to visit the Simmonses at the hospital. So, of course, my mother had followed Pat's progress. She and Priscilla Simmons often talked about it at school.

Pat had had a girlfriend at the time of his accident. Afterwards, the girlfriend had drifted away from him, and when Mrs. Simmons mentioned this to my mother, my mother's first thought was, Of course she did. Living with a quadriplegic is not for the faint of heart, and to expect a young girl to commit herself to that for a lifetime, to sign on to such a course voluntarily . . . well, who would? It's too much.

My mother thought of that the night of my accident, when she and Dad and Tobi and Keith and Maija were all waiting in the hospital. As I've mentioned, Mom's a pretty strong lady. The X rays had shown I'd broken—shattered—my fourth cervical vertebra, and the doctors had already told my parents that if there was permanent damage to my spinal cord at the point of the injury, which was probable, it was likely I'd be a quadriplegic, not having the use of my arms or my legs. In the next few days, the doctors would have a better idea of the extent of the damage, once the area was stabilized from surgery and the swelling began to go down. Sometimes the spinal cord shuts down from the shock of the initial blow to the spinal column, and, after a little time, movement and feeling begin to return. But right from the start, my parents had been told to prepare themselves for the worst.

My mother took Maija aside. They didn't know each other that well, but Mom, as is her nature, was direct. "Maija, you have to go on with your life," she said. "Do you understand? This isn't fair to you. You deserve a husband who can take care of you, who can give you children."

She was thinking of the girlfriend of Pat Simmons. Mom didn't want Maija to feel trapped, to feel guilt for deciding to leave. She was 18, a college freshman, and hadn't signed up for this. Mom didn't want to see two lives ruined by what had happened.

But Maija started to cry. Not at the thought of my injury, which was frightening and terrible enough. She didn't even know what the word *quadriplegic* meant—not exactly. But she was crying at the thought of having to leave, of being sent away and not being there to help take care of me when I needed her. "Mrs. Roy. I don't want to leave," she said.

My mom looked at her long and hard, then gave her a hug. They stood outside the waiting room, crying in each other's arms.

I remember so little of what happened in the next few weeks. So much is a haze, or a total blank. I was full of drugs to sedate me, with tubes running up and down my nose and throat. Coach Parker came to the hospital that first night after the game, but I guess I didn't want to see him. That's what I'm told. I don't remember. He saw me anyway. My father wasn't about to turn him away, no matter how I was feeling about it.

I can only speculate about what might have been going through my mind. In general, I wasn't wild about seeing anyone when I was so dependent on everything and everyone. I looked like hell, and didn't want people to worry. I didn't want people to go out of their way to look in on me, just as I hadn't liked it when I was lying on the ice being tended to by the paramedics, the reluctant center of attention. Whatever was in store for my family and me as a result of my injury, we'd deal with it. We'd be okay. That was all I wanted people to know.

But in the particular case of Coach Parker, I suppose I was also thinking I'd let him down. He'd recruited me, he'd counted on me, he'd put me on a terrific line. And my career had lasted exactly eleven seconds. I didn't want him to see me so helpless. I didn't want him to know, as I knew, that it was all over. Not yet.

Also, I didn't know Coach Parker that well. I'd always thought of him as this big, gung-ho hockey coach, with little else but hockey on his mind. I didn't want him coming to see me because he thought he had to. I didn't think I'd be able to relate to him, or talk to him, without the common ground of a hockey rink. To be truthful, I barely knew the man. But he kept returning every day, coaxing me, entertaining me, filling me in on the hockey team's fortunes, and I began looking forward to his visits more and more.

Within the first three days of the accident, I had become famous. Not that I was aware of it at the time. Locally, of course, the story was big. Hockey, in Boston, is a passion, and thousands of families have kids involved in the sport. It interested and alarmed those parents to think such an injury might occur on the ice during an absolutely routine play. All the Boston papers had news of my injury on the front of the sports sections, and updated developments daily. The sports talk shows discussed little else. In a way, I had become EverySon. Parents hearing of the accident, seeing the tape of the fall, thought, There but for the grace of God goes Johnny, or Billy, or Kathy—every kid who played hockey and dreamed of someday playing Division I.

What surprised everyone, though, was that my accident also attracted national attention. Because the game had been televised, my fall had been captured on videotape. ESPN showed it on *SportsCenter* the night of the game, and that made it a national story. Things snowballed from there. The evening news broadcasts picked it up—Peter Jennings, Dan Rather—and by Monday the morning talk shows were on the scene: *Good Morning America*, the *Today* show, and so on. My father was interviewed most often, and he was extremely moving—forthright and candid and, as is his nature, openly emotional.

Having a tape of the actual play made all the difference. To watch a young athlete's life change so drastically in a few seconds is powerful stuff. You saw me coming into the corner looking great, and then not coming out. It hadn't looked dangerous. It was the sort of thing that could have happened to anybody, which was part of its frightening allure. That, and the fact that it was the night BU raised the championship banner. Something about it seemed symbolic in our sports-obsessed culture, or tragically fateful. First shift of the first game of a 20-year-old freshman's college career, a Maine kid who'd worked his whole life to get there, living a dream for 11 seconds, then—bang—having his whole world turned upside down. That's a sad story, no question about it.

And there was the way my family dealt with it. That was a big part of the story. Maybe the biggest part. The human spirit is a rugged and beautiful thing. Right from the start, my family looked only at the positives. The day after the accident, my father spoke at a press conference at Walter Brown Arena and said, "My son will return to this arena. It may not be on skates, but he'll be back." He's so emotional that all the jaded reporters were crying right along with him. "The hand's been dealt," he said. "You just have to go with it. I hope the next hand will be a better one."

There was no blaming anyone or anything, no anger, no wallowing in self-pity. No grieving. Just courage and dignity. My family came across as simple, articulate, brave people. And very, very real. My father, a rink manager and coach; my mother, a teacher and school administrator; my sister, a nurse. How all-American could you get? Others saw them and thought, If it ever happened to me, I wonder if I could be so strong.

And there was still room for hope. My story was open-ended. While the prognosis was bleak, no one really knew how much feeling and movement I'd get back. That would take time. So the coverage continued for weeks, and even months. Three weeks after it happened, *Sports Illustrated* devoted 10 pages to my accident. Vice-President Al Gore came to visit me in the hospital, and that, too, made the news. I barely remember it. I was so drugged up I fell asleep before the vice-president had left the room—and wouldn't David Letterman and Jay Leno have had a field day with that one? Tens of thousands of prayers came our way, from President Clinton on down.

But I was unaware of all the fuss. Indifferent, I suppose, is a better word, for I'd become famous for all the wrong reasons. I was in my own little world, staring up at the cork ceiling of my hospital room, listening to the beeps and buzzes and unearthly breathing of the machines I was hooked up to, machines I could neither see nor understand. People came and people went. I couldn't speak, and I couldn't move. My life had become a waking nightmare.

I'd been transferred to Boston University Hospital, where I was scheduled to undergo surgery on October 23, three days after the accident. The surgery was to remove the broken shards of bone from my exploded fourth vertebra, and to stabilize the spinal column by inserting a two-inch plate between the third and fifth vertebrae. The surgery would not repair the spinal cord.

Modern medicine has not yet discovered how to do that. Rather, it would protect me from doing further damage to my spinal cord, which controls every nerve, every muscle, in the body. Until such surgery was performed, I had to be kept from moving my head.

To do that doctors literally bolted a halo-type contraption to my skull, attaching the device with small screws inserted in the sides of my forehead. Heavy weights were attached to the halo via a pulley to decompress the spine. I remember Tobi asking if the weights were bothering me. I told her I had no idea the weights were even there.

It was as if my head had been detached from the rest of my body. I had no movement or feeling anywhere below the shoulders. Tobi asked me if I could feel my bed moving. I couldn't. They'd put me in a rocking bed, one that swung from side to side like a hammock. The motion kept the fluids from settling and hardening in my lungs. I had no way to cough up these fluids, because the muscles of my diaphragm no longer functioned. I couldn't breathe for long periods without a ventilator. So doctors had put two tubes down my throat. The ventilator, which was the diameter of a Magic Marker, forced air in and out of my lungs. The second tube, the diameter of a pencil, sucked the fluids out of my lungs as they collected. Before doctors figured out a way to do that, most spinal-cord patients died of pneumonia. A third tube, for feeding, was inserted through my nostril.

It was torture. I kept gagging on the tubes, which I could feel running down my throat. I tried to remove the tubes from my mouth with my tongue. I had never felt so helpless, and I kept trying to thrash my head back and forth to work the tubes loose. I couldn't feel myself breathing. I couldn't feel my chest moving. It made me panic. I was groggy from the drugs I'd been given to calm me, and tried to communicate my desperation to anyone and everyone in the room. It was scary for Maija to see me like that. Scary for all of them. I kept trying to tell them to take the damn tubes out of my mouth so I could breathe, and they kept telling me please, please, for my own sake, to stop trying to move my head.

I gave up and tried only to sleep. I didn't want to wake up again and relive this nightmare. When I slept it would all disappear.

The night before my operation, a man introduced himself to my parents, and gave them a vial of holy water. He said his son had brought it back from the Gulf War. It was in an empty Advil container. He said if you were to put it on an ailing person, it would heal them, if not physically, then spiritually. The man wanted my parents to have it. He asked them to put the holy water on me.

My family is not particularly religious. I don't know. This experience has changed us all. But growing up, I'd have said we were not the type of family who believed in miracles. Or holy water collected from the Middle East. When something like this happens, however, you grab whatever hands are extended your way. It's natural. You have nothing to lose. So my family decided to try it.

I was asleep when they came into my room. On the CD player beside my bed, Pachelbel's Canon in D was playing. Maija had given it to me before the accident, and now I was listening to it 24 hours a day. I found the melody soothing. That, and sleep, were the only things in my life that were soothing. The music was always accompanied by the sound of the ventilator pumping air in and out of my lungs, in and out, like the breathing of Darth Vader in *Star Wars*.

It was dark in my hospital room, and the combined effect of that soothing music, the inhuman breathing, the near darkness, and the vial of holy water gave the moment a spiritual air. Almost mystical. I was lying there, inert, like the body at a wake. My father opened the vial. They weren't quite sure what to do with it. It's not like the holy water came with directions. But he started to sprinkle a little over my arms, then over my chest, over my legs, over my head. They were praying—Dad, Mom, Tobi, Keith, Maija—and they were all crying. They shook out the last few drops, so that none would be wasted. When it was gone they all kissed me and left me to sleep.

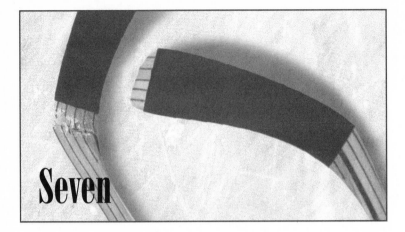

Seven

My family took turns sitting with me as I slept. I didn't like to be alone, and it made me feel safe to have one of them there. I was in a private room in the intensive care unit, my vital signs monitored by perpetually beeping machines. If something went amiss—if I temporarily cut off my air supply by biting down on my ventilator hose, if my intravenous saline solution was getting low, if the alarm system itself was malfunctioning—alarm bells would ring all over the floor. One would ring by the nurses' station, a second would go off outside my door, and a third alarm would cause a din inside my room. Other patients, too, were hooked up to machines that kept setting off alarms. There was never any peace. It was as if the whole intensive care unit was under constant attack. I would hear footsteps racing up and down the hall, and, if one of my machines was the problem, a nurse would quickly set it straight. Very seldom was it an actual emergency. I grew to hate those alarms. I grew to hate the beeping sounds of those machines.

Maija took that first week off from school so she could spend as much time as possible with me. Her parents were totally supportive. Not that they could have kept her away if they'd tried. But the important thing was that they backed her a hundred percent. Her whole focus, once she realized what I was facing, was to help me get through the ordeal. She dropped a course in mythology, her most time-consuming subject, which enabled her to be at the hospital from 2 to 10 P.M. every day. She spent her weekends in the hospital. She did her homework when I was asleep. She sat with me and read letters to me. She rubbed my shoulders and played with my hair, where I could feel the touch of her fingers.

Like everyone else in my family, she took her turn sleeping with me in my tiny, cramped hospital bed. It was cramped, that is, for whoever was sleeping alongside me in that narrow space. I was completely comfortable, because I had no sensation of anyone's legs and hips and arms touching mine. Even my father, all six feet two inches and 230 pounds of him, somehow crawled in beside me in my hospital bed when I asked him. Finally I signaled for him to get out, though. It was too much, even for me. And he was totally miserable. But Tobi, Mom, and Maija all took regular turns snuggling beside me in the bed. It meant the world to me to have them there. It made me feel safe when everything else was frightening.

Unless they laid a hand on my shoulder, or had their head pressed against my cheek, I couldn't feel them, however. When their legs were touching mine, or they rested a hand on my stomach, I wouldn't know it unless I happened to look down. When I mentioned that, it helped them understand my condition. It was easy for them to remember I couldn't move, but hard to get it into their heads I couldn't feel, either. Because, to them, I didn't look any different from the way I'd looked before, except for those tubes in my mouth. My body was still fit and strongly muscled.

My parents were told that if a miracle were going to happen, if my paralysis were temporary, it would probably show up in the first 48 hours after the surgery, once the area was stabilized and the swelling around the spinal cord, reduced by massive dosages of steroids, began to go down. After that, it was a question of degree. It was possible that for up to two years I'd continue to get certain muscle groups back—first the arms, then the wrists, maybe the fingers. Any movement in the legs fell into the "miracle" category. And, of course, it was also possible I'd never get back the use of any muscle groups below the shoulders.

Those first few days after the surgery, when I was asleep, Maija sometimes would dig her fingernails into my leg to see if I would flinch. To see if I'd wake up with a start, or show any signs at all of having recovered some feeling. Maybe my nerves were in a deep, deep sleep, but still functioned somewhere far beneath the surface. She'd press harder and harder, thinking, Come on, Travis, come on—trying to will me to open my eyes and cry out for her to stop. It was weird for her to dig into the still-living, still-supple flesh and get no response. Unbelievable, even. A couple of times she dug in so hard that she drew blood. She felt terrible about it afterward, and would wipe the blood clean and cover my legs back up with the sheet.

For an entire month, I kept going in and out of consciousness. People, I knew, were around me almost all of the time, but I couldn't talk to them even if I saw them. Coach Parker kept reappearing at my bedside. Coach O'Brien. Angus. Matt. Lots of Tabor and Yarmouth friends. Both of my grandmothers, Grandma Goodsell and Nana Roy.

It was the high point of my day when I saw either grandmother. Everyone loves Grandma Goodsell, who summers in Vermont and winters in Florida. She's very honest and says what everyone else wishes they could say. Nana Roy has always been the crazy grandmother in the family, dressing in outlandish outfits, looking and acting at least ten years younger than she is. She lives in Sedona, Arizona, with my step-grandfather, William Laird, who is the kindest, gentlest man. A tall, gray-bearded Westerner, he used to wear bolo ties to the hospital. When I was visiting them at age 14, he'd taught me how to shoot a pistol, and he used to wear a Stetson hat with the skin of a rattlesnake he'd killed himself around the brim. His presence was very comforting for me as I lay silently in my hospital bed. For some reason I always felt a little safer when he was around. A little more relaxed. He was always happiest when he was around the family, and maybe I connected with that.

The television in my room was on most of the time, but I didn't watch it. Time was a fog. A few hours became a few days became a few weeks, and in all that time, nothing about my condition changed. Not for the better, anyway. I did have several sharp turns for the worse. As expected, I came down with pneumonia. My temperature spiked as high as 105.5°. The steroids I'd been given left me with stomach ulcers. I began dropping weight, and my right lung partially collapsed.

Worst of all, though, I still couldn't talk. The tubes stayed down my throat for the first 17 days of my hospital stay, which was as long as they could be left in without causing permanent damage to my vocal cords. While they were in, I couldn't make anyone understand me. I'd want my left ear scratched, or the television to be turned off, and my family would gather around and try to read my lips as, fishlike, I worked them up and down against those godforsaken hoses. Glub-glub-glub, is what it looked like. They'd guess anyway, and I'd blink one time to say yes, two times to say no. It took forever. Even then, they seldom came up with what I was trying to say.

Frustrated, I'd start swearing at them. I knew they couldn't understand me, so I said anything that came into my head. It made me feel better to hurl unprintables at them without fear of offending anyone.

Finally someone came up with the idea of using a spelling board. They'd point to A . . . B . . . C . . . , and I'd blink when they got to the right letter. It was an arduous process, so I didn't try to write sentences that way. I'd try to spell a key word or phrase and let them guess the rest, like charades. I'm not a great speller in the best of circumstances, and being doped up on sedatives made the whole process an extraordinary challenge. Sometimes we'd be working two or three minutes trying to get a word, and I'd lose my place. Or I'd get confused what letter came next. Halfway through, I might suddenly realize I was misspelling the word. Now what? I couldn't tell them to go back and start over. I couldn't tell them anything. All I could do was blink. It was a time-consuming, imperfect method, but it was the only way I had of getting anything across.

Maija had given me a ring while I was in the hospital. It was on the middle finger of my left hand, and once, when she wasn't there, I wanted my dad to raise my hand high enough for me to look at it. He picked up the spelling board, and I carefully helped him spell out "ring."

"You want me to ring for the nurse?" my father asked, reaching for the call button.

I blinked twice for no.

"You want to make a phone call? Ring someone?"

Two more blinks.

"Do you have a ringing in your ears?"

Two blinks.

"Rink? Is it something about the rink?"

It was a maddening means of communication.

To get someone's attention, I couldn't yell out, or wave my hands. A call button was placed beside my pillow, which I could sometimes press with my head. But as often as not I couldn't reach it. Or if I reached it, it didn't ring when I pressed down. I finally figured out how to make a "prrrpp" sound with my mouth, despite the tubes, and within three days my "prrrpps" had driven everyone nuts. There was so little I could do for myself. Practically nothing.

A few days after my surgery, I had my parents pull out the spelling board. Patiently proceeding letter by letter, I managed to spell the phrase, "Is this it?"

I knew I was paralyzed. I'd already gathered I was going to be paralyzed for a long time. But I didn't know how long. No one had told me exactly what my hopes for recovery were. Tobi, who's a nurse herself and had been explaining hospital procedures all along, said, "We don't know if you're going to be able to move your arms and legs again. This is where the fight starts. Okay?"

I blinked once.

"Do you want to know more?" she continued.

I blinked twice. That was enough information for one day.

"Are you angry?"

I blinked twice.

"Are you sad?"

I blinked once. It was probably unnecessary, for my eyes were brimming with tears.

But I was sad. That's exactly the feeling that most often descended on me. Sad it had all ended so soon. Sad there was no second chance. Sad all of us could not go back to the wonderful lives we'd been living. To try to cheer me up, they'd rigged the television with a cable connection so we could get the BU hockey games on NESN. The team had been playing pretty well. But I didn't care to watch them. It caused me more pain than it brought pleasure. It just brought it home all the more vividly that my hockey career was finished, that it was impossible for me ever to play again.

I started having dreams. My dreams were so realistic they felt more like real life than my life did. Two, in particular, I had night after night, always dreaming either one or the other.

In the first dream I was back at BU. I was at the rink, putting on my skates, even though I knew I was paralyzed. Everyone else at the rink knew I was paralyzed, too. Yet I could tie on my skates by myself. And I could skate. It was wonderful. Then afterwards I knew I had to get back to the hospital, back to the intensive care unit, because I was paralyzed and that's where my family was waiting. I'd fight and fight to get back, but I couldn't find the hospital.

I'd get on a bus, or on the subway line, and the only way I could describe which hospital I was looking for was by describing the ceiling of my room. That's the only way I knew it. That's what I had memorized: a ceiling with cork tiles, painted white, full of holes. I'd cry out in my dream, calling for my parents, calling for Maija, but I couldn't get back. Then, when I awakened and found myself back in my hospital room, it was always a relief. I was glad to be there again.

In the second dream I was inside a video game. It was a game I'd created for my professor. I'd always find myself in the same difficult position in the game, where I'd be suspended across this ditch, or ravine. My hands would be on one side of the ditch and my legs on the other side, and I'd be looking straight up at the sky. I had to hold on so tightly to keep from falling into the ditch. My rear end felt like it was falling right through the bottom of the bed. It was like I was sinking deeper and deeper, losing control. It seemed like I was fighting for my life. All I could do was hang on until I woke up, but I couldn't get out of the dream, even once I knew it was a dream. I was stuck. When I woke up I'd be exhausted, and sweating, still muzzled by those horrible tubes going down my throat. But at least I felt safe again.

I started sleeptalking, which is the equivalent of sleepwalking without getting out of bed. One time my eyes flew open in the middle of the night, and I made my father get out the spelling board. I painstakingly spelled out "trash can." I'd been dreaming I was stuck, butt down, in a trash can, with my arms and legs helplessly waving in the air.

"Do you want me to empty the trash can?" my father, groggy with sleep, asked.

I blinked twice. Then I spelled out "Lift me out." I wanted him to set me free from that trash can. Then I closed my eyes and returned to my sleep. He must have thought I was losing my mind.

Another time I awoke and made my mother spell out "dancing shoes." I was dreaming that I was taking Maija dancing, but we couldn't go until we'd located my dancing shoes. I don't own a pair of dancing shoes, but I was frantic when my mother wouldn't bring them.

They were pumping me full of Valium, keeping me as sedated as possible. That was probably what was causing these hallucinations, or dreams. Whatever they were. Because suddenly they stopped, and my dreams became comforting ones. Great dreams, in which I was always mobile, running or skating, free.

When I was awake those first few weeks, I didn't dwell on my paralysis. It was surprisingly easy to block out. I didn't feel paralyzed when I was just lying there. Rather, I felt like I was lying in bed in a very comfortable position, since feeling uncomfortable requires feeling something. Comfort, it turns out, is the total absence of discomfort, just as cold is the absence of heat. Except for the tubes in my mouth, I was comfortable in my hospital bed. It wasn't until I tried to move that I was reminded of my condition.

Maija sometimes caught me lying in bed in the middle of the night with my eyes wide open, and she'd wonder what I was thinking about. She couldn't ask, because I couldn't speak. But it was always the same thing. I was thinking about what the rest of my life was going to be like. I wondered if I'd be bedridden, just as I was now. I assumed I'd be a vegetable, living at home, sitting in a chair, having to ask for everything I needed, just as I had to ask for everything now. That I wouldn't be able to go to the bathroom by myself, or bathe, or scratch, or feed myself ever again. That I'd never work again. Never even go outside again.

I wasn't suicidal. I didn't ever wish I was dead. The only reason I didn't want to die, however, was that I didn't want to leave my friends, my family, and Maija. They kept me going.

But I worried about what I was doing to them, about my parents and Maija having to deal with me. My paralysis was something I'd have been able to live with more easily if, somehow, I could have taken on all the suffering and pain myself. I didn't want to be a burden to my parents or Maija the rest of my life. Yet I didn't want my life to end.

There were so many things I missed. What I missed most, though, was being able to hug my loved ones, who were always right there by my side. I can remember Grandma Goodsell, who's very tiny, no more than four ten, pulling a stool up to my bedside so she could kiss me on the cheek. I wanted so much to reach out and hug her. Everyone loved her—all the hospital nurses, all my friends. In her direct, forthright manner, she was helping everyone deal with my situation, providing perspective, easing tension, staying composed and positive. She was such a great comfort to everyone in those first troubled weeks.

But the person I most wanted to hug was Maija. That was never far from my mind. I'm a person who, by nature, had always liked to touch people, and to be touched, and my favorite form of touching was a big hug. I didn't just drape my arms around a person. It was always a good firm hug. And I wanted to hug Maija so very badly. I wanted to feel her hands in mine, to cuddle with her while watching TV, to lay my head in her lap and look up into her eyes.

I couldn't imagine what my life would be like without her, but I knew that what was happening wasn't fair to her. That was the hardest thing. I wanted Maija to be happy. But I still wanted her to be with me. I didn't know how to resolve that. At night, I thought often about that, too.

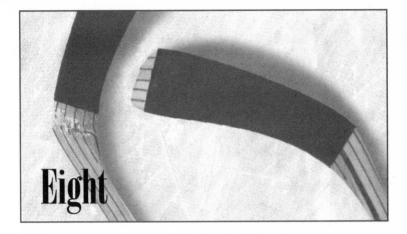

Eight

After 17 days of living with those awful tubes in my mouth, bound by my paralysis, gagged by the hoses that pumped air into my lungs and sucked the phlegm out, I was given a tracheotomy. A hole about the size of a nickel was cut in my throat, just beneath the Adam's apple, so the ventilator hose could enter my windpipe directly. Grim as that procedure may sound, the tracheotomy markedly improved my quality of life.

I stopped wrestling the tubes with my tongue. I was now able to move my lips, and people were able to read them. I could begin to taste things again, though I still wasn't allowed to eat. I sucked on ice cubes to appease my thirst, and, best of all, had lemon-flavored swabs rubbed on my gums and the inside of my mouth. My taste buds, numbed by their diet of plastic, found those swabs more flavorful than anything I could remember, more delicious than ice cream or steak. My mouth literally watered at the thought of a lemon swab.

I still couldn't speak. I still couldn't swallow food. Those hurdles wouldn't be overcome for another month. I still had to have my lungs cleared of the fluids that continually gathered in them, a miserable procedure I grew to loathe.

Every half hour or so, a nurse would come in and roll me onto my side, pounding my back so violently to loosen the phlegm my mother sometimes worried they'd break my ribs. Then my ventilator hose, which was hooked up to a valve in my throat, was replaced by a long suction tube that the nurse slid into the lungs. I could feel it tickle as it snaked down my throat. It was like one of those suction pumps used by a dentist, and it made that same sucking sound as it cleared my lungs of the mucus, like a straw slurping the last drops of a milk shake. My breathing, meanwhile, was done by a hand-held pump, sort of a minibellows, that the nurse operated. It wasn't painful, but it was torture. Every half hour, all night and all day. Wakened, pounded on, shaken, then drained by a hose. I made Maija get out the spelling board one night, and I wrote out, "I hate this."

If I'd been getting better, all of these aggravations and indignities would have been inconsequential. But I wasn't. I had no more movement a month after my accident than I did fifteen seconds after it had happened. My family tried their best to keep my spirits from flagging. They could see a better future for me than I was able to see for myself. They could envision a time when I'd be in a wheelchair, having a life that was worth living. My father kept talking about how we could watch hockey games together on television as soon as I could sit up. How we could eat dinner together as a family. And I'd be thinking, Are you kidding? I'm supposed to get excited about this? Watching a game on TV? Sitting around talking? This is what I have to look forward to? I'd give him my thousand-yard stare, then would go back to sleep.

Someone sent my parents a parable called "Footprints," written on a bookmark, that my mother saved and read to me once. I don't remember exactly how it went, but the gist was that a man dreams he is lost in the desert. He is dying of thirst, and prays for help and deliverance. That's the last thing the man remembers. He survives, but has no memory of how he escaped his desperate plight.

An angel appears before him. "How did I get out of the desert?" the man asks the angel.

"Come with me," the angel replies. The angel takes the man back into the desert, where his footprints are still visible in the sand. Some of the way there are two sets of tracks, side by side, but at other times only one set of footprints is visible for long stretches.

The man asks the angel, "Are those your footprints in the sand next to mine?"

"They are," says the angel.

"What about the stretches where there's only one set of footprints? Why did you leave me alone in my time of greatest need?"

"I didn't," the angel says. "That's when I was carrying you."

My mother refers to that story when she tries to put into words how we got through the months immediately following my accident. Angels came into our lives. Human angels. Everyday people who reached out to us in our time of need. Big people and small people, friends and strangers, young and old. The world carried my family out of the desert. That's what got us through to the other side.

Every day it was something. Some small kindness. My parents were staying in the Boston Harbor Hotel when my accident happened. After a few days, it was clear I was going to be in the hospital quite a long time—months—and my parents packed up to move to a friend's house in a nearby suburb. It would mean a longer commute—the hotel was just down the street from the hospital—but they really didn't have an option because of the expense.

As my parents tried to check out, the hotel manager, Paul Jacques, asked if there was some problem. He knew, by then, who they were. Who I was. The only problem, they explained, was that they didn't want to wear out their welcome, and they weren't sure who was picking up the tab. He signaled to the porter and told him to carry their bags back upstairs. They weren't to worry about the expense, because there wasn't going to be any charge. And they could stay as long as they liked. Furthermore, he upgraded them into a suite.

They ended up staying another three months. Mr. Jacques's gesture was more important than you might think. To be able to return to a nice room, to get a good meal and a good night's sleep after the strain of spending all day in the hospital with me, meant everything to my parents. It rejuvenated them. It was the one time in their day that wasn't a trial.

Dad couldn't buy groceries. He'd be standing in a checkout line and someone would recognize him, and that someone wouldn't allow him to pay. It was a small gesture, but always so sincere that he couldn't say no. People wanted to do *something* to help. Anything. There was a lady who walked into the waiting room of the intensive care unit and handed my mother an electric toothbrush, a toothbrush I use to this day. "Mrs. Roy? I want you to have this for Travis. People in these situations ignore their teeth."

One watches the evening news, or reads the newspapers, and it's easy to forget about all those millions of people who aren't violent, who aren't greedy, who don't hate—the ordinary folks who quietly go through life as good citizens and good people. Well, my family won't forget. Not now. We saw mankind at its best. It's a large price to pay, I'll grant you, but it's still a good thing to have seen. It changes your thinking. It alters your angle of regard to know there is, in fact, a family of man. To know that the generous side of human nature, the fine, unselfish side, is around us all the time, waiting to emerge when the need is truly there.

A sports talk-show host in Boston, Dale Arnold of WEEI, aired a program about me the Monday after my accident. Actually, he didn't intend to talk about me the entire show. The Patriots were playing the Buffalo Bills that night, and he thought most of his callers would want to talk about the big Monday night football game. But they didn't. Most of them wanted to talk about me, about Boston University hockey, and about spinal-cord injuries in general. Darryl Stingley, a Patriots wide receiver, became a quadriplegic a number of years ago as a result of a hit he took during a game. Actor Christopher Reeve's accident had happened about five months earlier. So there was plenty of material for discussion.

At the end of the show, Dale decided there was something to my story that had touched the heartstrings of the community, and that instead of just talking about it, he'd do something to help. Something concrete. He set about organizing a marathon call-in fund-raiser, enlisting the help of John Maguire, the vice-president and general manager of both WEEI and WRKO, two of the largest radio stations in New England.

The average medical expenditures over a lifetime for a person with my type of injury are something like $3.5 million, and that does not include the cost of home care. Fortunately, my insurance coverage is about as good as anyone's. Between my mother's insurance policy at the high school and the NCAA's policy, and BU's, my medical bills have been completely covered. For home health care, I get $100,000 a year, which can be adjusted upwards if necessary, to pay for personal-care attendants and nursing aides. That sounds like a lot, I know, but I need someone with me 24 hours a day when I'm at school. A registered nurse costs about $35 an hour; a personal-care attendant around $12 per hour. Last year I went through that $100,000 in 198 days.

For a quadriplegic to function with a measure of independence in the world, there must also be expenditures for special wheelchairs, special vans, special beds, special telephones and computers and environmental control units and elevators, and other items that help increase independence. Plus common, everyday expenses associated with living and raising a family, which I someday hope to do: mortgages, groceries, clothes, schooling, recreation . . . on and on and on.

It all takes money—the kind of money my family didn't have. I hope to get a good job when I get out of school—certainly I'll do some sort of work—but the hard facts are that 75 percent of paralysis victims are on welfare. Within days of my accident, the Travis Roy Fund was set up, to give me a decent start financially. The fund-raiser organized by John Maguire and Dale Arnold at WEEI became the single biggest source of contributions to that fund. Dale was the first snowflake in what became an avalanche of support.

The original idea was to have a four-hour show on November 9. But calls started coming in from stations all over New England asking what they could do to help. The format changed to a 12-hour show, with the idea being to start taking calls at 6 A.M. and to shut off the phones at 6 P.M. Boston University donated a building in which volunteers could stand by to answer the phones, and Bobby Orr, who did promotional work for NYNEX, got NYNEX to install 30 phone lines into the building for free. The entire Boston sports community got behind it. Members of the Celtics, the Bruins, BU hockey players, my roommates—all of them volunteered to answer phone lines and to go on the radio to drum up support.

When the day arrived, John Maguire picked up my father at the hotel at 5:30 A.M. and drove him to the building BU had provided as command central. Even at that hour it was already surrounded by five or six television news trucks, there to cover the event. "How much money do you think we're going to raise today?" Mr. Maguire asked my dad.

He had no idea. Pressed, Dad finally said he'd be delighted if we could raise $10,000. Mr. Maguire said he'd be disappointed if they didn't raise $100,000.

"Are you wacko?" my father said.

The phones started ringing at 5:45, before the morning commute, and they kept ringing with such persistence that it was more than 15 hours later—at 9 P.M.—that the radio station finally closed up shop. They'd passed Mr. Maguire's $100,000 mark by nine in the morning. They passed $200,000 by midafternoon. Things picked up again during the evening rush hour and again after the radio-athon was covered on the evening news, so when all the receipts were finally tallied late that night, they'd raised $452,000 in cash and $150,000 in services on my behalf.

Angels, carrying us along. My family was overwhelmed. Not just by the final numbers, but by the selfless nature of some of the gifts. One child broke open his piggy bank and pledged $7.23. A family who had saved $4,000 for a trip to Austria for Christmas—perfect strangers—had voted instead to donate that money to me. They gave up their vacation. How do you explain something like that?

Up in Maine, the Friends of Travis Roy was formed, since no one in the Yarmouth area wanted to send their hard-earned money down to the rich swells in Massachusetts, where the Travis Roy Fund was based. And they raised over $100,000. A bottle drive in Yarmouth (population 3,000) raised $3,000 in a single day, which means that 60,000 bottles and cans were collected—20 for every man, woman, and child in the town.

Ed Anderson, who was owner of the Maine Mariners when I worked as a stickboy, donated the proceeds from three exhibition games of his current team, the Providence Bruins, to the Travis Roy Fund. He also helped Bobby Orr and Mike Eruzione organize an invitation-only auction that was held at the Trattoria Il Panino, a restaurant and club in Boston's North End. There were signed jerseys donated by every NHL team, plus memorabilia and collectibles donated by any number of NHL stars: Wayne Gretzky, Eric Lindros, Mario Lemieux, Paul Coffey. There was a signed Cal Ripken jersey. Basketballs signed by Larry Bird and other members of the Celtics. Dozens and dozens of items.

But Bobby Orr pointed out that that was the easy part, getting things donated. The trick was to get an A-list of people who would bid, and bid generously, to buy them. I don't know how he did it, but Bobby called in some favors and, despite a major snowstorm that kept some high-rolling out-of-towners from attending, the event raised $240,000. One old New Englander told my father that the only time he'd seen anything like it was the night they first opened the Jimmy Fund for cancer-stricken children. Typical of the spirit of the evening, a StairMaster with a retail value of $2,400 went for $9,600 with Bobby acting as auctioneer. A golf weekend with Bobby at his vacation home in Florida went for $24,000, the biggest-ticket item of the night.

All those stories you hear about what a terrific person Bobby Orr is, humble and caring and genuine, are true. Another angel. In addition to his fund-raising efforts, he became a real friend, regularly visiting me in the hospital. He had a direct phone line put into the room and arranged for the delivery of my first hands-free telephone.

A trading card company, Pinnacle, had been after Bobby to do a special card for that year's NHL all-star game, which was being played at Boston's new FleetCenter. They were offering him $25,000. He'd repeatedly told them he wasn't interested, but after my accident he changed his mind. He went back to Pinnacle and said he'd do the all-star-game card on two conditions. First, he insisted that it be a Bobby Orr/Travis Roy card, with a picture of him on one side and me on the other in my Boston University uniform. Second, he upped his fee to $50,000.

Bobby donated that fee to the Travis Roy Fund. First, though, he talked to Coach Parker to make sure that my family wouldn't be offended by his gesture. Can you imagine what it meant to my dad? Not just the money, but to have his son pictured on a trading card with the greatest defenseman, arguably the greatest player, of all time?

Human angels. Carrying us out of the desert.

There was Bob Taylor, a computer software salesman living in

Dallas. In *Dallas*. He'd read about my story in *Sports Illustrated*. What triggered his involvement, though, was the night in December he was listening to a hockey game between the Dallas Stars and Boston Bruins. Bob's a Stars season ticket holder, and in fact is one of those vociferous—read: obnoxious—fans who sits behind the visitors' penalty box and taunts opposing players. He's good at it. Persistent. Three separate times, he's been escorted by ushers from his seat, once for climbing the glass to go after a player who'd squirted a water bottle at his wife, Susie. Bob's a doer. A hands-on guy. Anyway, that night the announcers were talking about how the Stars players had taken a collection among themselves before the game and raised $1,200 for the Travis Roy Fund. It was a terrific gesture, but Bob Taylor thought to himself, That's not enough. The people of Dallas can do more than that.

The next day he met with the Dallas Stars management. They gave him permission to collect money for the Travis Roy Fund at the next three Stars games. Then he called Ed Carpenter, BU's sports information director—another angel, by the way—and asked him if he knew of anything in particular we needed. Ed mentioned a van, one that was equipped with a hoist for a wheelchair. That's what Bob latched on to.

He got together 25 or so friends, and they went up and down the aisles at the next two Stars games with five-gallon water jugs, collecting quarters, dollars, fives—whatever people threw in. Texans raising money for a Boston kid no one had ever heard of two months earlier. Those first two games, he collected $15,000. But a van that was outfitted for a wheelchair cost about $50,000. He wanted to deliver it to us at the NHL all-star weekend in Boston in mid-January, so Bob was running out of time. He went to the new owner of the Stars, Tom Hicks, and Hicks agreed to make an announcement at the next game promising to match whatever was gathered in the water jugs that night. That turned out to be $9,500. The matching grant by Hicks brought the total to

$34,000, and individual corporate contributions the next week put Taylor over the top.

He and his wife, Susie, picked up the van, factory new, with every possible option—leather seats, a television, a CD player, radar detector, wheelchair hoist—and drove it to Boston themselves. They'd only talked to my father over the phone twice before handing him the keys at the Boston Harbor Hotel. They threw four Dallas Stars leather coats into the bargain. And the Taylors are still involved in our lives. Bob is one of five board members for the Travis Roy Foundation, which raises money for other paralysis victims.

At the hospital, every day something new would arrive in the mail, or somebody famous would call. Mike Milbury, who was coach and general manager of the New York Islanders, flew up to see me on a day off. Former Bruins tough guy Lyndon Byers came by. Race car driver Ricky Craven, who's a longtime friend of my dad's and mine. I received a Lou Holtz autographed football. Signed magazine covers and posters. Boxes and boxes of letters.

It was more fun for everyone else than it was for me. To be honest, I couldn't have cared less. But for my parents, Maija, Tobi, Matt, Angus, and all my uncles and aunts and cousins and buddies from Tabor who'd taken over the waiting room of the hospital, it broke up the dark tedium of the days. They got a big kick out of seeing what would come next.

I didn't like people thinking of me that way: as a quadriplegic. I just didn't. I was in a state of denial, of nonacceptance, still hoping to wake up one day with my movement miraculously restored. We got letters from people who went six months before something twitched, and they'd tell us how now they were walking—even running. That was what I wanted to hear.

More often, though, I'd heard more realistic scenarios. Over the first couple of months, four or five quadriplegics came to my room at the BU medical center to visit me. I didn't even want to talk to them, to be honest. But they wanted to help. Or maybe they'd been asked to help. They'd tell me that they'd found life does go on. That, in fact, their lives were pretty good, and mine would be, too.

But we were in two completely different mind frames. I'd just had my accident, and these guys would roll in and start talking about how good my life was going to be. It was frustrating. It didn't cheer me up at all. I couldn't understand how life would be okay living in a wheelchair. Not for me. I was a Division I hockey player. And I'd be more depressed after they left.

Then my family would say, "What did you think, Trav?"

And I'd meticulously say, so they were able to read my lips, "I don't want to be like that."

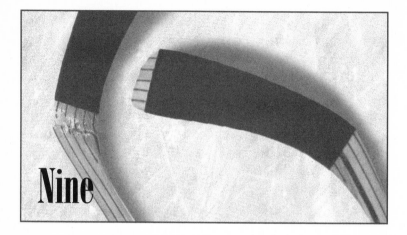

Nine

It was a big event when, on November 20, I was moved from Boston University Hospital's intensive care unit to its spinal-cord unit, where I would begin my therapy sessions. I was afraid of the move, for some reason. In my four weeks in the ICU, I'd become used to the doctors and nurses, used to those alarms and the beeping of the monitoring machines. I didn't think I was ready for a change.

But the doctors did. And everyone in my family was excited, since it represented some form of progress. The goal, right from the start, was for me to be out of the hospital and living at home in time for Tobi's wedding on April 27. Between now and then was the proverbial journey of a thousand miles. This was a single step.

My new room was a little brighter than my old one but, beyond that, materially unchanged. The beds were the same, the ventilator machine was the same, I had a view of the same ceiling tiles. A little more light came in through the window, but from my bed, with a neck brace to keep me from swiveling my head, I could barely see out. I could just get a glimpse of a brick wall and a tiny sliver of sky. I knew I was closer to the street, because I could hear more: sirens and, once winter came, snowplows.

I'd gotten a bedsore, or decubitus, in the intensive care unit. That's a common problem for paralysis victims, since they lie all day and night in the same position, and it significantly slowed down my therapy. The sore was directly on my coccyx, and I was unable to sit in a wheelchair without aggravating it. The only way to cure the bedsore was to keep me off my back. So the nurses constantly rolled me from side to side—every hour during the day, and every two hours at night.

Shortly after changing rooms, I began getting sharp, intense pains in my lower body, somewhere around my abdomen. The pains, which were more acute than any I'd ever known, seemed to be unrelated to my bedsore. Any loud noises, unexpected sounds, or small jolts brought them on. People laughing. Doors shutting. Someone accidentally bumping into my bed. Just the noise of my doctors talking in their normal voices sometimes brought me close to tears. It was agonizing. People had to whisper when they came in the room. Coach O'Brien, who used to tap me on the forehead when he visited by way of saying hello, nearly made me faint when he tapped me during this period. I gave him such a nasty look I later called him to apologize.

The doctors couldn't figure it out. Everything in my body was out of whack, basically, so a symptom in one part of my body might really mean there was a problem elsewhere. In the same way my brain couldn't send messages to most parts of my body, my body couldn't send warning messages to my brain. My body's thermostat didn't work, for example. When a healthy person gets cold, he or she gets goose bumps. When a healthy person's hot, he or she sweats. Quadriplegics neither get goose bumps nor sweat below their level of injury. So when my body has something wrong with it—an infection, a broken bone, a kidney stone, a full bladder—it finds other ways to communicate to the brain. High blood pressure. Rapid pulse. Fever. Dizziness. Headache. Abdominal pain. This is called autonomic dysreflexia.

My doctors theorized these pains brought on by loud noises had something to do with my nerves being traumatized and supersensitive. Poor little lost souls, they'd been turned into a gang of juvenile nerve delinquents. Those may not have been the doctor's exact words. But as I understood it, my nerves, angry and confused at having been cut off from the mother ship—the brain—were screaming their bloody heads off at the slightest provocation, seeking guidance and direction: "Hey Travis! What the hell about *us!*" Then they'd zap me in the lower abdomen.

Just as suddenly as the pains started, they went away. It took about two weeks. There are still times when I get similar, but more moderate, spasms when I'm startled. It's like my whole body jumps internally, the way it used to when, as a kid, someone leaped from behind a door to frighten me. It happens to me sometimes when Maija says something in the middle of the night, when I'm not expecting it—just a quick flash of pain, below my injury level. It's the only thing I *can* feel below my shoulders. I have to remind her: Please don't startle me.

From my new quarters, I began to go down to therapy every day at 11:30 in the morning. I was the only patient from the spinal-care unit who arrived in a bed. Everyone else was in a wheelchair, but my bedsore still prevented me from sitting up.

My contribution to the sessions, at first, consisted mainly of providing body parts for the physical therapists to work with. They'd stretch me and range me, taking each finger and flexing it back and forth ten times. Then they'd proceed to the wrist, the elbow, the shoulder, the trunk, and so on—until each joint in the body, even my neck, had been wriggled and wiggled and flexed. It took about 45 minutes every day. The purpose was to keep my joints in working order and to prevent my unused muscles from binding up. Without the ranging and stretching, my fingers would have curled up into claws.

Then the therapist would check my progress by asking me to try to move in certain ways. Right from the start, my doctors expected me to be able to move my shoulders. A little, anyway. It's all predicated on where the spinal cord has been damaged. The higher up the spinal column one's injury is—the closer to the brain—the greater the extent of the paralysis. It's pretty straightforward. A C_1–C_2, which is what Christopher Reeve is, has damage to the spinal cord between the first and second vertebrae, which means he has no control over respiration and breathing. A C_3 is able to breathe and to move his neck. A C_4 also has control of his or her shoulders and upper chest. A C_5 can also move his or her biceps. C_8 is the demarcation point between being a quadriplegic and a paraplegic. For doctors specializing in spinal-cord injuries, how much movement a patient is able to recover after an accident is a fairly exact science.

That's important to know. Recovery from a spinal-cord injury has nothing to do with how hard a patient works, or how dedicated he or she is to walking again. Everyone who's ever been paralyzed will do anything to walk again. But for most of us, we may as well be trying to fly. The spinal cord is like a superhighway for millions of nerve fibers, or axons, that carry messages from the brain to the muscles. If you were to enlarge the spinal cord 10,000 times, it would look like a cable television line, with the nerve fibers represented by all those little strands of copper. Once that cable line is cut, or broken, it can't be repaired by medical science. Not yet, anyway. And how much movement and feeling one still has, where the paralysis starts and stops, is contingent solely on where the injury occurred. If the brain's messages aren't getting through because of a roadblock at Point X, nothing below Point X works.

I'm a C_4–C_5. The fourth vertebra from the top of my spinal column was shattered, and the spinal cord was damaged between there and the fifth vertebra—about the level of my chin. I've seen X rays of the area, and a dense white dot, about the size of the eraser on a pencil, shows up on the spinal cord where the damage has been done. That's the roadblock. Above and below that point, the spinal cord appears translucent. But that eraser-sized white dot prevents any messages from my brain from getting through. Above that white dot, all is well. Drill a hole in my tooth, and I'll feel it as assuredly as I ever did. The doctors, therefore, definitely expected me to be able to move my deltoids, which are the thick, triangular muscles covering the shoulder joint that raise the arm from the side. And they hoped I'd be able to move my biceps, which flexes the elbows, since the biceps are at the C5 level. The wrist and the fingers, which are controlled at the C6 level, they weren't as optimistic about.

So after stretching and ranging me, my therapist, Amy, would ask me to shrug. Bring your shoulders up and down, she'd say. Almost immediately, I was able to do it. It didn't surprise me very much. I remember thinking, Big deal. What good is it to be able to shrug? From a practical viewpoint, however, it meant that I might also someday get back the use of my biceps. If a C4–C5 can't move his shoulders, he'll never regain the use of his biceps, either. They work together. But no one explained that to me at the time.

For a couple of weeks, shrugging was the only thing I could do. Amy would say, "Travis, move your biceps." I'd try. Nothing. She'd raise my arm up and ask me to resist her. Nothing. It was like asking a noodle to flex.

It was disheartening. I was convinced I was never going to get better. There were times—many times—when there was nothing going on inside me mentally. I seemed to have lost my will.

Then one day, when Amy asked me to flex, she felt something. Not much. Just the slightest twitch in the right arm, so minimal I didn't feel it myself. But she did. She called another therapist over. She, too, felt a twitch. They got far more excited than I did, congratulating me as if I'd scored the winning goal in overtime.

When Maija came by that afternoon, Amy greeted her with, "We got the biceps back."

Maija burst into tears and ran to call her mother. As it turned out, that was a slightly premature diagnosis. Only my right biceps came back. My left one didn't, so my left arm, even now, is unable to move. But having the use of my right arm has enabled me to feed myself, to control the joystick on my wheelchair, to scratch my nose, even, when I want to. It's made all the difference in the world.

I didn't see it that way then, though. Everyone seemed to grasp the possibilities more clearly than I did. "Aren't you excited?" Amy asked.

I nodded. But I wasn't. I didn't even mention it to my parents when I saw them later in the day. I was thinking, What do I have to be excited about? A twitch? If I wasn't going to be able to walk and skate again, the rest of it didn't matter. The little things just didn't do it for me. Now, of course, I realize how much some quadriplegics would give to have the little biceps movement I do.

It was a week after Amy had detected that first twitch in the biceps before I could visually see my arm trying to move. Even then, it was just a tiny flickering of the muscle, easy to miss, not really enough to give me any sense of progress. After a couple of these miniflexes, the third try would be hopeless. My arm would go completely dead, as if someone had unplugged the juice. That's how weak I was, how little movement I had. In the left arm, I didn't even have that.

They finally began to wean me off the ventilator in late November, a process that had been delayed after I'd come down with a second case of pneumonia. For six solid weeks, the machine had been breathing for me, and the longer I depended on it, the weaker the unused muscles of my diaphragm became.

At the beginning they had me breathe on my own for five

minutes at a time. Then 10. Then I worked up to 30. It felt like I was breathing through a straw. When I tired, I'd start taking very short breaths and panting like a dog.

I began to talk when I was off the ventilator. Not fluidly, or continuously. I could speak only when I exhaled. Since my breaths were so short, that meant saying only one word at a time: "Hi . . . (breathe in) . . . Doc . . . (breathe in)." It didn't sound at all like my voice. It was very high and boyish, as if the words were coming from a different person entirely. Still, this was something about which I could get excited. Being mute for nearly seven weeks had been my greatest source of frustration, besides the accident itself.

I worked up to two words at a time: "I want . . . (breathe in) . . . to get . . . (breathe in) . . ." By December 11, I felt strong enough to try to make a call to my father, who'd gone back to Maine for a few days and still hadn't heard me speak. Mom was with me. She dialed, and was holding the phone for me when my father picked it up. I paused. "Hi, Dad," I said.

It didn't sound like me. But he knew. He got it. My father began to laugh and cry at once. I honestly had never heard him get more excited. It was, he later told me, a little like I'd come back from the dead. It was the first genuinely happy emotion he'd felt in seven weeks.

My next call was to Coach Parker. The secretary in the hockey office, Sue MacDonald, answered, and said that he'd just left. I said, "Sue, this is Travis."

She gave a little yell and said, "Hold on! I'll go catch him."

When he got to the phone, I said, "Hi, Coach." He was so excited that he, too, was laughing.

That night he came to the hospital, as he did just about every night. I'd grown to look forward to his visits so. He said he'd told the guys in the locker room that he'd spoken to me on the phone, and that everyone was excited and had passed along their hellos. Coach Parker was great about keeping me filled in on what was happening with the team. He'd tell me things even the players didn't know. Who was playing well and who wasn't. Line combinations he was going to try. Power-play changes. Who was starting in goal the next game. Things that no one knew besides the two of us, and maybe the assistant coaches. He let me into his inner circle.

I told him I had a favor to ask. Maija's birthday was coming up in mid-December. Months earlier, before the accident, she'd commented that she'd wanted a BU hockey jersey with my name and number on the back. You could have them made up at the Boston University bookstore. I asked him if I could give Maija my real game jersey, the one I was wearing the night I was injured. I didn't think I'd be needing it again.

"You got it," he said.

I'd developed a deep emotional attachment to Coach Parker. He was always quick with a joke. He'd threaten to put me through a quick round of Russian circuits if I didn't cooperate with my therapists. He knew when to just listen and when to say the right thing to cheer me up, to keep my spirits up. I don't know how he did it, because this was all new to him, too. He'd never had a player go through an injury like this. He became like a second father to me in the coming months.

I talked to him about things I was reluctant to get into with Dad. About hockey mostly, and how it had been such a big part of my life. Like a third hand. How it ached not to be able to get back onto the ice. My father and I didn't need to talk about those things, or want to, because Dad was feeling and experiencing the same sort of emotional loss as me. As much as I loved playing hockey, Dad loved watching me play it. We both knew how the other felt, and he was hurting, too. For both our sakes, he always tried to get me to look ahead to other things.

But I could talk to Coach Parker about how much I missed the whole scene. I had a bit of my mother in me, too, and she needs to talk about things. It hurts, Coach, I would tell him. Then I'd describe how it felt like there was this big hole inside me that I knew would never be filled. I had always made sure there was more to my life than hockey, but I knew for certain I'd never be able to find anything to replace it. That nothing would ever excite me again like hockey did. And I knew how close I'd come to having everything work out just the way I'd always dreamed.

I'm a crier, and if I feel like crying, I cry. Coach Parker would say to me, "Trav, just let it out," when he saw I was holding the tears back. He'd shed a tear or two, as well. That surprised me. I never would have expected that from him. But there were a lot of things I never expected from Coach Parker.

Afterwards, he'd wipe my face dry. And he'd wipe his own face dry. I always felt better, then, and I'd tell him that. I didn't want him worrying about me more than he already did, and I'd thank him and assure him that I was going to be okay. And this one time, when he turned to go, I said, "I love you, Coach."

I'd wanted to say it to him for a long time. My relationship with him had deepened that intensely.

He came right back with, "I love you, too, Trav."

I have a great deal of respect for that word. It was like I'd said in that speech I gave at Tabor on my twentieth birthday, that there are many different kinds of love. Love for family, love for friends, love for girlfriends. Love for coaches. And, as he's shown me, love for players. The next time Coach Parker came to see me, it was he who said as he was leaving, "I love you, Trav."

For me, that was a very emotional moment. "I love you, too, Coach."

And that's how we say good-bye to each other now, every time.

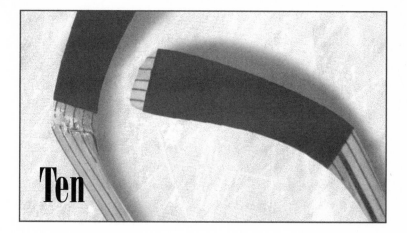

Ten

I tried hard, very hard, to hide how sad I was from my family. To have them believe that, psychologically, I was getting better. Adapting to my circumstances like a good soldier. It wasn't until later, when I was down at the Shepherd Center in Atlanta, that I realized I wasn't fooling anybody, that everyone knew my frame of mind.

I had known I wasn't fooling Maija. Every night I told her how sad I was. She was the only person I let down my pretenses around. She'd been my sounding board, the person I told everything to, the good thoughts and bad thoughts. I didn't tell my parents much of anything by comparison. She mostly just listened. She wasn't as emotional on the outside as I was. I cry very easily anyway, and just about every night, I cried. Maija hardly ever cried with me.

Sometimes that bothered me. The few times Maija did cry was when we'd speak of the things I'd miss out on because of my injury. Hockey was number one. She knew how much that hurt me, how much I'd enjoyed playing. She'd liked watching me, too. She cried when I told her how much it bothered me not to be able to hug her. It felt so good to give her a good hug, to have my arms around her and squeeze tight.

I asked her why she kept staying with me. I couldn't understand it. What did I have to offer her now? Why didn't she just leave and get on with her life? I'd understand. Was it that she felt trapped?

She said, "If I loved you any less, it would be impossible."

There was never a time when she sat down and asked herself, What am I going to do? Not once. She followed her heart, not her head. Subconsciously, I suppose, she must have faced that question, weighed her options, and decided that as bad as my injury was, as difficult as it was making our lives, it was not as bad as losing the one you loved.

But I couldn't bring myself to believe her. So every night I'd ask her again. What do I have to offer you? Why would you want to stay with me? How can you go on without physical contact? Ten times a night I'd ask her these kinds of questions. And she'd always respond perfectly. She'd give me an answer when I didn't think there was an answer.

Maija told me she didn't fall in love with me because I was an athlete, because I could run the mile fast or could skate like the wind. She said the things she loved about me before were still in me today. That what we had now wasn't better or worse than what we had before. Just different. Where before we had hugs, now we had head hugs. We'd put our heads together and she'd squeeze them closer for a long time with her hands. So I could feel the warmth and softness of her cheek. She said the head hugs were just as meaningful to her as a real hug. And I believed her. She gave me no reason not to believe her.

Sometimes with Maija I'd try to figure out why this had happened, what was the greater purpose. If something terrible had to happen, couldn't it have been quick and painless, like death? I used to compare them in my mind. Which would be worse? Death or being quadriplegic? I tried to weigh the pros and cons.

LEFT: *As far back as I can remember, I was always a hockey player. (Author's collection)*
BELOW: *I'm all smiles on the ice. (Author's collection)*

RIGHT: *I was a two-sport star at Tabor Academy, where I also played soccer. (Author's collection/Courtesy of Tabor Academy)*
BELOW: *Standing with my parents the day I graduated from Tabor in June of 1995. (Author's collection)*
BOTTOM: *Mom, Dad, and Maija offer me love and support. (Author's collection)*

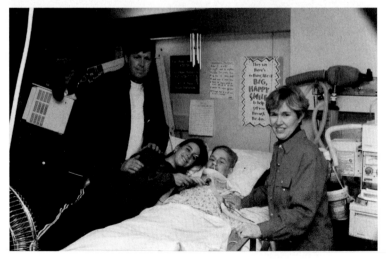

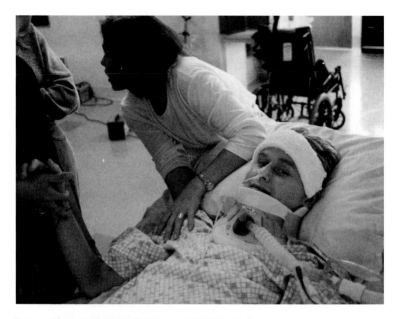

ABOVE: *During the early stages of my recovery. (Author's collection)*
LEFT: *I return home on a snowy April 13, 1996. (Author's collection)*

ABOVE: *There's no place like home. (Author's collection)* **BELOW:** *Practicing my unconventional painting technique. (Author's collection)*

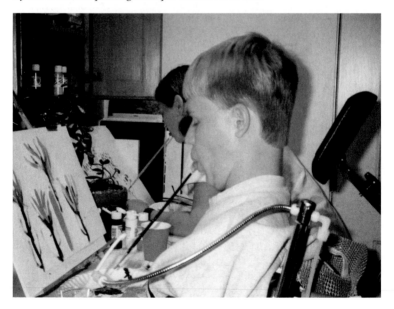

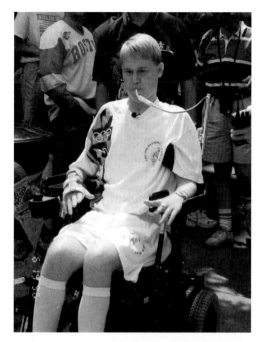

LEFT: *Carrying the Olympic torch en route to Atlanta for the 1996 Olympic Games. (Author's collection)*
BELOW: *Dressed to the nines at my sister Tobi's wedding in April 1996. (Author's collection)*

ABOVE: *Maija and I returning from an L.A. Kings fund-raiser in September 1996. (Author's collection)*
RIGHT: *Celebrating Christmas at Bob Taylor's house in Dallas. (Author's collection)*

LEFT: *Maija and I at the Mount Washington Inn last summer. (Author's collection)*
BELOW: *The Roy family Christmas card, 1996. (Author's collection)*

ABOVE: *Maija congratulates me after my speech at the* Globe All-Scholastics Banquet. *(Author's collection/Courtesy of* Boston Globe*)*

Thank you very much for
Your care and support.
I am home again, and
You have helped me to
face the challenges
which lie ahead.
          Sincerely
          Travis Roy

Was anything worse than this? But every time, I'd decide it was better to be quadriplegic. It was harder, but better.

Sometimes Maija would purposely walk through the chemotherapy ward on her way to visit me. There were a lot of worse things than being paralyzed, and you didn't have to look very far to find them. It made her realize—made us both realize—how lucky we were. "I don't do pep talks," Maija told me one time when I was feeling sorry for myself. "It's easier to find solutions."

She was my own private angel, carrying me through the desert.

I had a nurse in the morning, named Steve, who became a great friend, helping me through those early, difficult times. He'd do my bowel and bladder care, bathe me, and feed me. The whole experience at first is very much like returning to infancy. One day I was a 20-year-old Division I hockey star; the next day I couldn't feed myself, couldn't clean myself, and had no control over my bowels or bladder. It readjusts your thinking rather dramatically.

The routine is this. Each morning, upon waking, I'm given a suppository to trigger a bowel movement. That takes about an hour. I'm catheterized to empty my bladder, which takes about fifteen minutes. (The catheterization is repeated again at noon and a third time at night.) I'm bathed, dried off, and dressed, which takes at least another 45 minutes, depending on the strength of the person doing the dressing. So before I'm presentable, I'm two hours into my day.

One morning, after we'd gone through all that, Steve saw that it was snowing. He is a sensitive, compassionate man, with a wife and three beautiful daughters. I would love to be the kind of father he is someday. He was always doing things for other people that were above and beyond his job description, and Steve asked if I wanted to go outside. He thought that a little excursion might be good for my soul.

Of course I said yes. I hadn't been outside the hospital since my accident. This was just before Christmas. He rolled my bed onto the elevator, and we descended to the lobby level. Steve covered me with a thick blue comforter and pushed me out into the parking lot.

It was snowing hard but there was no wind, so the big, light flakes were falling straight down like white spiders dropping from webs in the clouds. I tried to catch the flakes in my mouth, snapping at the air, feeling them tickle my face. It was something I remember doing as a kid, remaining on my back after making a snow angel, opening my mouth so the flakes would descend into the terrible dark cavern of my mouth, lying so silently I could hear the flakes land against the nylon shell of my parka. When I'd catch one, there'd be this tiny wet burst of delicious cold in my mouth, like a bubble.

I wouldn't let Steve take me in. Grinning with delight, content to be alive, I stayed outside for close to an hour, long enough for the snow to have gathered in the folds of the quilt and for my pale, dry cheeks to have turned red from the cold. Maija, driving into Boston from Holy Cross, found us like that in the parking lot: me lying beneath that blue puff, stretched out on my hospital bed, trying to catch snowflakes in my mouth. It's an image she tells me she'll always remember—the first time since the accident she'd seen me happy.

It was not a happy Christmas that year, however. First Maija tried to decorate my hospital room. She asked two different nurses if it was all right. Then she went out with her father and bought a small tree, set it up in the corner, and decorated it with lights and ornaments. The balsam smelled tangy and wonderful in that sterile, antiseptic environment. But the head nurse, when she got wind of my tree, made them take it away because it was a fire hazard.

The hospital staff did allow me to go to Tobi's apartment to celebrate Christmas Day. The fact that Tobi was a registered nurse made all the difference. Everyone was excited, because it meant we could all be together on our favorite holiday in a place outside the hospital. And I think my family needed *something* to get excited about. It had been two months of hell, when you came right down to it.

They got me dressed, which was an adventure in itself, because it was the first time I'd been dressed in anything besides a hospital gown since the accident. Then they transferred me from my bed to a stretcher, and from the stretcher to an ambulance. That brought back all sorts of memories, none of them very pleasant. I lay on my back staring up at the ceiling, just as I'd done two months earlier. I was just as helpless, just as immobile. I could see the bright lights on the roof, feel the little bumps on the road, listen to the people talking around me. It all brought back the night of the accident, which didn't put me in a very good frame of mind.

There were piles of snow along the sidewalks, and it took the ambulance attendants some time to find a place where they could push the dolly stretcher from the ambulance to a cleared part of the sidewalk. Tobi and Keith lived on the first floor, fortunately, but it is still a few steps up from street level, and the ambulance attendants had to carry me up. It was about 11 A.M., and they said they'd be back at six that evening.

Tobi and Keith had tried so hard to make everything perfect. Our family had always had happy Christmases, and we'd hoped that, despite everything, this would be another. The apartment smelled so good. They put me on a bed that was covered with three soft quilts, to protect my bedsore. Tobi had set up a huge tree in front of the window, and a toy train was going around it. She was so looking forward to my reaction when I saw the train set, but from my position on the bed, I couldn't look down. I couldn't see the brightly wrapped presents around the tree. All I could do was stare up at the ceiling from my back and listen to the train going around.

I'd done no shopping, and at Christmas that's my favorite

thing to do. I'd much rather buy nice things for someone else than get them. I'd done no decorating. I'd sung no carols. So it seemed like just another day, except that I was out of my hospital room.

Keith's parents, Mr. and Mrs. Van Orden, were there, too. And they had a black, curly-haired puppy that climbed all over me. It made me think of my springer spaniel, Effie. I hadn't thought that much about Effie, and I suddenly missed her. They'd brought her to see me one time at the hospital, to try to cheer me up, but Effie hadn't recognized me. To her, I was just some body lying in a weird-smelling room who didn't even scratch her. I didn't look like Travis, I didn't sound like Travis, and I sure as heck didn't act like Travis. So Effie had ignored me, which didn't cheer me up very much.

Everyone had bought me presents, of course. I tried to show my appreciation. It's a challenge to buy something for me these days. You've got to be really creative. Clothes are pretty much the only option. Tobi got me a fleece sweatshirt from Eddie Bauer, and when she held it up everyone was saying how cozy and warm and soft it was. But I couldn't feel how soft it was. Its softness didn't matter much to me. I wondered if they'd thought about that. They got me some shirts, and a set of red, one-piece jumpsuit long johns. It was neat, but just try getting me into it sometime. It was all really great stuff, but none of the presents were very practical. At least that's how it seemed to me.

My father hadn't done any Christmas shopping that year. He said he hadn't had time for it. He's like me. He'd much rather buy nice things for someone else than receive them. But he told us right off that he hadn't been in the Christmas spirit, and he made no apologies. It was kind of sad, because we all knew it was his favorite time of year.

We tried to enjoy the holiday as best we could, though. Keith's mother made a delicious beef Bourguignon, which filled the apartment with the most wonderful aromas while it was cooking. It was so nice to be away from all the beepers and buzzers of the hospital, just to lie in an ordinary bed with soft pillows. That was the best part of the day. But it wasn't Christmas. What was good about the day had nothing to do with Christmas. What was good was the opportunity to get out of the hospital and spend time in a quiet atmosphere with my family. I didn't want to leave when it came time to go back.

Eventually we came to the conclusion that we could be getting better care than I was receiving at Boston University Hospital. My family came to that conclusion, rather. My weight, which had been 173 pounds at the time of the accident, had plummeted to 120. I was just bones and skin. Even after I was finally able to chew and swallow solid foods, I had no appetite. The doctors decided to put a feeding tube directly into my stomach, which was like eating an extra meal a day. That got my weight up to 130, but it also sent up a red flag about the level of attention I was getting. The hospital bed, we later learned, should have been on an incline as long as the food tube was in. Otherwise the food could have gone up into my lungs if I vomited as I slept and caused all sorts of problems, including asphyxiation and possibly death. It was not until the third day that anyone on the hospital staff noticed.

It wasn't the first sign we'd had of such oversights. Once I was due to have testing done on my ulcers, which required me to be anesthetized. For 24 hours before anesthesia, you're not supposed to eat, but my breakfast came the day of the testing, same as usual. It wasn't until my dad said something about it that the nurse looked up the schedule and took the food away.

And there were the continuing problems with my bedsore. By early January, the doctors at BU finally thought my decubitus was sufficiently healed for me to be put into a wheelchair. I hadn't been making any progress at all while doing therapy from my bed. I'd been there three months, and I still could only move my arm six inches, and that effort was so exhausting I couldn't move it again for half an hour.

So they brought a regular wheelchair to my bedside—one without a special cushion for my sore—and an orderly put me in it by a method referred to as a "football transfer." He lifted me out of bed by putting me under his arm, with my head leaning forward, like a man lugging a football. Or a football dummy. I hated it, and am at some pains to describe how awful and helpless a feeling it is to have your body flopping around beneath someone's arm, as if your skin is stuffed with straw. I felt like a suitcase. The orderly plopped me into the chair, propped me upright, and strapped me in so I wouldn't tip over. After three solid months of lying down, I was so discombobulated that I immediately became nauseous, began to dry-heave, and then passed out.

That went on for three days. Then, for the third time, the decubitus split wide open. That was the straw that broke the camel's back. My parents decided to look for another hospital for me that specialized in spinal-cord care.

As it happened, my mother was visiting Grandma Goodsell in Florida in early January. On the way home, Mom had to change planes in Atlanta. She got stuck there because Logan Airport in Boston was closed due to a major snowstorm. Mom waited out the two-day delay with my cousin Bill Roy. While there, she made some phone calls and was able to book a tour of the Shepherd Center, Atlanta's state-of-the-art, 100-bed hospital that provides specialized care for people with spinal-cord injuries.

She came home all excited. She had returned with a video about Shepherd, which showed some of the advanced equipment and technology that hospital had that were unavailable at BU. Shepherd had a swimming pool that patients used for therapy, and a gym. Mom mentioned several times that it had a pool table and a Ping-Pong table, as if that would tip the scales in Shepherd's behalf. "How the hell am I going to play Ping-Pong?" I asked her.

"Well, someone can help you play it," she said pleasantly.

It passed through my mind that Mom knew even less about Ping-Pong than she did about hockey, and I tried to tell her you couldn't play Ping-Pong with someone else holding your hand.

But she's a determined and persuasive lady when she gets something into her head. Shepherd sent up an evaluator to go over my records, to see if they felt they could help me and determine whether our insurance would cover the costs. It did. Once that was established, we had a family meeting around my bed to try to decide whether or not I should go.

I was given the opportunity to speak first. I was against leaving. I wanted to stay in Boston and remain close to my family and friends. I always had visitors: Angus, Matt, Ian Conway, Tony McNaboe, who was a kid I'd grown up with at Yarmouth. Coach O'Brien. Coach Parker. Maija's mother and sister. My cousins from Sudbury, from Belmont, from Vermont. My parents and Tobi and Keith. Every night someone would come in. It kept my mind off things. It was, frankly, the only thing getting me through. I especially wanted to stay close to Maija. She had been my backbone, the one listening to my problems each night, and I was afraid to leave her. I was in tears long before I was done. In no uncertain terms, I wanted to stay.

My sister was next. Tobi was concerned about the attention I was getting at BU. She cited the foul-up with the feeding tube. The continuing breakdown of my bedsore. And a couple of other less dramatic but troublesome incidents. She thought I should go to Shepherd.

Then came Maija. One of the biggest strengths about Shepherd, beyond their modern facilities, was the emphasis they placed on getting patients back into society. They took excursions out into the real world: to the mall, to movie theaters, out to dinner. There was no program even remotely like that at BU. Maija felt that, if I was going to get weaned off hospital life, if I was ever going to get involved in everyday life again, this was the best way to do it. She thought I should go. That surprised me, and upset me a little. Hers was the one vote I thought I'd get.

"Come on," I said. "Someone support me."

My mom followed. I already knew what she thought. Shepherd had originally been her idea. My father spoke last. He also thought I should go. My rehabilitation just hadn't been proceeding as well as it could have. The first six months after a spinal-cord injury are by far the most important in terms of recovering movement, and we'd already lost half that time.

So the vote was 4–1. But going into it, my family had made it clear it was my decision. It was up to me. If I didn't want to go, no one would force me.

Everyone left the room but Maija. We kept talking about it, and I kept returning to the one thing that worried me most: not being able to see her. She said, "Look, Travis, you can't be concerned about the distance between us. You have to be concerned about one thing and one thing only: getting better."

"Will you forget about me?" I asked.

"What makes you ask something like that?"

"Will you?"

"Of course not."

"Will you visit me?"

"Every weekend."

"Really?"

"Well, I haven't really thought about it before. But I will. I'll find a way. I mean it."

So I told her that if she promised to visit me every weekend, I'd go. Perhaps that sounds selfish. Perhaps it was. But that's how much I'd come to depend upon her, how much I loved her, and how much I feared losing her. She'd spent practically every day with me for the past three and a half months, getting me this far, and the thought of seeing her only on weekends was traumatic enough.

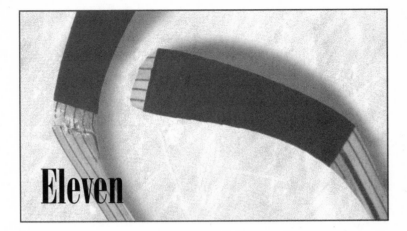

Eleven

On February 5 a medevac Learjet took me, my mother, and my aunt, Sandra Collins, to Atlanta. It was a two-hour flight, and I was strapped onto a stretcher with my nose about six inches from the ceiling of the plane. I didn't talk the entire flight, and the others thought I was asleep. It gave me a chance to think about the changes happening in my life. About being away from Maija. About the prospect of finally getting into a wheelchair. I was happy to be leaving the BU hospital. It felt almost like I was getting a fresh start. But I kept wondering why I was going all the way down to Atlanta. What could Shepherd do for me that couldn't be done closer to home? I still wasn't convinced that this was the right move.

From the Atlanta airport, it was a half-hour ride to Shepherd by ambulance. The hospital is located on a busy section of Peachtree Road, in a fashionable part of the city called Buckhead, a few minutes from the heart of downtown. It was a modern brick-and-glass building, with wide, well-lighted halls brightened by artwork. Within a minute or two of arriving, I was taken off for a fresh set of X rays. Then they showed me to the room that would be my home for the next nine weeks.

It was spacious and attractive, a single with its own large bathroom. It had a big window overlooking a garden with trees, which was a pleasant change from the brick walls I'd had for scenery in Boston. Looking at the bright blue sky and the sun and the leafy trees from my room made me almost feel like I was beginning to grow again. It was therapeutic. Everything I could see from my room in Boston had been dressed like winter—cold, gray, dormant, lifeless. In Atlanta the warmth and colors of spring raised my spirits by reawakening my senses.

What may have impressed me most about my new room, however, was a small detail emblematic of Shepherd's focus. Multicolored butterflies were painted on the ceiling of my room. For the past three and a half months, my entire world had been viewed while lying down, and here at last someone had acknowledged that simple fact. They'd made an effort to brighten my horizontal angle of regard with something more stimulating than white corkboard squares.

The room also had a television that swung around in front of my face, which, since my accident, was literally the first thing I was able to work on my own. That was huge. The controls were hooked up to a flexible, adjustable arm with a plastic straw attached to its end. This straw was called a sip-and-puff device. If I took the straw in my mouth and puffed, the television would turn on. If I sucked hard on the straw, it would turn off. If I drew air in softly, the channel would change. There were 12 different channels to choose from, and being able to change them without assistance altered my whole way of thinking. Suddenly I realized there were things I'd be able to do for myself, more things than I had ever imagined. For the first time since my accident, I didn't feel like I was six years old. If my mother and aunt wanted to go back to the hotel to go to bed, as they did that first night after dinner, I could stay up and watch television as long as I liked. You have no idea how good it felt finally to be able to assert some independence.

I had a second sip-and-puff device that was attached to my telephone. If someone called in, I could sip on the straw, and the speakerphone would click on. I could talk as long as I wanted, and when it came time to hang up, I sipped on the straw again. If I wanted to call out, I puffed on the straw, which connected me to a preprogrammed Sprint operator. He or she then connected me with whichever number I wanted. My phone bills at Shepherd were immense until I was given a complimentary calling card from Sprint. I called Maija, or she called me, every night.

A third sip-and-puff straw allowed me to buzz the nurses' station. After I sipped, a nurse would answer over the intercom, "Hi, Trav, what do you need?" No more banging on a clicker with my head, as I'd had to do at BU.

And so every night, the last person to leave—who was usually my father, who stayed in Atlanta with me as soon as Mom had to return to her position at Deering High School—adjusted all three sip-and-puff straws so they were inches away from my face, where I could easily reach them. I felt like a one-man band. Just having that much control of my life raised my spirits immeasurably. That alone was enough to justify my move to Shepherd.

It didn't take long for me to realize how special a place Shepherd was. Each morning I was awakened at 6:30, and my aide would put me through my bowel and bladder program, get me dressed, and feed me breakfast. I'd be rolled down to therapy around 8 A.M., for an hour and a half of stretching and ranging. My shoulders had begun to curve in unnaturally from those many weeks of lying on my side at the BU hospital, so a lot of the early therapy involved getting my clavicles properly positioned again. The therapist would gently pull my shoulders back, which was great because I could feel it. It took about six weeks before they were back to normal.

Around 10 A.M. I would be taken to Shepherd's technology

department, where I was introduced to everything from sip-and-puff wheelchairs, to voice-activated computers, to voice-activated environmental control units, or ECUs. An ECU costs about $7,000, and can control every electrical appliance in a room. I named my ECU Jim. He understood about 150 words.

"Jim," I would say, to get his attention.

"Yes," Jim would answer.

"Television." Like every other electrical appliance in the room, the television was plugged into Jim.

"Yes."

"On."

"Yes." The television would go on.

"Channel seven."

"Excuse me?"

"Channel seven."

"Yes." Click to channel seven.

Jim was not much of a conversationalist, but he had excellent manners. Jim could set the temperature controls on the air conditioner, activate the fan, turn on the computer and printer—a wonderful, clever fellow to have around. And no backtalk.

I had my first shower three days after arriving at Shepherd, and that, too, had a buoyant effect on my mood. At BU I'd had only sponge baths. Taking a shower was a lot more complicated. First I had to be rolled onto a nylon hammock that was then clipped to a metal frame. The frame, with me aboard, was wheeled down the hall and into the shower. To test the water temperature, my aide would aim the nozzle at my shoulders, where I could feel if it was too hot or too cold. But it was weird, because the spray would also be hitting my lower body, where I had no sensation whatsoever. It was like taking a shower in a rubber wet suit that stopped at the shoulders. The nurse would begin to scrub my feet and legs with soap, but she might as well have been scrubbing the floor, for all I could feel. The only part of the shower that was the way I remembered it was when she would wash my hair. It felt absolutely great to have the warm stream of water hitting my scalp, dripping down the back of my neck, and the nurse's fingers working the shampoo through my hair. It was heaven.

They were determined at Shepherd to get me into a wheelchair as soon as possible. My bedsore was pretty much healed, and to make sure it didn't break open again, the therapists fitted my wheelchair with a large, square gelatin-filled cushion that had a V cut out where my sore had been. That solved the problem.

Instead of putting me into the wheelchair by the "football transfer" method—guaranteed to dizzy and nauseate a patient who had been bedridden for 110 days—the attendants at Shepherd used a device called a Hoyer lift, which hydraulically hoisted me from my bed into the chair by means of a sling. It made the whole process smoother and nicer.

To help patients get accustomed to the feeling of being upright, Shepherd used reclining wheelchairs. I'd start out at something like a 45-degree angle, and they'd elevate me little by little until I asked them to stop. If I came too close to vertical, I'd get a queasy feeling throughout my body and my eyesight would go blurry. But every day I made progress. Every day I could comfortably be raised a little higher, though it was probably four weeks before I was able to sit upright in my chair.

I remember the first time Maija came down and saw me in the wheelchair. It was tough. All of a sudden it hit her: This was what life would be like. This was the reality of living with a quadriplegic. Maija had never known anybody in a wheelchair before. She'd never even seen a quadriplegic, that she could remember. So seeing me like that was hard on the eye. That big, cold chair showed the reality of the situation more graphically than anything she'd seen before.

"What do you think?" I asked her. But the reality of the situation had hit me, too, and I got tears in my eyes. Happy as we were to see each other, we both started to cry.

Prior to that meeting, whenever Maija had seen me, I'd always been in a hospital bed. It had been easy for her to believe I was sick, temporarily incapacitated, and that when I got out of that hospital bed, I'd be the same old Travis. That's what usually happened, right? When people got out of the hospital, they were cured. But the wheelchair brought it all home. She told me, "It takes some getting used to, seeing you in a wheelchair."

"For me, too."

"But this is you now," Maija said, managing a smile.

"It's me." I smiled, too. "Ta-daaa."

"It's big," she said, wiping the tears from my cheeks with the palm of her hand. "It's bigger than I pictured."

"You don't want to know how much it weighs," I said. "Go ahead and guess."

"I have no idea. A hundred pounds?"

"Four hundred and fifty pounds with me in it."

Maija's eyes flew open in disbelief. "Come on."

"It's true. Four hundred and fifty pounds."

"No wonder it looks big." She was examining it. I thought she might kick the tires. "It's still you," she said. "It's like a new part of your body."

"A movable part. Watch. Stand back."

I took the sip-and-puff straw into my mouth and gave it one hard puff. That shifted the chair from neutral into drive. Another hard puff started it forward. A soft puff turned it to the right, and as long as I kept blowing, it kept turning. With one breath I was capable of getting it to turn two 360s, if I so desired. I could pirouette. A soft sip, and the wheelchair turned to the left. A hard sip, and it stopped. Another hard sip put it into reverse.

It took some getting used to, to put it mildly. At Shepherd, they had us learn in the gym on a full-sized basketball court, where there was plenty of room for error. It took about a month before I was very accomplished, and until that time they put small yellow hubcaps on my wheelchair to show people that I was a rookie driver. As long as those hubcaps were on, you were not allowed to go anywhere by yourself without supervision.

Even so, there were near disasters. When the wheelchair is heading someplace you don't want it to go, the tendency is to blow harder and harder as your anxiety starts to build. You panic. But to turn, you have to blow softly. To stop, you have to sip. The first accident I had, I hit a door frame when I was coming in from the garden, wedging my two left fingers between the door and the wheelchair. I panicked and forgot that I had to sip hard in order to back up the wheelchair.

The second time was a near-death experience. I was on the sidewalk beside Peachtree Road with my father. The sidewalk angles slightly toward the road, perhaps for drainage purposes. To keep my wheelchair going straight down the sidewalk, I had to give my chair continuous soft puffs to realign it. I fell behind and got pretty near the edge, then started to panic. Instead of puffing softly, I puffed hard. That kept the wheelchair going straight toward the busy road, and my mind froze up. I kept puffing. I completely forgot how to stop. Suddenly I was right in the middle of a traffic lane on Peachtree Road. My father jumped in front of the chair and was physically trying to push against it before I toodled across all six lanes, but 450 pounds is a lot of weight to muscle around. Finally I regained enough composure to sip, and we reversed course and got the chair back to the sidewalk. We both looked at each other wide-eyed for a moment before speaking.

"That was scary," my father said.

Once the initial shock wore off, Maija got used to my wheelchair quickly. It was, after all, my entry back into the real world. Today, if she goes to touch me, she is just as likely to rest her hand on the back of my chair as she is to lay it across my shoulders. It's like the chair is part of me. She touches it as affectionately and possessively as she touches other parts of me. If another girl—some friend—absentmindedly puts her hand on my chair, or rests a foot on my footrest, Maija reacts the same way she would if that girl put her feet in my lap, or held my hand right in front of her. No matter how innocent it is, it makes her jealous.

I was so excited to be able to show her around Shepherd. It was so obviously a happy environment, a place where hope was restored. People were always zooming around in their wheelchairs with smiles on their faces. The staff felt good about their work. It was, simply put, a very positive place.

"Where Life Begins Again" is one of Shepherd's mottoes, and it was clear to both of us that it had been the right decision for me to come down. The weather was part of it. It had been such a brutal winter in Boston that year, and that first weekend Maija visited it was perfectly beautiful in Atlanta. Even in February, flowers were growing. We were able to sit outside in the garden to have lunch, talking and trying to figure out how things were going to work out between us. The birds were singing, the sun was out, the temperature was warm. Maija was feeding me my sandwich, and she said, "Trav, things really aren't that bad."

"I know they're not," I said.

True to her word, Maija came down just about every weekend, plus an entire week for spring break, using her father's frequent-flyer miles. I hadn't expected her to keep her promise. And it was kind of exciting because every time she returned, there were a few more things I could do.

As part of my therapy, several times a day I was hooked up to a machine that sent electrical impulses through my muscles, stimulating them to flex. Mainly they were concentrating on my biceps, both left and right. But only my right biceps was responding. Gradually, I began to regain some strength in that one arm. My occupational therapist, Marcie Sapir, would ask me to raise my arm two or three inches off my armrest and hold it for two or three seconds. Gravity was the barbell, and it was every bit as formidable as the 35-pound disks we'd used while doing Russian circuits at BU. I was so weak at first I couldn't raise my arm from my lap to my armrest.

I had a lot of fun with Marcie. She was in her midtwenties, about five feet eight inches tall, with light blond hair, very attractive, but she hadn't dated anyone seriously in about a year. She'd say, "Travis, can't you find any of your friends for me? He has to be Jewish and tall." By the time I left, nine weeks later, she'd dropped all the restrictions: "He has to be breathing." When ESPN and the *Today* show came to film how I was progressing, the other therapists were holding up signs in the background with arrows pointing toward Marcie: LOOKING FOR BOYFRIEND. It was the standard joke around Shepherd.

Marcie had two goals for me. First, she wanted me to be able to feed myself. Second, she wanted me to be able to operate my wheelchair with a joystick. I didn't believe I'd be able to achieve either one, but it gave me something concrete to work toward.

The biggest hurdle wasn't so much my lack of strength as it was my limited range of motion. I could move my right arm up— first a few inches, then a few more. Gravity would bring it back down. But I could barely budge my arm when I tried to go from side to side, or forward and backward. Just the friction made it impossible for me to slide my arm forward on the armrest. I'd have to overcome that if I were ever going to accomplish those two goals.

We started by doing a lot of my therapy in a swimming pool, which effectively eliminated gravity and friction. Marcie would attach a flotation device to me, then I'd paddle around in circles on my own, pulling and pushing my right arm through the water. Forward, backward, side to side. Up. Down. Forward, backward, side to side. I could do wonders in the pool. There's a serious difference between exercising with gravity and exercising without it. Sometimes I stayed in for up to an hour.

It was strange, though, when I was initially hoisted into the water. I'd see my feet go into the pool, then my legs, then my waist—but I couldn't feel anything. If I'd had my eyes closed, I wouldn't have known I was even wet. I'd be up to my chest, finally, and still have no sense that I was in an element that was different than air. I wouldn't know if the water was warm or cold. I wouldn't experience that wonderful silky sensation the cool water makes upon your skin. It was frustrating until I got up to my shoulders, which was when, suddenly, I could feel the wetness. And the cold. Even though the water temperature was always at least 85 degrees, it always felt cold to me. It took me several sessions before I got used to these things.

In the afternoons Shepherd held classes to educate us about our injuries and to answer our questions. They encouraged family members and loved ones—anyone who would be involved with your care—to attend the classes with you, and my parents and Maija did.

The Shepherd instructors went over bowel and bladder care, detailing the various options that were available to us. For our bladder program, we had chosen catheterization. A simpler method is to have a superpubic tube inserted directly into the bladder. That eliminates the whole need for catheterization. The bladder is constantly emptying into a small bag attached to your lower abdomen. Over time, however, the bladder starts to shrink up, because it's never distended. It's never contracting and expanding. Once the bladder shrinks, it never regains its original size and elasticity.

That isn't a problem unless there's a cure for paralysis. And I know there's going to be a cure. I know it. That isn't even a question in my mind. So, to me, there was no debate over which method to choose: catheterization versus a superpubic tube. It is short-term pain over long-term gain.

We learned more about dysreflexia, how the body communicates its distress to the brain after the spinal cord has been damaged. We learned how to prevent bedsores and skin sores, which tend to occur on the elbows and ankles of quadriplegics, since our arms and feet are always resting on an armrest or footrest. I learned to wear shoes that were at least two sizes too large, so my feet—always inert, always the lowest part of my body—would have room to swell comfortably. We learned about the different kinds of wheelchairs, the pros and cons of wet- and dry-celled batteries.

To know what was going on with my body, to have a working understanding of all the various procedures and options, was so important for my peace of mind. I no longer felt like a broken vessel in the hands of the doctors, totally dependent on their attention and care. I could begin to make informed decisions by myself.

Little by little, Shepherd also began to expose me to some of the recreational opportunities available to quadriplegics. A couple of times a week I took an art class, where I learned how to mouth-paint. I'd always enjoyed ceramics and sculpture, and had done some painting at Tabor. I'd found it a welcome diversion from the pressures of academics and sports. Mouth-painting was much the same. It, too, was a diversion from the pressures of my everyday life. The teacher would stick a brush between my lips, set the easel and the paints within range, and turn me loose. My mind, temporarily anyway, would get lost in the painting process and the scene I was trying to create.

I used an ordinary paintbrush that had tape wrapped around the handle. The more creases and bumps in the tape, the easier the brush was to grip. I painted with acrylics, and primarily tried to do landscapes—although I did do one picture of me in my Boston University uniform, and another of Maija's dog. But realism was difficult. I couldn't maintain full control over the brush, so painting straight lines was pretty much an impossibility. My mouth would get tired and sore, and things wouldn't come out exactly like I'd planned. So I was more or less forced into an abstract mode. Just the process of reaching all four corners of the paper was a challenge.

What I found, though, was that the mistakes sort of made the paintings. I stopped seeking perfection when I was drawing flowers, or rivers, or trees, because perfection just wasn't going to happen. So I tried to adjust to what *was* happening on the canvas. Being able to work with my mistakes, making them into part of the piece, even essential to the piece, was what maybe, just maybe, made the painting better than I had intended it to be. It was almost like a metaphor for life, because you're going to make mistakes in life no matter how hard you try to be perfect. It's how you cope with those mistakes that's important.

We watched films about other activities available to quadriplegics, too. I'm not much for blood sports, but I watched a videotape on hunting from wheelchairs. You got all decked out in camouflage gear in a blind, same as other hunters. The rifle was mounted on a bracket attached to the chair, and you aimed and fired it by means of a sip-and-puff. We saw pictures of former patients with dead deer in front of them. Gross, to my eye, but sort of amazing.

The important thing was to enable paralysis victims to enjoy whatever hobbies they'd had before their accidents. Someone had invented a device that held a fishing rod to a wheelchair, and you reeled line in or let it out with the press of a button. There was a film on quadriplegic waterskiing, which showed the skier sitting in some sort of basket on top of a water ski that looked like a cross between a snowboard and a surfboard. I'd done some waterskiing, so that looked like something I might someday be able to try, if I could muster up the courage.

One activity I did try at Shepherd was scuba diving. They put me in a wet suit, held a regulator up to my mouth, and once I was comfortable breathing through it, they took me down to the bottom of the pool. Then they kind of pulled me around so I could admire everyone's legs from below. But it was easy to imagine how much fun it would be to do the same thing along a coral reef in the Bahamas.

The point they kept drilling into us at Shepherd was that everything now would take a little more time and a lot more planning—but things were do-able. Flying in an airplane was do-able. Going to movies was do-able. Shopping was do-able. Going to work was do-able. So was going to school.

Unfortunately, quadriplegic hockey does *not* appear to be do-able. They haven't figured that one out yet. From experience, I can tell you 450 pounds of wheelchair skidding on ice would not be a pretty thing to be near.

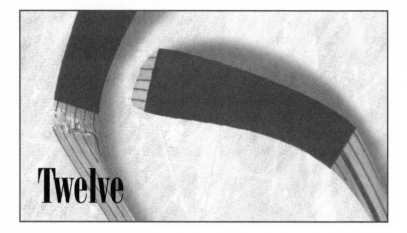

Twelve

About three weeks after coming to Shepherd, I went to a restaurant for the first time, and from that point on, we always ate out twice a week. A group of us would pile into a bus in our wheelchairs, anywhere from four to eight in number, and off we'd go. It was pretty comical. But most of the restaurants in the area were used to it.

The first time, though, was tough. It was definitely one of the low points of my recovery. My parents accompanied me to a place called the Black-Eyed Pea, which is only a couple of blocks from Shepherd, and as soon as I arrived I began to feel self-conscious. The bus pulled right up to the handicapped access outside the restaurant's door, and I was unloaded on a big lift. Then, once inside, the hostess looked at me and asked, "Are you Travis Roy? I've read all about you."

I couldn't believe it. My first trip into the real world, and the first person I meet recognizes me. She seated us in the middle of the room, and immediately I could see there was going to be a problem. My wheelchair was too high to fit under the table, so I was sticking way out into the aisle. Waitresses and patrons had to detour around me. The only way my mom would be able to feed me was by standing up from her seat. I was too far away for her to reach me otherwise. Everyone in the restaurant was watching us anyway, because of the chair, and possibly because some of them recognized me. All I wanted was to fit in normally. To be invisible. Then it suddenly came to me: This was what life was going to be like.

I lost it and burst into tears. It took about five seconds from the time we'd been seated. My mom began crying, too. We didn't have to say anything. We all were thinking exactly the same thing. And then I thought: I'm never going to go out again.

Everything I did those first few months was like a brand-new sheet of ice. All the experiences were new ones, and I couldn't foresee which would be easy and which would be difficult. I didn't know where the pitfalls lay. The things I'd learned in my first 20 years, the things I was good at before, were no longer of much use to me. It was like being two years old again. I was starting from scratch.

By the end of the meal, things had gotten better. We switched tables so at least we were seated in a corner, where I didn't feel like I was the main attraction at a freak show. My mother sat next to me and could now feed me while sitting down. But it wasn't enjoyable. It wasn't close to enjoyable.

Each time I ventured into public, however, things became a little bit easier. I learned, for example, to have my food cut up in the kitchen, so when it was brought to the table it was already in bite-sized pieces. We learned to ask to be seated away from foot traffic. It's an interesting phenomenon, but we noticed that the hostess or maître d', who ordinarily would confer with the man when a couple arrived at a restaurant—Smoking or no smoking? Table for two?—always ignored me and, instead, conferred with Maija. When it came time to give us the check, it was the same thing. It was as if my status in society had gone down because I was in a wheelchair. So Maija, on the suggestion of a woman who had gone through the same thing, learned to say, "You'll have to ask him," with a deferential nod in my direction.

As part of my reorientation to society, I went with a group to a shopping mall with a list of four or five things to do. I had to buy a greeting card, make a phone call, check out a bathroom, order food, take an elevator. All of those things required planning, but they were do-able. I had to keep my money in a pocket that was accessible to either a shopkeeper or my attendant. I had to ask the greeting-card store owner to read me three or four cards so I could select the one I wanted. I had to have a quarter handy for the phone. Planning was the most important element of these trips.

We took a field trip to the airport, too. As one of the Shepherd volunteers told me, if you can take a plane by yourself, you can go just about anywhere. A couple of Delta personnel showed us how to do an actual transfer from our wheelchairs—which were too big to fit down the aisle of a plane—to the dolly that flight attendants used to take wheelchair-bound passengers to their seats. You needed to take along an extra seat belt, which would be fastened around your chest to keep you from tipping over forward. You have no control over your torso, you see. But it was actually pretty simple to fly commercially, as long as you planned ahead and gave yourself extra time. Certainly I've flown more since my accident than I ever did before.

I'd become a pretty close friend to Steve Sheline, one of the other Shepherd patients, and on that trip to the airport we started doing figure eights in the terminal—not an easy thing when you're working a sip-and-puff device. It was the most pure fun I'd had since the accident, and watching us zoom around like a couple of kids put a smile on the faces of the passengers walking through the Atlanta terminal, too. Steve was a fun-loving guy, about 25, who'd been injured in a car accident one night with a friend he was living with, Pat Hogan. Both had broken their necks at the C5 level in the crash. It was a pretty amazing coincidence. I spent a lot of time with them during my stay at Shepherd.

Steve was a comedian. He always brought a smile to my face. Every Saturday night Shepherd showed a movie in the common room, and one time Steve and another patient named K.C. planned this big practical joke. They decided to steal the bowl of potato chips that were put out for everyone to enjoy as a movie-time snack. Not exactly the Great Train Robbery, but a pretty daring coup for Shepherd.

K.C. was a mountain of a man, with rolls of blubber stacked on his primary layer of blubber. The plan was for K.C., who was a paraplegic, to take his shirt off at the start of the movie as a diversion. I'm telling you, General Robert E. Lee had nothing on these guys. While everyone howled and guffawed and gagged at K.C.'s bare torso, Steve slipped away undetected with the bowl of chips. He made a beeline with the booty into my room, where my dad and I were watching television. We'd missed the whole thing. Steve, though, was happy to fill us in on the details of the heist. This was big entertainment for Shepherd, definitely a highlight of the week. He was pretty pleased with himself.

Finally my father said, "Great job, Steve. Now how're you going to eat them?"

Dad had that little wry look on his face, that twinkle I remembered seeing when he needled kids on our Mites team, back when I'd been a Mite for life. I laughed when I saw Steve's expression. His injury was such that he could move his arms sufficiently to lift an entire bowl, but he couldn't pinch his fingers together well enough to grab an individual potato chip.

My father reached over and plucked out a couple of the chips for himself, thanking Steve for his thoughtfulness. After enjoying his joke, Dad relented, of course, and fed Steve and me the chips. They were delicious. Steve had a theory that food always tasted better when it had been stolen.

*   *   *

On one of our outings from Shepherd we went to an Atlanta Knights game, which was a minor league team that played in the International Hockey League. A small group of us sat in the handicapped-access area, and I explained the rules of the sport to my cohorts, most of whom had never seen hockey before. That was icing, that was off-sides, that was a penalty. It was the first time I'd been in an arena since the night I'd been hurt.

My first reaction upon seeing it again was that hockey was an unbelievable sport. A wonderful, wonderful treasure. It takes the best aspects of a bunch of sports and combines them into one. Handling the puck in your feet like soccer. Contact like football. Finesse like basketball. The speed. Nothing has the speed of hockey. That alone sets it apart. Quick turns. Starts and stops. Crossing over.

I missed it. That was my second reaction. I'd forgotten how much I missed it. It wasn't the competition I missed as much as physically being on the ice. I kept trying to remember how the skates felt on my feet. The actual feeling of skating. The contact of the skate blade on the ice, the feeling of the edges cutting into the ice. It's an amazing process, when you think about it. A hockey blade is only 1/8 of an inch wide, and since it's rounded lengthwise, shaped like a bow, the portion of the blade actually touching the ice at any given time is no more than two inches. I don't understand the science of it—how two inches of metal blade can propel a 200-pound man as fast as Carl Lewis can run, then allow him to stop on a dime on a substance as slippery and hard as ice, without ever losing his balance. That a tiny length of steel on your feet is able to create such speed and grace and power is pretty miraculous.

I began thinking of the hours and hours I'd spent alone at night in my dad's arena. Just me and the sounds of hockey. The sound of a hard turn, of the blades carving chunks out of the perfect, smooth surface. The sound of a quick stop that sends the shavings up into tiny flakes. Of the puck hitting the boards in an otherwise silent arena. I don't know if I now relate more to the sounds of hockey than to the feelings because the sounds are still there and the feelings are gone—but I do. I relate to the sounds of the game that I so loved to play.

I want to re-create them. And I want to re-create the feelings that I associate with those sounds. I want to re-create a shot, twisting my body and following through the way I did so many thousands of times. I want to re-create the feelings of putting on my skates, of the laces stretching taut against my knuckles. You don't just lace up your skates and tie a knot. Oh no. You literally pull the laces as tight as you can between each pair of eyelets. Then you go on to the next pair of eyelets and pull tight again. Up and up, until you make a knot at the top that seals the boot of the skate to your feet. They become one. You cannot tell where the foot begins and the boot ends.

The process of lacing up those skates as tightly as I could, day after day, practice after practice, would rub the hair off the sides of both my hands. It would take all summer for the hair to grow back again. My hands were always dry and callused, from the lacing, but also from shooting buckets and buckets of pucks. The palms of my hockey gloves would wear out every couple of months, and I'd tape the palms to cover the holes. And the palms of my hands would blister, and then callus, and those calluses would stay on until summer.

I thought about those calluses as I looked down at my hands, and saw they were soft as a baby's skin, with hair growing on the backs and sides. Never in my life had my hands looked the way they did now. I thought about all those things while pretending to watch the Atlanta Knights game with my friends, the sounds triggering the memories, the memories triggering a longing that I had repressed.

That night, I returned to my room, and for the first time since the accident, I prayed to God. Religion was never a big part of my life. I believe there is Someone looking out for us, who will take care of us when we pass on. But I was never one to pray every night.

But this one time I asked God in my prayer: Why did it happen? I didn't understand why God would take everything I had going for me away. I wasn't angry. Or bitter. I just lay in my bed searching for an explanation.

I'd always believed I was a good person. A person who hadn't taken his blessings for granted. I spoke of that in my speech at Tabor, how lucky I felt to have the family and the friends I did, to be doing the things I was doing. I'd always believed that as long as I took note of how fortunate I was, nothing bad would happen to me. I don't know why I believed that, but I did. So I remembered to count my blessings. I distinctly remember doing that four or five times a week, when I was walking back to my dorm from soccer practice, looking around at Tabor's beautiful campus, realizing how lucky I was to be there. Or walking from my room in Shelton Hall to Keith and Tobi's apartment, thinking how great it was to be going to college in Boston, playing for the defending national champions. I didn't have a name for Whoever or Whatever I was trying to communicate these feelings to, but I wasn't just saying it to myself.

Sometimes I explain the way things have turned out this way: This life I'm now leading is not necessarily my own. It's not the life of the Travis Roy I was when I was growing up in Yarmouth. This is another Travis Roy. You understand? My personality has changed. I don't have the goals I had, or the excitement I had, or the confidence I had. I certainly don't have the fun I had. There are very few things I do that can be described as fun anymore. It's like I'm living my life as much for everybody else now as I'm living it for me. I've become something of a living reality check; I'm in a wheelchair so people will realize how fortunate they are. So people will realize just how much they have if they have their health. So people will, maybe, help out others like me a little more.

I don't like talking to someone like a minister about these

things, having someone probe into my spiritual side. I'm comfortable with my beliefs. I know that God could not do this to somebody, could not take away what's been taken away from me, without there being more to it. There has to be another side to this nightmare.

I know—and don't ask me how I know it, but I do—that when I die, I'll go back to the eleventh second of that game when I was paralyzed. *I know it.* I'll go back to that precise instant, only this time I'll finish my check properly, as I'd intended. I'll finish my shift. I may even score a goal.

The instant I die, I'll go back to that moment, and I'll pick up again with the life I was supposed to have lived. The life Travis Roy was supposed to have lived. The Travis Roy who grew up in Yarmouth, not the one who was born on the ice eleven seconds into his first college game. I'll be flesh and blood. It won't be my spirit that does the reliving. It'll be me. I won't remember that any of this ever happened. I won't have known the quadriplegic Travis Roy ever existed, and neither will anyone else.

I don't know if life goes on and on like this—dying and returning, dying and returning—until you somehow get your life right. It's possible. Maybe that's the explanation for déjà vu. When you *know* you've already done something, or been somewhere, but there's no way you can explain it, except by allowing that a tiny part of your brain or your soul remembers that you lived through it once before.

I first started thinking about all this after talking to my friend Tony McNaboe, from Yarmouth. When he was 14 or 15 years old, he got in a car accident with a friend. Neither one had a license, and they skidded off the road in the pouring rain, taking out a telephone pole, crashing into a drainage ditch, then flipping over into a driveway. They both lived. Tony blacked out but then walked away unscathed from the accident. But if you had seen the car, you would have sworn there was no way he could have survived. No possible way.

Tony and I talked about it later. This was long before my accident. He believed that he had really died in the crash, which was when he blacked out, but at the instant of his death he slipped into something like a parallel universe. It was *that* Tony who walked away unscathed from the crash. So the Tony I know now, my friend Tony, is living out his destiny.

At the time Tony was telling me about all this, it made a little bit of sense. Because you should have seen that car. There was no other logical explanation for someone walking away from it. But it was nothing I was going to believe. I mean really *believe*, whether it made a little sense or not. I mean, I wasn't crazy.

But I believe it now. Now it makes plenty of sense. Because I just don't believe an accident like mine could happen without there being more to it than Travis Roy spending the rest of his life in a wheelchair. That's what's impossible to believe. God wouldn't do that to somebody without there being another side to it somewhere down the road. Life has twists and turns in it for all of us to learn from: some put there for our benefit, some put there for the benefit of others.

I remember the first time I told all this to Maija. She listened to me thoughtfully, and then said, "So what are you doing? Getting all psyched up to die?"

I told her no. I'd live out this life and continue to learn from it and make the best of it. But I do look forward to my next life. My real destiny.

But Maija didn't like the whole theory. She asked me, "What does that mean for the rest of us, those who are part of your life now? Don't we matter? Aren't we real? Will we be part of this parallel life of yours, too?"

She's worried that I think this life, my life as a quadriplegic, doesn't matter to me, since it's not the life I believe I was meant to have. But I also believe the life I have now will eventually make sense on its own terms. Which is how I'm now trying to live.

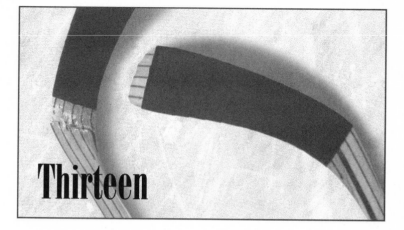

Thirteen

We had so many individual interview requests from news organizations that wanted to update my story, we decided to schedule a press conference at Shepherd for March 15.

During the week leading up to it, I did a series of one-on-one sessions. *USA Today* was the first to publish pictures of me in a wheelchair. After that story ran, Bob Hope sent me a nice letter along with an autographed picture. My father still teases me about that. After I read it, I asked him, "Who's Bob Hope?"

CNN came down. The *Today* show. *Good Morning America.* ESPN. All the biggies, doing follow-up reports on my progress. The most common questions were: What do you remember from the accident? and What have the last five months been like?

The interviews all went pretty well. I was calm. I just tried to be myself and answer the questions as sincerely and naturally as I could. There were something like 15 television cameras at the press conference, so I don't know why I felt so relaxed. It just didn't seem to me like a big deal. I still didn't really understand why they were so interested in me, since there are some 10,000 new spinal-cord victims every year. I had no concept of the millions of people who had been following my story. I remember the last thing I said was that I was looking forward to being home for my sister's wedding, and that they could all help my family by leaving us alone on that occasion. They did, too, which was nice.

So many friends came down to Shepherd to visit during my stay. Mr. and Mrs. Muther, my dorm parents from Tabor, flew down for four days with their daughter, Sam. Mr. Muther was my soccer coach and assistant hockey coach. Angus flew down with his girlfriend, Shannon McGrath. Matt Perrin. A friend from Yarmouth, Chad Drew, who was going to college at Brevard in North Carolina, came to Atlanta almost every weekend. We used to play street hockey together for hours on end—he lived right down the street—and had regularly destroyed his mother's flower bed beside their driveway. We hadn't seen much of each other through high school, and now Chad and I had a chance to renew our friendship. We had Easter brunch together at my dad's hotel, and Chad was still the entertaining kid I remembered, always quick with a joke.

I was excited for my friends to see me now, so they could tell for themselves how much better I was doing. None of them had seen me in a wheelchair before, and I enjoyed being able to go out with them to lunch or dinner, rather than trying to carry on a conversation while lying in a hospital bed. I didn't have to pretend to be in a good frame of mind, as I'd had to do at the BU hospital. I loved hearing them say, "Trav, you're looking good again." I'd gained back all the weight I'd lost, and before I knew it, my face started looking pudgy. I began getting a little double chin like my dad.

And best of all, Coach Parker surprised me by coming down one day for a visit. He arrived around noon, spent most of the afternoon hanging out with me at Shepherd, and was genuinely excited to see me doing better. He had relatives in the area, so he had dinner with them. But then he came back for about 45 minutes in the evening to say good-bye before flying home. It was clear that my accident had affected him deeply, much as it would have if it had happened to a member of his own family. Which I was, in a way. I was a member of his hockey family.

Coach Parker asked if I was coming up to the NCAA regional championships in Albany. Boston University was playing against Clarkson, and the University of Vermont was playing against Lake Superior State. A win over Clarkson would mean a trip to the Final Four, which was going to be held the following weekend in Cincinnati. It had always been in the back of my mind to try to make it back to a BU game before the end of the season, and the regionals now gave me that chance. After six weeks of progress at Shepherd, I felt I was up to making the trip.

My dad and I flew up the Saturday morning of the game. I left my sip-and-puff wheelchair behind and was given a manual chair that weighed only 40 pounds. That turned out to be a blessing when we discovered the Albany airport had no jetway. Two hefty ground-crew personnel had to carry me down the stairs. But even with that little surprise, my first commercial flight was a success, as routine as the Shepherd people had told me it would be when we'd practiced.

Dad rented a van, and we drove to the place where the team was having its pregame meal. I was nervous, but also excited. I didn't know if they were expecting me or not. As soon as Dad wheeled me in, all my teammates, the assistant coaches, Coach Parker, the trainers and managers—everyone—stopped eating and stood and clapped. It was so great to see them, but I really didn't like that. I didn't want the special attention. I just wanted to be part of the team. And naturally once the clapping started, the tears started flowing—most of them mine and my dad's. So many memories came flooding back. I wanted to jump right out of my chair and give every one of my teammates a hug. My linemates, Chris Drury and Mike Sylvia, came over to say hi. The captain, Jay Pandolfo. My roommates, Dan Ronan and Michel Larocque.

I'd lift my right hand up from the armrest so they could squeeze it, and tried to act as natural as possible. "How's it going?" I'd ask. Or "What's up?" They had a big hockey game to play that night, and I didn't want to be a distraction. Those guys had enough on their minds.

After the meal Coach Parker asked me what I'd like to do before and during the game. I was still part of the team as far as he was concerned, and short of asking to center the power play, I think he'd have gone along with almost any request I made. I told him I wanted to be in the locker room before the game. I knew it would be hard. I knew there was a good chance I'd get emotional. But I wanted to try it, to see if I would still get enjoyment from being around the game and around the team.

It felt strange arriving at the arena two hours before game time in a wheelchair. I already knew how much I missed playing the game. Watching the Atlanta Knights game had reminded me of that. But I'd forgotten how much I missed the locker-room scene. Just the ordinary stuff. The preparations leading up to game time. Taping your sticks, taping down your shin pads. Feeling the pressure nice and snug against your legs. The banter and the slowly building tension.

I'd never been on a road trip with the Terriers before, and this was so much bigger and more exciting than anything I'd ever experienced. The NCAA play-offs. I'd always dreamed of them. Lose tonight, and the season was over. Everyone seemed to know exactly what they were doing. Three or four trainers scurried about their business. The coaches walked nervously back and forth, reporting on the progress of the UVM–Lake Superior game. The players quietly stretched and talked in twos and threes, or sat off by themselves, mentally preparing for the game. It was like a big family.

But it was a family I no longer felt part of. No matter how hard Coach Parker tried, how hard the guys tried, how hard I tried, it was a little awkward for everyone. I hadn't spent that much time with my teammates before my injury. I was hurt in the first game of the season. I'd missed the entire year. The other freshmen—my roommates, Dan and Michel, Albie O'Connell, Brendan Walsh—weren't like freshmen anymore. They were equals. They'd proved themselves to their teammates, and now everyone was on the same level. I hadn't been there long enough to prove myself, to make the sorts of friendships one makes as part of a team, the friendships that never go away. Hearing the way they talked to each other and kidded each other made me realize how far they'd gone without me in the last five and a half months. How far I'd been left behind. I was an outsider. A guest.

Then Coach Parker came into the room, and the whole atmosphere changed. His presence in a locker room was huge. The players hung on every word he said. His energy, and the energy of the guys, started to build. And the more it built, the more I remembered that incredible feeling. The oneness. The sense of going to war together, knowing that in a few hours, there will be a winner and a loser, and how you handled yourself in the interim might make the difference. The sense of responsibility you felt to the man beside you, the man across from you. The singleness of purpose shared by every person in the room. I missed it. I missed being a part, *really* a part, of it. Which is when I realized I was going to lose it. I was just so sad to be missing out on this. Sad that it had all ended so soon.

The coach saw it coming. He came over and gave me a hug. I wasn't uttering a sound. My face was as expressionless as I could make it. But I was weeping. The tears were rolling down my cheeks. I couldn't stop them.

"This sucks, huh?" he said.

I nodded. He got behind my chair and pushed me out of the locker room. Dad met him in the hallway, just as we were going out the door. I tried to compose myself as quickly as possible. I wanted to wish them luck on their way out to the ice, and the last thing I wanted was for the guys to be worrying about me before their play-off game.

It was such an emotional day for me. The University of Vermont ended up winning the first game in overtime, and I wanted to go in and congratulate them. I was so pleased for the team, which had never made it to the Final Four; so proud of my dad's alma mater. And I was right there in the hallway outside their room. Plus I'd been recruited by the coaching staff, and knew a couple of their players. But almost as soon as I went in, I got choked up again, and sort of lost it in the midst of my congratulations. It took their mind off the game pretty quick, I know that. Real quick. Seeing me made them all realize there's a lot more to life than winning a hockey game.

I was emotionally drained before the BU-Clarkson contest even started. I wanted BU to win, of course, but nothing really meant that much to me. Nothing registered. It was almost surreal: 15,000 people watching my teammates play hockey, and me sitting motionless in a wheelchair. I was in a fog the entire time. I didn't follow the strategy. I didn't feel any anxiety. No adrenaline. That's another thing I lost when I was injured—my adrenaline glands no longer seem to work. Things happened, and I watched them without thinking about them. It was like I was in a glass room by myself watching everything go past.

The Terriers won, 3–2. But what I remember best about that game was that it became clear to me—painfully so—that I'd never enjoy watching hockey the way I enjoyed it before. I used to study the game, to watch for individual skills and subtle moves I might be able to incorporate into my own game. There was no point in doing that anymore.

Worst of all, every time someone got hit, or went into the boards a little funny, I'd cringe. I'd watch to make sure they'd get up. I wouldn't follow the play. And it happened all the time. They went into the boards funny all the time. So I couldn't help wondering, Why doesn't it happen more often? Why aren't there more injuries like mine?

I've learned since then that serious cervical spine injuries are more common in hockey than you might think. Certainly more common than I'd been aware of, and more common than they used to be. My father, who's been around hockey his whole life, had never heard of a single permanent spinal-cord injury before mine. But in 1995, the year I was injured, USA Hockey statistics show I was one of four players who became quadriplegics as the result of an on-ice injury. A fifth player became a paraplegic. In Canada the numbers are even more alarming: Hockey is responsible for creating an average of four quadriplegics every year for the past 15 years.

Chris O'Sullivan, who had scored the first goal of the season in the game in which I was injured, fractured one of his vertebrae his freshman year, but was fortunate not to suffer any damage to his spinal cord as a result. Less than three months after my injury, there was another terrible incident in Walter Brown Arena, not 20 feet from the exact spot where I'd broken my neck. A Suffolk University player named John Gilpatrick compressed his spinal cord when he banged his head on the ice, and he, too, is now a quadriplegic. His is a very rare kind of quadriplegia. John has the use of his legs, but not his arms, torso, or shoulders. He also ended up at Shepherd, and we crossed paths there my final three weeks.

No one knows quite what to do about this terrible trend. USA Hockey officials are trying to teach kids to get their heads up if they're going to crash into the boards, so you hit the boards with your face mask rather than the top of your helmet. That way the neck tends to bend to absorb the blow, rather than straighten and become compressed. That probably would have saved me. Not that I had any time to react. Things happen so fast in hockey, the players are skating so hard, and so much of the action is near the boards, that you wonder if they'll ever be able to eliminate these tragic injuries entirely.

A lot of people, including Coach Parker, think that the face masks themselves are a big part of the problem. Ever since they were made mandatory in the early 1980s, kids who play hockey have grown up without any healthy fear of the speed, the sticks, the elbows, the puck, or the boards. They're not afraid of playing out of control. Of going funny into the boards. Of crashing into the net. They feel invincible.

All I can tell them is, they are not.

Probably the best thing about that emotionally draining weekend, for me, was seeing my mother again. She'd missed out on so many of the good things that had been happening to me in Atlanta. Mom had been sitting up there in Maine all by herself, coping with a difficult situation at her high school. A new principal hadn't worked out, and my mom, in her capacity as one of two assistant principals, took on many more responsibilities. As if she didn't have enough on her mind.

She'd put in a long day at school and go back to that cold, drafty house at night by herself. She was in the midst of having an addition put on the house, overseeing the tearing down of our barn to make room for a wing that would accommodate my special needs. Mom was working with Alan Mooney, an architect, and the many, many other volunteers who put in hours of their own time to get the addition done in time for my return. Excavators and builders and roofers and painters—more angels carrying us along. We ended up sending 45 separate thank-you cards to people who'd donated time or supplies. Most of it while Dad and I were in Atlanta.

We'd call home just about every night, and Mom would be alone eating take-out pizza. She never complained, but it must have been so tough for her to hear about everything that was going on over the phone. We almost tortured her with details of how much better I was doing. She would much rather have been down in Atlanta with me and Dad, but someone in the family had to start living a normal life again. I was just beginning to appreciate how extraordinarily capable she was.

My release date from Shepherd was fast approaching. One of the first things they had done after I got there was give me a date—April 11—when I'd be going home. The average stay was eight weeks, but I was scheduled to stay nine. By that time, they figured they would have done as much for me as possible, and there was a long waiting list of new patients for every open slot.

I was not yet feeding myself, nor was I using a joystick to steer my wheelchair, but I had definitely gained strength and range of motion in my right arm. Marcie, my therapist, believed that by the end of the summer I'd be doing both those things by myself. It seemed like all the other patients there had improved more than I had. My friend Steve, a C5, had continued getting back more feeling and more movement his entire stay at Shepherd. His progress was truly extraordinary. When I went back for my eight-week checkup, in fact, he not only had a full range of motion in both his arms, he was using his fingers a little bit. By then he could have eaten that whole bowl of potato chips, no problem.

My father asked me if it bothered me to see everyone recovering more movement than me. But I was happy for them. Genuinely happy. They were going to have a better life with each muscle group that came back, and knowing that made me feel good. My own situation had nothing to do with theirs.

Leaving Shepherd was bittersweet. I couldn't get out of Boston University Hospital quick enough, once I'd decided to leave. But with Shepherd it was completely different. I'd loved my time there. When I thought about going home, of not having a professional nurse to call to on my sip-and-puff, it scared me. I'd felt safe my entire time at Shepherd. I was never sick while I was there, never had the flu or a cold or an infection. I was always getting better. It was a healing environment.

The night before I left, Steve came down to my room to talk.

What a good man he was. One of the best people I've ever met. A young girl, 15, had come to Shepherd three weeks before my release date. She'd been in a car accident, and now was a paraplegic, and one of only two female patients in the hospital. She was very young, very immature, and very negative—a squeaky, high-pitched nuisance, in my book.

"I'm not going to do therapy" was her attitude. Day after day we listened to that. It drove me nuts, and I wasn't going to have anything to do with her.

But Steve reached out to her. He used to go down to her room to talk. He took her under his wing and made her look at things more positively. By the time I left, she'd already changed her outlook, and today, believe it or not, she's walking with a cane. A paraplegic, and now walking with the help of a cane. Hers was one of those cases where it turned out the spinal cord had only been bruised.

I wonder, though, if that girl would have gotten where she is now without Steve's help. His cheerful nature had been such a joy to all of us during my stay, and he'd been helpful to me, too, when my spirits wavered.

That last night he told me something that took me by surprise. He told me I'd helped him, too. He said he'd learned a lot from me, that my attitude had helped him to stay positive about things.

It made me feel good. You don't always realize that what you're doing, how you're behaving, is affecting other people. So we ended up thanking each other. I was going to miss him. I do miss him.

But I was also ready to leave. I wanted to get home. I'd spent enough time in hospitals—nearly six months. As comforting as Shepherd was, I'd done everything there that I could, and they'd done everything they could for me. It was time to face the real world again.

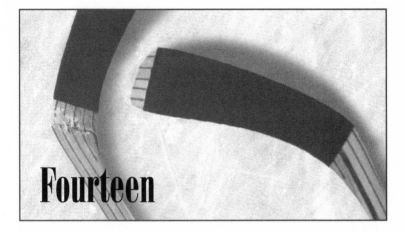

Fourteen

We were hoping to arrive in Boston without any fanfare, but someone at Delta released my flight information, and when my dad and I got off the plane at Logan we were met by the rest of my family and every news camera in the state. I gave an impromptu press conference, saying how great it felt to be back in New England, and that I was doing fine. I thanked everyone for their encouragement and support.

When we checked in at the Boston Harbor Hotel, the bellboys all greeted my parents by name. "Great to have you back, Mr. Roy, Mrs. Roy." It was a beautiful spring day, and while the van was being unloaded, I was sitting out on the sidewalk in my chair, letting it all soak in. I think two cars went past before the third one honked and the driver waved. Then another car slowed down, and the driver rolled down his window and called out, "Welcome back, Travis. You're an inspiration." A pedestrian stopped and said, "You're Travis Roy," as if I were suffering from amnesia instead of paralysis.

"Yes. I am," I confirmed, not quite knowing what I should say next. It was beginning to register that, whether I liked it or not, I was a recognizable face.

We had to hustle to get down to Bourne, on Cape Cod, where the Tabor alumni were playing a team of Boston Bruins old-timers in a benefit hockey game for me. I was excited. I looked good and felt good, and it was obvious to everyone that things had changed for the better since I'd left Boston nine weeks ago. On the long drive down, I just closed my eyes and listened to my family talking.

We arrived at the game near the end of the second period. The place was packed. The rink seated 1,200 people, and they'd sold something like 4,000 tickets. I watched from a little passageway beneath the stands where the spectators couldn't see me, and the players participating in the benefit didn't know that I'd be there. So it was a pretty big surprise when, at the presentation after the game, I drove my chair onto the ice with my sip-and-puff. A roar of recognition broke out, and everyone stood up and clapped, long and loud. It was another extremely emotional moment. A lot of the players were in tears. One of the Bruins alumni—I didn't know most of their names—took my hand, and then three or four other players followed his lead. It's tiring for me to shake hands, and pretty soon the players were just grabbing my hand as it stuck out from the armrest and giving it a shake. Then they presented me with a check for $24,000. I couldn't believe it. One small benefit game in one small rink. It was just another example of how human angels were carrying us along. I never knew, and still don't know, how to properly thank all the people who have helped me and my family.

My Tabor coach, Tim Pratt, was one of the people I saw at the game. His wife, Kerri, was expecting their first child any day. He called me a few days later from the hospital.

"Good news, Trav," he told me. "Devon Travis Pratt was born this morning."

"You're kidding."

"Nope. I'm not." It was the greatest gesture that Tim, a new father, could have made to show me what I meant to him. That first year Mr. Pratt was head coach at Tabor, we had been through a lot together. He wasn't naming his son after me because I was a good hockey player. It was the way I'd handled myself away from the rink, the way I'd tried as hard as I could academically, the way I'd treated other kids, the way I'd tried to help him out with the team off the ice, too, that made me someone special to him. It really made me feel good to hear that.

We had a full schedule those first few days in Boston. I'd been invited to throw out the first ball at a Red Sox game, and a couple of hours before it started I went to Fenway Park to meet some of the players in the locker room. Roger Clemens made a point of coming over to talk to me, and he gave me a pair of cleats and his warm-up jacket. Mo Vaughn and Jose Canseco each gave me a signed bat. Everyone was extraordinarily kind.

When it came time for the ceremony, the crowd—and it was a full house—gave me a standing ovation when I was introduced. This celebrity business was all new to me, and enjoyable as it was to be noticed, and to meet all these famous people, I'd gladly have traded places with anyone up in the crowd. In a heartbeat. I never forgot for a moment *why* I was a celebrity.

I couldn't actually throw the ball, naturally. I couldn't even hold one. So they'd taped a strip of Velcro to the baseball, and another strip of Velcro to the wrist brace that supported my right hand. That gave me a grip that was the envy of the entire Red Sox bullpen. Thus outfitted, I sipped and puffed my way to home plate, turned my arm over, and the catcher, Don Haselman, caught my best gravity-propelled sinker. Play ball!

That night I took Maija to the Chart House, which was our favorite restaurant in Boston. The last time we'd been there was before the 1994 Christmas ballet, *The Nutcracker*. It was just the two of us. When calling for the reservation, I'd asked for a table on the ground floor that was wheelchair accessible. So everything went without a hitch, thanks to all the practice we'd had going out to eat from Shepherd. I can't tell you how enjoyable it was to be doing something somewhat normal again. Then the waiter gave us a nice surprise by telling us not to worry about the check. Bit by bit, I was beginning to understand the impact my story had had.

Of course I'd been aware of the thousands and thousands of letters that had been sent to me. Boxes and boxes of them, many with small contributions to my fund. When we were in Atlanta, my father spent hours every day answering them. But for some reason, I hadn't realized it was the common, everyday working people who were writing me. I'd assumed most of the letters were from grandmothers with nothing else to do, or people in the hockey community, or religious people, or friends, or relatives of friends.

But it was everyone. Right across the spectrum. It was union workers, presidents of corporations, men, women, of all races, religions, and walks of life.

That message was further reinforced the next day when I went to the Copley Place mall with the whole family. All the other shoppers were turning around and looking at us. "That's Travis Roy. . . ." I could hear them saying. Some would come up and talk, telling me how admirable they thought I was. Or that I'd been in their prayers, and that it was good to see me out of the hospital. Some would just stare as they passed by. It was such a weird experience having people know who I was.

I liked it, though. I liked that people knew what I'd been through, because from where I was sitting it felt like I'd been through a lot. I also liked the idea that, because of me, some people were more aware of spinal-cord injuries than they'd ever been, and could see that a quadriplegic was able to go out and about and didn't have to stay under constant care in a nursing home.

The next day it was back up to Maine for my big homecoming. It was snowing and wet and gross—a typical April day during mud season. On the lawn outside my house was a big board that read: WELCOME HOME, TRAVIS. But I hardly noticed it.

The barn that had always been attached to the side of the house was gone. In its place was a huge extension, fronted by a wheelchair ramp that zigzagged into the middle of the yard. I couldn't get over how big the whole thing was. The original house was built in 1840, and the addition looked twice its size, with two stories and a full basement.

The cellar was the idea of a friend of my father's from Harrison, Maine, named Gary Searles. It's another one of those angel stories. He'd pumped gas with my dad in the summers when they were both in high school, 1963–64, but they'd gone their separate ways and hadn't seen each other half a dozen times since. Mr. Searles had never met me in his life. But when he heard about my accident, he wanted to do something to help. Once he found out we were tearing down the barn to put on an addition, he told my father, "Good. I've found something I can do."

He owned a construction firm, and said he'd send some trucks down to cart away the barn. When he got to our house, he took a look at the construction plans for the addition and asked my mom why we weren't putting in a full cellar. Too expensive; hadn't really thought about it, my mom replied. Mr. Searles figured out it would give us something like 30% more space in the living quarters to have a full basement, so with Mom's okay, he had his crew dig the foundation. Then he arranged for a friend of his to put in the forms. Someone else donated the cement.

It was a house unto itself, with room for a full kitchen, a dining area, a living room, an upstairs bedroom, and a large, handicapped-accessible bathroom. With the help of volunteer labor and donated supplies, the whole thing had been built for well under $100,000.

But as grateful as I was—and still am—for the addition, it made me sad the first time I saw it. I liked our house the way it had been. I liked the barn. All my hockey sticks had been stored in that barn, all my dad's tools, and the shell of the Porsche he was always working on. It had always been chock full of junk, but it was the kind of fun stuff that one always finds in a barn. It was where we kept our woodpile. The last thing I did before going to BU as a freshman was to fill the woodshed in the barn all by myself. That was my project, my share of the work that had to be done around the house before I went to college. Now that woodpile, too, had disappeared.

I had somehow imagined that when I got back into my house, everything would start returning to normal. It was just one more shock to find that the home I'd lived in for 20 years wasn't the same. It was as if everything in the world that had been important to me had changed. The doorways inside the house had been widened to accommodate my wheelchair. We had to move carpets around, and tables, because I was banging into furniture right from the start. We had to get rid of 150-year-old doorsills because they'd set off muscle spasms when the wheelchair rolled over them. We had to cut the corner off the kitchen counter so I could maneuver around it. I found it very unsettling to have to re-arrange the scale of that old house.

And, worst of all, my springer spaniel, Effie, still didn't recognize me. I was hoping that now that I was out of the hospital she'd see I was the same old Travis. I'm definitely a dog person. I played with her more than anyone else. But I didn't smell the same or look the same or talk the same, and I couldn't scratch her or rub her ears the way I used to. I was just some stranger in a big awkward chair.

That first night home was terrible. My parents got me undressed and ready for bed—they had done all my personal care since I'd come back from Shepherd—and after they walked out of my new bedroom, I couldn't help myself. I was having a hard time believing this was how things were really going to be. I started to cry. Why would you make anyone go through this? I wondered in a silent prayer. This can't be real.

I was beyond depressed. My dad came back in and saw me lying alone in bed crying, and he broke down, too. Really broke down for the first time since my accident. It was as sad as I'd ever seen him. We talked about how shitty this was, how it sucked, using those exact words, which I remember because my father and I rarely swear. He hugged me. And we lay there in each other's arms, crying. Everybody had been so strong throughout the whole ordeal, and my dad had been the strongest. He deals with his problems by himself. He doesn't share them. But now he was letting it out. I cried myself to sleep that first night home.

The next morning my new care attendant came. My mother walked through everything with her, showing her how we did things. But that, too, was difficult, having a stranger come in from outside and do all my personal care—my bowel care and bladder care and bathing and dressing and feeding. Knowing that was the way life was going to be from now on. Which it is. And while you never quite get used to it, you learn to live with it because you have no other choice. But the first time for everything is tough.

Dinnertime, however, I loved. Being in my own house for a home-cooked meal. The food and the smells of it cooking, which you never get in a hospital or hotel. Eating off familiar dishware, the light brown ceramic plates we'd had for years, hand-thrown in Freeport, with small flowers in the center and a blue border on the rim. I never appreciated before how much of a difference dishware made. I never appreciated so many small things that now are the joys of my life. I remembered how my father had told me way back when I was in the BU hospital how great it would be to sit around the dinner table with the family. And I'd thought, That's what I have to look forward to? But he was right. It is great. I look forward to dinnertime every day.

Effie began to suspect I might be someone familiar. Maybe. The first sign of recognition came a few days after I'd returned home. My room was at the opposite end of the house from my parents' room—too far away for them to hear me calling. So my parents got one of those baby monitors, putting the transmitter in my room and the receiver in theirs. If I needed anything in the middle of the night, I'd call out, and the monitor would pick it up.

One night, shortly after I'd returned home, my father turned off the monitor so he wouldn't overhear the phone call I was making to Maija. I used to call her at Holy Cross every night. He went to bed without turning the monitor back on.

During the night, my blankets slipped off my shoulders. Since my shoulders are the only part of my body I can feel, when they're cold, all of me is cold. I had no way of readjusting the covers. I tried to put the chill out of my head, but it was useless. So I finally called to my parents for help.

They couldn't hear me. The monitor was off, the door to the addition was shut, and I was at the absolute opposite end of the house. I can't shout very loud anyway, since my diaphragm is only about half the strength it was before my accident. But I kept trying. And the more I tried, the more helpless and frustrated I felt. I screamed at what, for me, was the top of my lungs. Over and over, I shouted into the darkness.

It was just loud enough for Effie to pick up on. She came running downstairs barking. I heard her scruffling around outside the door, letting out an occasional yip. "Come here, Effie. Come on, girl. Good girl."

Some overgrown path in her brain must have beckoned, a path she recognized as having once known and loved. I like to think so, anyway. She hadn't paid me two seconds of attention since I'd been home. Maybe it was just the fact that something—anything—was making noise behind that door. I could have been a cat or a raccoon. But Effie pushed the door open and came flying into the room.

"Good girl, Effie. Come here. It's me. Remember me? Travis." Just having her in the room eased my panic, and I began to relax.

Hesitantly, she came closer. I could hear her sniffing. Then I felt Effie's cold nose brush against my shoulder and cheek. "That's it. Good girl, Ef. You remember me." I began calling out again for my parents. Effie stayed, but kept her distance. With the door open, they were finally able to hear me. My mom came down and pulled the blankets over me and tucked me back in for the night.

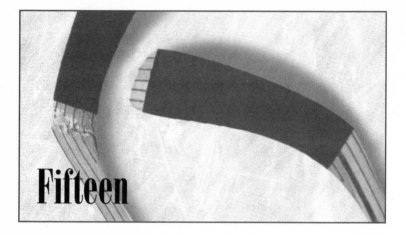

Fifteen

April 17 was my twenty-first birthday. A year ago exactly I'd delivered my "10 Rules of Life" speech to the student body at Tabor, and one of my goals was to return on my birthday to give another speech, thanking the community for all they had done. It was one of my favorite places on earth.

Just a few teachers knew about the plan, plus my family and Maija, and a few friends like Matt, Angus, and Ian Conway, all of whom came back from college to be there.

Maija and I were waiting behind a curtain in the auditorium. The students thought they'd assembled to hear speeches from the candidates for school elections. But the headmaster, Jay Stroud, announced they had a special surprise. That was my signal, and I rolled my wheelchair onto the stage. It seemed like they clapped forever.

I told them how great it was to be back. I knew about three-quarters of the student body, and my speech came straight from the heart:

"As some of you may remember, I stood before you exactly one year ago. Today, on my twenty-first birthday, I sit before you. That's one of the few things about me that's changed.

"As you may recall, following the example of Moses and the Ten Commandments and David Letterman's nightly Top Ten list, I delivered Travis Roy's 10 Rules of Life. I'd like to begin where I left off last year, with rule number 10. It went something like this: 'I'm a 20-year-old high school senior, and I'm wise enough to know my life is just beginning and there will always be more lessons to be learned.'

"Little did I know what a difficult lesson was just around the corner. At that time, my life was in good order. I'd just been accepted by Boston University on a full hockey scholarship. I knew it was important to set goals, and two goals that I'd worked for hardest were about to be realized. I was going to get a quality education, and I was going to play Division One hockey for the Terriers. Both dreams were about to come true.

"Today, one of those goals has changed. Hockey has been taken away from me. I could never have imagined that life could change so dramatically. My life, as I knew it, came to an end October 20. I am now faced with dealing with life from an entirely new perspective.

"There are several 'Rules' from my last speech that I would like to bring up today, as they seem to apply more than ever to life as I now see it.

" 'Never take things for granted' was my second rule. I am so grateful I realized this before my accident. I have no regrets, and feel very lucky about the life I had. It has taken a while, but I am realizing how lucky I still am today. I still have my family, my friends, and my pride. Those are three more of my 'rules' from last year. Tabor is where I made my best friends, and my friends have not let me down. They have actually become even closer. They have listened, laughed, and cried with me, and always have been there to support me. My most important relationship is the one I have with Maija. She has been at my side since the accident, and I have admired her strength and courage throughout this entire ordeal.

"My family, as always, has been a source of strength for me. My mother and father have become my arms and legs. My sister, Tobi, who is here today, and her fiancé, Keith, have become closer to me than ever.

"Along with old friends, I have also made new friends and acquaintances, some of whom I've never actually met. I received a letter from a respiratory therapist in Sioux City, Iowa. He enclosed a speech given by the late Jim Valvano a few years ago, delivered at the ESPY awards. Mr. Valvano was the basketball coach at North Carolina State when they won their national championship in the early eighties. He was dying of cancer when he delivered the speech. There are some points in it I found relevant to my situation, and I'd like to share them with you.

"Coach Valvano said that each day we should find time for laughter, for thought, for emotion. Through my family, friends, and fellow patients, I have found many opportunities to laugh. I recall an outing in Atlanta when a group of my fellow patients visited the airport to learn about the new challenges of flying. My friend Steve and I played follow the leader, doing loops, turns, and figure eights through the concourses in our wheelchairs. We had a ball amusing not just ourselves but a number of onlookers as well.

"Another time I called a friend with my sip-and-puff–operated phone. I had a muscle spasm, lost reach of the sip-and-puff control, and couldn't hang up. I ended up talking to his answering machine for 20 minutes until a nurse came in and rescued me. So always remember to be able to laugh at yourself and laugh with your friends.

"Coach Valvano also wanted us to take time for reflection every day. Mentally dealing with my injury has been the hardest part about the last six months. There are times when it's been very easy *not* to see past the negatives. Not being able to open doors.

Not being able to hug people. Not being able to pat my dog—these are some of the negatives. To dwell on these, however, just brings me down and leads to self-pity and unwanted sympathy. I've had to learn to have a more positive outlook. I can still kiss people. I can still breathe and talk on my own. I can still think for myself, and reflect. So I'm asking you to think, stay positive, and take advantage of the things you can do, rather than dwell on what you cannot do.

"The last thing Coach Valvano felt was important was to be able to show emotion. I have cried more times than I can count with Maija. I have cried on national television. I have cried with friends and family. These tears have come from both joy and sadness. There have been times when I've held back the tears, and times when I've let them flow. Every time I cried, I've felt much better. So I'm telling you today, don't be afraid of your emotions, and don't be afraid to let them show.

"So what is my message? We must continue to chart a course for our lives. Set goals and live every day to the fullest as we strive to achieve them. If life takes an unexpected turn, hang on to the goals that are still realistic, and reassess those that are not. Our value systems remain unchanged. It is these core values that provide the foundation for setting a new course. That course may lead us in directions that we never anticipated, or even dreamed of. But that new course may lead us to making contributions and accomplishments that are of more value to society than those we had originally planned for ourselves.

"I am still in the process of reassessing and figuring out exactly how my life will work again. I know that it will be a good and happy life, however, and one of which I will be proud. Lastly, I'd like to thank the Tabor community for making me laugh so many times. For making me think and, ultimately, become a wiser person. And for allowing me to express my emotions in both good times and bad."

The speech went pretty well. I had the audience's attention, that's for sure. It was a special day for me. I had probably grown more in my two years at Tabor than in any two years in my life. Afterwards everyone got a chance to practice what I'd preached by showing their emotions, and if the tears shed were any indication, a lot of the students had listened and learned. A number of them told me later it was a day, and a speech, they'd never forget.

That same week I went to Boston to get fitted for a tuxedo for Tobi's wedding. Naturally the rental store on Newbury Street wasn't handicapped accessible. Fortunately, it was a nice day, and the tailor came out on the sidewalk to take my measurements. It was a pretty comical scene, actually. It was a four-step operation just to measure my leg, but he was pretty handy with that tape of his and didn't waste any time.

The wedding was to be in Yarmouth. The church we usually attended was already booked for that weekend, so Tobi chose to have the wedding in the old meetinghouse in the middle of town—a beautiful and simple building with a steeple, a raised altar, no cross, white walls, clear glass windows, and wide, uneven floorboards. It was built in 1796 and is now run by the historical society for special occasions. It was unheated, and the one fear Tobi had was that if it were cold on April 27, it would be uncomfortable. So Mrs. Van Orden had some blankets made up with the date put on them, which would be handed out in the event of cold weather. The classic, antique feeling of the church was slightly modified for the occasion by a temporary aluminum ramp that was added a week before the wedding to make it handicapped accessible.

Maija was a bridesmaid, and I was an usher. My role was to greet people when they entered the small lobby, then, when the time came, to seat my mother. The aisles were too narrow for me to turn my chair around in, so I wasn't going to be seating anyone else, that was certain. It was pretty tricky just handling my mom.

There was no center aisle, so I had to come down the left-hand aisle, seat her, then take a right-hand turn and continue all the way across the front of the hall, taking my place at the end of the line of ushers, beside the piano.

The rehearsal dinner and reception were at the Black Point Inn, a lovely, rambling seaside inn on Prouts Neck—home of the great painter Winslow Homer—a half hour from our house. That's where Maija and I and the rest of the wedding party were staying. It was a lobster dinner, with a first course of fresh hot mussels, so it seemed more like a clambake than a wedding, very festive and informal. The seafood was a treat for the guests from Philadelphia, which is where the Van Ordens live. Not for Tobi, though. She's one Maine girl who hates lobster—there are many—so the bride-to-be ordered chicken instead.

The weather was perfect the day of the wedding. My care attendants came to the Black Point Inn to get me up, same as usual, which is not exactly the way I'd always imagined starting the day of my sister's wedding. They'd only been with me two weeks, and I still wasn't used to them. That was a downer. It was fun being part of the wedding party, though, watching Maija and the other bridesmaids get ready. And, wonder of wonders, my tuxedo actually fit.

From a personal standpoint, I was looking forward to showing my cousins, uncles, aunts, and the many friends who hadn't seen me that I was getting around well and looked ten times better than I had when I left the BU hospital. About 150 guests were coming, among them Coach Parker and his wife, Jackie, and Ed Carpenter and his wife, Susan. Coach Parker's secretary, Sue MacDonald, would be there. The events of the last six months had altered the invitation list. Bobby Orr had been invited, but at the last minute he couldn't come. He called, though, and sent Tobi and Keith a wonderful gift.

Keith was a little nervous, for sure, but it looked like he was going to go through with it. He'd gone to college with Tobi at

Syracuse, and when I first met him, I guess I'd expected him to be more of an adult. He was about six four, lean and lanky, very social and young at heart. His athletic ability was best demonstrated on the ski slopes. He was quite intelligent, with a good sense of humor, an all-around hardworking and dedicated guy. He now works for Putnam Investments in Boston.

He took on a big role after my accident, basically serving as the family's PR man during the whole recovery period. Keith coordinated all the newspaper and magazine interview requests, the talk-show appearances, and helped with the fund-raiser on WEEI. It was a huge job, and it gave my parents the ability just to focus on and worry about me. As a result my whole family's gotten closer to him than we might have otherwise, and the wedding was something everyone felt very good about.

I got to the church early, along with the other ushers, and met people as they came through the door. Most of the guests had never seen me in a wheelchair, and I think they were shocked to see how good I looked. "It's the tuxedo," I told them, laughing. But it was my sister's day, and they knew not to huddle around me and talk.

When it came time to walk my mother down the aisle, she took my right hand, and I used my sip-and-puff to start us on our way. It took quite a bit of concentration to keep the wheelchair straight on those slanted aisles. I sure didn't want to take out any of the pews, and all the guests in them, with a single wayward sip. I later found out that, watching from the foyer, all of the bridesmaids were crying. Tobi and Dad were crying. It was a bittersweet moment for all of them. They were proud to see how far I'd come. But they were sad, too. Seeing my mother on the arm of me in a wheelchair, well, it wasn't the way any of us had imagined my sister's wedding day.

Mom and I were the picture of composure, though. I felt pretty good about getting her to her seat without causing a disaster, and as she let go of my hand, letting it fall back onto the arm-rest, she said, "Thank you, Travis. I love you."

"I love you, too, Mom."

I took the right turn and continued across the floor, and waited with the rest of the ushers as the bridesmaids filed in. Last was the ringbearer, my six-year-old cousin, Brendan Collins. Then the wedding march began, and I watched my father escort Tobi down the aisle.

I kept waiting for my father to cry, but he never did. Maybe he was all cried out from watching me and my mother walk in. I hadn't known about that. But I found it amazing to see him look-ing so dry-eyed and happy since he's usually the one who gets weepy and emotional at family affairs. I think he just felt so good about Keith, and happy that I was out of the hospital, that he was in a great, almost giddy, mood. When the minister asked, "Who gives this woman to be wed?" my father answered, "Her mother and I do." Then he turned to shake hands with Keith and said, "No take-backs."

It cracked everyone up.

My mother didn't cry either. And neither did I. That was probably a first for our family at any wedding, ever. I remember thinking how absolutely beautiful Tobi looked in her wedding dress, which was simple and classic. It was satin from the waist up, sleeveless, with long satin gloves to match. The bottom was very puffy and billowy, layer after layer of a fine starched netting that matched her veil. It looked like a gown Cinderella might have worn, with 25 buttons down the back, each one covered by a tiny bow.

Watching her take her vows, my mind drifted back to when Tobi had come to my Tabor graduation. She had inexplicably started to cry, and it confused me at the time. So I asked Tobi to come with me, and we took a walk away from the rest of the fam-ily. It was just the two of us. I asked her what was the matter.

She said, "I feel like I've missed everything." She explained that she'd either been away at college or away at work the entire time I'd been in high school, and had basically missed that period in my life when I'd gone from being a kid hockey player to a young man capable of playing at the Division I level for the best hockey program in the East. She hadn't seen me—her younger brother, her only brother—grow up. We hugged, and I told her she'd have lots of opportunities to see me play in college. It was all just beginning. That was a big point in our relationship. It was a bonding the two of us hadn't felt since we were kids.

That summer she and Keith had moved to Boston from South Carolina, and she was so excited that we were going to have a lot of time together again, and that she'd finally be able to see me play. The first month and a half of school, I'd been to their apartment all the time. She'd helped me type papers. And we reestablished that special brother/sister relationship we'd lost when she went away to college.

Then the accident happened, and Tobi, the nurse, was by my bed every second she could get away from her job. She took on a huge role, and spent many nights with me in intensive care. To talk to and cry with your sister is a whole different feeling than to do that with your parents. She was the one who explained the whole tracheotomy procedure to me, and told me it was nothing to worry about. Any medical questions I had, Tobi explained.

It was so important to her that I be at her wedding. And to me. From the first day I went into the hospital, that had always been my goal, but for the longest time it seemed like it wasn't going to happen. Now I'd made it. And seeing her standing there in her wedding dress, looking so lovely, well, it was extremely emotional for me. I was so proud of her, grateful for all she'd done for me, and happy to see her getting married to a guy everybody liked. A guy she loved. I thought about how much had passed between us in the past 12 months.

The reception was at the Black Point Inn, a buffet of lobster tails, roast beef, chocolate-covered strawberries. I remember the only thing my dad was worried about was whether there'd be shrimp left when we finally got out of the receiving line.

Everything went great until the first dance, the traditional waltz between the bride and groom. Keith and Tobi, of course, started it off, and everyone stopped what they were doing to watch them. Then my parents cut in. Then Keith's parents joined them.

It started to go downhill quickly for me then. My whole family was up there, except for me, and then they were joined by other members of the wedding party. I knew I was going to lose it, and tried to make my way out of the room before I started to cry. I didn't make it. And to work my sip-and-puff while crying was more than I could handle.

Tony McNaboe, my old friend from Yarmouth, got behind me and pushed me through the door, looking for a quiet place where he could console me. But Coach Parker intercepted us as we were leaving. "What's up?" he asked.

Tony left us alone. Coach Parker took me into the inn's sunroom, a quiet place where we could talk away from the others. He's new at dealing with quadriplegics, but he knows how to handle all sorts of people and situations. Mostly he just listens, and in the process gets me to let everything out that's been building up inside me.

Out it came. I told him that nothing was like I'd pictured it would be. I'd been so looking forward to my sister's wedding day. I'd thought about it so many times. Then with the aides coming to get me up that morning at the inn, things had started off on the wrong foot, and had never really got back on track. I'd always pictured myself dancing at my sister's wedding, throwing rice and rose petals at her when she left. All that corny stuff I'd never done, and now would never be able to do. I wanted to *do* things, not just sit there and watch them.

Then to break down in tears that way, to take away from Tobi's day, which was the one thing I'd sworn I wouldn't do. I was disappointed in myself on top of everything else. A wedding was an occasion when everyone was supposed to be happy for the bride and groom, not feeling sorry for themselves. And everyone but me was happy. It made me feel guilty as hell that I couldn't be happy for Tobi's sake. I couldn't understand why I wasn't able to control these fits of depression.

Coach Parker told me he thought I'd handled everything admirably. I told him, "I don't want to be 'admirable.'"

He didn't ask what I wanted. He knew what I wanted. It wasn't going to help either of us to hear me say it.

We talked for half an hour. I felt better afterwards, as I always did after talking to him. "We better get back out there," I said.

"Sure. See if they've left us any of that cake."

"I don't want to miss that whole garter belt thing."

"Better duck, Trav, or you'll be the next victim."

Maija found us as we were heading back to the party. I thanked Coach Parker. Maija asked how I was doing, and we went back to her room to talk. I hated thinking that my sudden exit had bummed everyone out, but she said that once my parents had seen I was with Coach Parker, they went right back to the dance floor. Nothing was going to keep them from having a blast at Tobi's wedding. And Tobi hadn't noticed a thing.

I started to feel better. I wanted to try to enjoy the last part of the wedding, at least, and I'd been gone long enough. When Maija and I returned, the other bridesmaids all came up and started encouraging me to go out and dance. I'd thought about it before, actually, and had sort of planned on dancing with Tobi somehow. But I had mixed emotions. I mean, it's a big wheelchair. It doesn't exactly blend into the background, and I didn't want to be out there knocking people down.

But I kept thinking about it, and a few more people told me not to worry about the chair. And finally I figured, Why not? Do it for Maija. Give it a try. So I asked her if she'd like to sit in my lap and go spin around a little bit. I didn't know if it was going to be enjoyable or not—frankly, I had my doubts—but I pushed myself to do it. She didn't think twice. She said she'd love to.

The other members of the wedding party made a big circle—I needed a lot of the dance floor—and Maija, smiling broadly, threw one arm around my neck and held on to the chair with the other. I did a couple 360s—soft, continuous puffs that you have to hold and keep holding—and a couple of back-and-forths. Ah-one and ah-two. Soft sip to go left; soft puff to go right. It definitely wasn't to any rhythm. But Maija was beaming with delight, laughing out loud, and seeing the smile on my love's face, knowing I had put it there, made me feel so good. So comfortable. Clearly, she was having a great time.

I worry a lot about not being able to do things, or trying to do things from a wheelchair. But Maija doesn't think twice about it. Whatever we do to substitute for what we did before is just as enjoyable to her. She tells me that all the time. It's not better or worse. She doesn't compare them that way. It's just different. Dancing at my sister's wedding was something she enjoyed just as much as dancing before. And that was a huge lesson for me, understanding that about her.

After a few loops around the floor, I took a little rest. It's harder than you think to dance in a sip-and-puff wheelchair. You get out of breath. I was contentedly watching the others dancing from the side of the floor, feeling this huge sense of relief, when someone came up and grabbed my hand.

It was Tobi. "Can't say no to the bride," she said, her eyes shining with happiness.

Back onto the dance floor we went, Tobi holding my hand as I spun my chair around. I think I was leading. I'm not sure. But I liked that a lot. It was a perfect substitute for my dream of actually dancing with my sister at her wedding. Dancing with Tobi and with Maija made the wedding for me. It brought everything together. It made everything not just okay, but excellent.

Which isn't to suggest that it was at all natural. Not for me.

Not for anyone else. It was strange and surreal, like I've found so much of my new life to be. For me to dance in a wheelchair was a big deal, and everyone watched and applauded and cheered because I did it. But I wish I could just go out and dance with Maija with no one watching.

That would be a big deal to me.

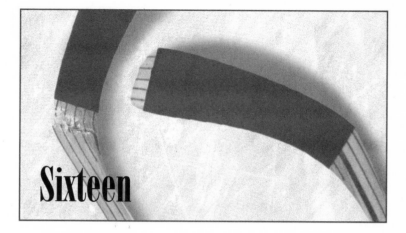

Sixteen

I accepted three paid speaking engagements over the summer, the largest of which was before the *Boston Globe* all-scholastics gathering, which attracted about 1,000 people. I'd always had a summer job, so these appearances were a nice way for me to earn spending money for Christmas presents, dinners, and such. The Travis Roy Fund was there to support me the rest of my life, so I wasn't going to touch any of that.

I could have done a lot more of those kinds of engagements, but we wanted to concentrate on my therapy. Three times a week I went to the New England Rehabilitation Outpatient Clinic in South Portland, which was about a 20-minute drive from our house. Chad Drew usually drove me back and forth. He was my one friend who was around Yarmouth all summer, and he was the best because he *made* me get out of the house. He'd nag me to go with him to the movies, or to a summer hockey game at my dad's rink. That was the best thing he could possibly have done for me, because I felt safe at home, protected, secure in the knowledge I wouldn't have to face people for the first time and talk about how I was doing. I didn't like going out and dealing with all that was involved in being the new Travis Roy. But once I was out, especially when I was with Chad, who was easygoing and quick with a joke, I always enjoyed it. It was just great to be able to be with a buddy my own age to whom I didn't have to explain everything.

It didn't take me long to find out that the therapists at the New England Rehabilitation Outpatient Clinic weren't quite at the level of Shepherd's. They'd ask, "How are the fingers? How are the wrists?" If you're a specialist in paralysis, those aren't questions you have to ask a C4-level quadriplegic. A week later, they'd ask it again.

The building didn't have automatic doors, which is pretty unbelievable for an outpatient clinic specializing in rehabilitation. One day, as I was entering the building and my dad was holding the door open, I had a muscle spasm, which caused me to involuntarily blow into the sip-and-puff and send the chair bolting forward. My footrest crashed right through the Sheetrock in the opposite wall.

So after about a month I switched to a different clinic, Orthopedic Associates of South Portland, where one of our neighbors, Frank Gentile, was a physical therapist. Most of our efforts at that point were focused on building up the strength in my right arm, and every week I could feel a difference. The clinic had a swimming pool, and my therapist, Pat, would put a life ring around my neck and a webbed glove on my hand, almost like a flipper, to create more resistance. She'd have me swim around like that for half an hour. By the time I got out, I was so spent I couldn't lift my arm off the armrest. I loved that feeling of having worked out to exhaustion, like I used to do every day in hockey. I loved knowing I'd gotten everything out of what I had.

I was well aware that, as hard as I worked, I wasn't going to walk again without a medical breakthrough. But I wanted my right biceps to get as big as it could get. In my mind I imagined I might be able to have this huge right arm, the size of Arnold Schwarzenegger's, so I could lift just about anything. But as time went on, I learned more and more about my injury. I was thinking that the biceps was sort of like a TV: If it's plugged in, it's either on or off. There's no such thing as getting half a picture because of a lack of juice.

But a biceps isn't like a TV. No muscle group is. Thousands of cords have to be plugged in for muscles to work properly, and I had only a few of those cords operational. I don't have my triceps, for example. I can lift my arm up, but only gravity can bring it down. I don't have wrist extensors, which are the muscles that lift up your hand. If I don't wear a wrist brace, I have no control of my hand. And I have nothing at all in my left arm.

Most likely, none of that is going to change. I've talked to some quadriplegics who've gotten a muscle group back years after an accident, but the doctors will tell you it won't happen.

I was still working toward the goals that Marcie had set for me at Shepherd, and it was early in the summer when I met one of them by feeding myself for the first time. I don't know what I was thinking, but I decided to start with grapes, which have to be the most impossible thing in the world to eat with a fork.

Still, I always liked a challenge, and it provided huge entertainment for the family members who had gathered in the kitchen that afternoon. A good crowd was in attendance: Mom and Dad, and my uncle Frank and aunt Lolita Bishop. I was armed with a special fork Marcie had given me that slipped into the wrist brace of my right hand. It was four-pronged, and three inches longer than an ordinary fork. The handle was bent almost at a right angle to accommodate my limited range.

But even with such an engineering marvel on my side, the grapes presented quite a challenge. The rubbery texture of their skin resisted piercing, and they kept squirting around on my plate like tadpoles in a wading pool dodging a child's grasp. Several flew off the plate and onto the floor, where Effie was waiting to dispatch them.

Finally I discovered the grape's Achilles' heel: the little hole in its stem. After about a half hour of trying, I managed to stick a prong into that hole—hold still now, my precious, this only hurts once—and fed myself my first postparalysis grape. It brought a smile of triumph to my face and cheers from the assembled throng.

A man could build up an appetite eating like that. I was exhausted. Eventually we figured out that if the grapes were cut in half, they were a lot more susceptible to skewering. But who wants the easy way out?

It was a nice accomplishment, but from a practical standpoint, it didn't make much difference in my everyday life. I still only feed myself one meal a day, and that meal has to be carefully cut into bite-sized pieces. It's not like I was ready to peel a banana, or hold a sandwich, or stick my fork into a firm piece of steak. I still can't do any of those things. When I go out to a restaurant, I can't get my chair close enough to the table to reach my plate, so I still have to be fed. I'm conscious of those limitations every day.

I continued to work toward driving my wheelchair with a joystick. To increase my range of motion, my therapist had me using a skateboard-type device that reduced both friction and gravity. She'd lay the skateboard on a table, then put my right arm on the skateboard, and would ask me to push it forward and backward for five to ten minutes. Those ten minutes felt like a three-hour workout. It took everything out of me to move the skateboard a foot four or five times. On some days—good days—I moved it six or seven times. The difference between the ease with which I accomplished the first up-and-back with the skateboard and the effort the fifth one took was, in its own simple way, similar to the difference between a hockey player's skills in the first period of a game and in the third period. It was a vivid example of how quickly fatigue affects performance.

But I was getting stronger. I could see the results. To this day, I'm still getting stronger, but not like that first summer, when every week I could do a little bit more.

In early July, my therapists added a joystick to my wheelchair so I could actually begin to practice. Pat would take me out to the parking lot—far, far away from any parked cars—and run me through my paces. I could go left and right pretty well, but I was moving at a snail's pace because I had difficulty pushing the joystick forward. Off the tarmac, on grass or dirt, I couldn't get the chair moving at all. In the tight quarters of my house, I was always running into things—which wasn't safe for me, the furniture, or poor Effie, whose paws I ran over twice. So indoors I stuck to the sip-and-puff, which I'd grown quite attached to, and we saved the joystick sessions for wide-open spaces outside.

I was worried that Effie might never get used to me, this strange immobile Travis I had become. But she began to recognize me more and more as the summer went on. I finally figured out how to bribe her. I'd have my mom give me a bone, which I'd put in my mouth. Then I'd maneuver the wheelchair near a piece of furniture so Effie could jump up and take it. I did that a number of times. It got to be quite a little game for Effie. By the end of the summer, when I returned home after a few days away, she'd jump up in my lap, put her paws on my shoulders, and give me kisses by licking my face.

My father had spent quite a bit of time with me since my accident—virtually every day for the first six months. That summer he started back into his normal routine. He was going to the rink more and more, running his hockey camps. That was tough, though, because for the past five summers, that had been my job, too. We would get up together, have breakfast, and go to the rink to tackle these various projects. I'd repair the Plexiglas, paint the locker rooms, assist my dad when he put in the ice. I'd drive the Zamboni and coach skills at his hockey camps. I used to be his top gun. Now I was being left behind at home, and my place was taken by a young man named Jason Currier.

Quiet and polite, Jason was from Calais, Maine, a small town four hours to the north. He'd been a boarder in our home for the past three years, while he was going to North Yarmouth Academy, which helped us afford my Tabor education. He was a year behind me in school, and Jason and I had always had a good relationship. He was very respectful of me and of my family, and everyone felt pretty close to him.

After my accident, my dad offered him the summer job I used to have. He was staying in Tobi's room, which is in the main, old part of the house. At night sometimes he'd go to the rink and skate by himself, just as I used to do, and afterwards lock up. He was going to Villanova that fall, which has a Division III hockey team, and he was getting himself into shape, just as I had done the previous summer. In some ways, it seemed to me Jason had taken my place in the family.

My young cousins, Brendan and Patrick Collins, who attended Dad's hockey camp, would come back at the end of the day gushing about how hard Jason could shoot the puck. How fast he could skate. I thought to myself, I could shoot the puck a lot harder and more accurately than Jason. You guys should have seen me a year ago.

But I couldn't. Not even to Brendan and Patrick. I was taught not to be egotistical, to let my actions speak for themselves. And, on a hockey rink, they always had. Hockey was a source of great confidence for me. But now I *only* had words, since my actions had fallen mum. As a result a lot of my self-confidence was gone. I'm not the same person I was. As much as I liked to be recognized as a well-rounded person, hockey had been the core of my self-esteem.

If it had been anyone else but Jason—who was so polite and so respectful of me, both as a person and an athlete—it would have been unbearable. He knew what I was thinking, I suspect. We never really talked about it.

One day Jason came in and asked if it would be okay for him

to borrow my mountain bike. He was very cautious and deferential when he asked. I had a nearly brand-new Cannondale, and he wanted to use it for aerobic training. He always respected my belongings and if it had been anybody but him, I wouldn't have let him use it. The only people I let borrow my things are my family. I told Jason I appreciated him asking, and to go ahead.

My mom saw him carrying it up from the basement later, and she confronted him: "What are you doing with Travis's bike?"

He explained that he'd talked to me about it. She knew it was a very symbolic and meaningful thing that I was letting Jason use my equipment, and, frankly, it bothered her more than it bothered me. She talked to me about it later. It made her sad to see someone else using my stuff.

I haven't given any of it away—not the bike, not my golf clubs, not my new tennis racket, not my skates—because I know I'll use them again. It's not something I dwell on, but I know it. There's no question in my mind. There'll be a medical breakthrough. It'll be a little while, but I will use those things again. My faith in that helps keep me going.

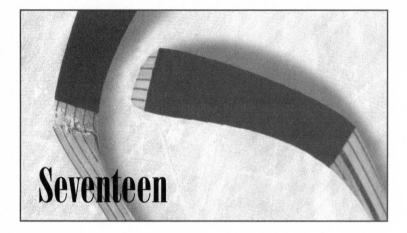

Seventeen

On the July Fourth weekend we went to my family's place just north of Burlington, Vermont, to a peninsula on Lake Champlain called Goodsell Point in the town of Colchester. My mother's maiden name is Goodsell. Her grandfather bought the land, which is on Malletts Bay, and gave each of his daughters and his son lots on which to build. So now there are four houses on the point, plus a fifth one—my great-grandfather's—that everyone shares. Only one of the houses has passed out of the family.

It's just about my favorite place to go in the world. Three generations on my mother's side still use it, and I'm very big on family. We'd spend two to three weeks there every summer, and it was like summer camp. The cousins would organize Wiffle ball and soccer games in the field between the houses, or play croquet. We'd go snorkeling, canoeing, sailing, or bass fishing from the rocks. It's the kind of place where you make your own fun, not much different than it was a half century ago. The television only gets one channel. There's only one phone line servicing the five houses, and each house has a different ring.

I really wasn't too excited about going up there this time, however. I wouldn't be able to do all the things that had made it fun. Plus I was feeling poorly for the first time since leaving the BU hospital, getting terrible chills on the drive across Maine and New Hampshire with my mother. It was about 95° outside, but every time my mom put on the air conditioning, I'd start freezing. Just the tiniest bit of cool air would make me feel I was immersed in a tub of ice. As a result, Mom just about boiled to death.

The second night in Vermont was rainy and cold, and I lay shivering in my bed. I had my parents cover me with blankets, but my temperature was 104°. So they took off the blankets and called Dr. Haile, our family physician back in Yarmouth. He couldn't explain from their description what was going on. The left side of my body was freezing. I felt like I was naked and lying on my left side in the snow. My right side, though, felt fine. It was so weird to have your body divided up like that, but I was getting used to my body doing strange things.

I was headachy, dizzy, and ice cold. Finally, around 2 A.M., I asked to go to the hospital. It was only a ten-minute drive. Obviously my body was trying to tell us something, but we couldn't figure out what. We came in the door of the emergency entrance, and the lady behind the desk was out of her chair in a snap.

"Travis Roy!" she gushed, her loud, cheerful voice clanging like a hammer against an anvil inside my head. "Great to meet you. I've been following your story. What can we do for you?"

She meant well. But there's a time and a place for it to be great to meet someone, and 2 A.M. in the emergency room is not one of them. The first thing they tested for was a urinary tract infection. That's a common problem for quadriplegics because of the frequent catheterizations. They took a blood sample, hooked me up to an IV to rehydrate me with a saline solution, and kept me overnight for observation. My fever had come down by the morning, and the chills on my left side had disappeared. So without really having discovered what the problem had been, I was released.

The next night, the same thing happened. Fever, chills, excruciating pain in my left side. This time, instead of waiting till two in the morning, I started asking my parents to take me to the hospital around 10 P.M. They thought I was overreacting, and were reluctant to go back for another all-night vigil. My dad's attitude of "Get up, you're not hurt" didn't just apply to hockey.

"They're not going to do anything, Trav," he said. "They'll just give you saline solution and tell you to go home."

Mom agreed with him. She thought the hospital was like a security blanket for me. All I had to do was show up and I'd feel better. She thought the symptoms were mostly in my head. But I continued to feel worse and worse. I was yelling and screaming—even swearing—at them. "Why don't you listen to me?" I shouted. "I've never been a whiner. I've always been a tough kid. You both know that. Just take me to the hospital, if for no other reason than it'll make me feel safe."

It took an hour and a half to finally convince them. Dad drove me in, and there was a different doctor on duty this time. He looked at my chart from the night before, and asked without any clear conviction, "What do you want me to do?"

At the very least I wanted something to help me sleep. I was still shivering with cold. My teeth were literally chattering. I'd started to calm down, though, reinforcing my mother's belief that the hospital was like a protective haven that calmed all my fears. So the doctor gave me some Valium, and Dad and I drove back out to camp. When the drug kicked in, I slept for 24 straight hours.

The symptoms were gone when I awoke, and this time, they didn't return. I felt fine. It was like whatever had ailed me had been cured by sleep. We wouldn't learn that it hadn't been for another six weeks.

Soon I was able to fall back into the familiar rhythms of vacationing in Vermont with my family. My concerns about not enjoying a return to that wonderful spot had been unwarranted. No, I couldn't play ball with the cousins, or soccer, or croquet, or go fishing and snorkeling. But I discovered that what I loved more than all of these activities was spending time with my extended family, the 16 cousins and four uncles and aunts who came to Goodsell Point. That was, by far, the most important element of our trips to Vermont.

Everyone helped with my care. But my 13-year-old cousin, Courtney Collins, took a special interest in looking after me. She's a pretty girl, tall and thin, who lives in Rutland, Vermont. She was always right by my side, and would feed me, put on my suntan lotion, and run any number of errands. Her brothers, Brendan and Patrick, stitched *T.R.* on the sleeves of their new hockey jackets. It made me feel good that they still looked up to me, even when I was in a wheelchair. I'm very much like an older brother to them, and I love that role. The uncles built wheelchair ramps into three of the four houses so I could go visiting by myself. It gave me a sense of independence and freedom I hadn't felt since my accident. We'd stay up late and talk—about boyfriends, girlfriends, hockey, junior high stuff—and in the mornings I'd sleep in.

Then we picked up one of those pontoon party boats, which we'd had custom designed to accommodate my wheelchair. It could carry as many as 12 people at once, plus Effie, and was fast enough to waterski behind. It was one of the few things I found I could get truly excited about. One of the few things that was actually fun. My cousins would drag my chair through the sand to a neighbor's dock, where the pontoon boat was able to pick me up. They'd strap the chair down in the middle of the boat, and off we'd go, Maija driving, the wind blowing through my hair, buffeting my neck and my face. It gave me a sensation of speed that was the closest thing yet to skating. It made me want to laugh out loud, plowing through the clean, fresh air.

We went out seven days straight. It was the best week of the whole summer.

L ater in the month I was invited to carry the Olympic torch twice, once in Maine and once when it came through Boston. It was quite an honor, of course. I don't know if anyone else in the country carried it two different times. But it was an honor I felt awkward accepting and still feel ambivalent about. All these crazy things were coming my way because of the accident, because I'd broken my neck, not because of me. Sometimes, honest to God, I felt like Forrest Gump. Vice-President Al Gore came to see me, and with all my medications I wasn't able to stay awake. Wayne Gretzky visited me after a hockey game. Bobby Orr came to my hospital room. I threw out the first ball at a Red Sox game, and was asked to carry the Olympic torch. I was interviewed by *Good Morning America* and the *Today* show and ESPN.

It was exciting and it was an honor to meet these people and do these things, but on every occasion, I couldn't help but wonder where my life would be if I hadn't broken my neck. All I really wanted to do was go back to being an ordinary college hockey player whom nobody knew.

But everyone around me was very excited about my carrying the torch, all my family members and friends. Even the newspapers, since Maine was not originally scheduled to be part of the Olympic torch relay. It wasn't something I was prepared to turn down. So when the torch flew to Maine, I was in a car at the airport to meet it with Joan Benoit Samuelson, the 1984 women's marathon winner and probably Maine's greatest Olympian. As we'd been driving in, the people lining the route had been cheering loudly for me, more so than for Joanie. I was thinking, I'm not deserving of all this attention. I was embarrassed, to tell you the truth. Here was this great Olympic champion, and people were yelling, "Go, Travis. . . . You're an inspiration, Travis!" I'd had aspirations to be an Olympian one day, too, to be cheered for and admired as an athlete. But not like this.

The relay officials attached the torch to my wheelchair, and I carried it a third of a mile. Drove it a third of a mile. It took quite a long time. To be honest, I was thinking, This sucks. I'd much rather have been one of those people standing there watching and cheering. I'd have given *anything* to be one of those people. And they were probably thinking, I'd give anything to carry that torch. And after I'd finished, all the members of the media asked me how it felt. Sincere expressions. Microphones. What does it feel like to carry the Olympic torch, Travis?

Thanks for asking. It sucked.

You see? You can't tell the truth sometimes. So I tried my best to sound excited and emotional. But that's not what I was feeling inside.

It was much the same down in Boston, the biggest difference being that the television news magazine *48 Hours* was covering me when I carried the torch. They were preparing a whole segment on me. My leg lasted five to seven minutes, and afterwards, when the reporter from *48 Hours* interviewed me, I felt like I was supposed to say that carrying the Olympic torch was the greatest feeling in the world. That's what he wanted. But it wasn't the greatest feeling in the world. Not to me. The greatest feeling in the world would have been to stand up out of that chair and hug Maija.

So I got around it by saying, "The emotions you feel inside when you're carrying the torch are not something words can describe." That was pretty much the exact quote. It was true, too. At least this time I didn't lie. Because there were no emotions inside me while I was carrying the torch. It felt empty and hollow. That's why words couldn't describe them. It sparked no emotions at all.

In August I spoke down at Bridgewater State College, which wasn't far from Maija's home in Duxbury. She drove me down from Maine. It was one of the first times we were alone together, out in the real world, without nurses or care attendants or friends or parents. Just driving in the van with her was fun.

Maija's house wasn't handicapped accessible. Very few houses are, which is why I so seldom go to other people's homes anymore. It doesn't take much to turn me away. A six-inch step is sufficient. Since my chair weighs 450 pounds with me in it, you need two pretty strong guys to lift me up. Also, a lot of houses don't have front doors that are wide enough for my wheelchair, which is 28 inches across.

When I do come inside, there's a lot of rearranging that has to be done, unless you don't care about your furniture. I need an eight-foot radius to turn the chair around without parallel parking. Doorsills and rugs can be a problem. Tables and chairs are always in the way. Having me to dinner is not an easy project all around, so when I visit I usually do so in nice weather and hang out on the front lawn.

I made a hotel reservation at the Sheraton in Plymouth, about 10 miles from Maija's home. There's a lot of extra baggage when traveling with me, and I seriously doubted that Maija could handle it all by herself. But every time I doubt she can do something, she proves me wrong.

I travel with a special air mattress, which keeps me from getting bedsores. It comes with a motorized pump that readjusts the air pressure in the mattress every three minutes, so a different part of my body absorbs my weight. It's almost like I'm shifting position. I also need to take a 35-pound battery charger along for my wheelchair. Plus a 50-pound portable aluminum ramp—8 feet long, 30 inches wide—for getting into and out of places that are not handicapped accessible.

Maija had no problem with any of that stuff. It was getting me into and out of bed by herself that was the real test. I'd have bet anything she wouldn't be able to do it.

Maija weighs 115 pounds. I'm 155 pounds of dead weight. No, worse than 155 pounds of dead weight, since my body is clumsy and awkward and always going in different directions. It's also fragile. Just because I can't feel anything anymore doesn't mean I can't be injured.

Here was the drill: To get into bed, I had to park my wheelchair directly beside it. Maija then removed the armrest and placed a 30-inch board between my seat and the edge of the bed. Next she had to slide me across that bridge, a performance we should have taped for *America's Funniest Home Videos.*

She placed my hands in my lap, then locked my knees between her knees to stabilize my lower body. She then tipped my head forward, so it hung over her shoulder, and she grabbed me by the hips. Once we were thus joined, she began to slide me across the board. She took her time, and did an incredible job. We made it to the bed in three slides.

But her work was just beginning. She still had to get me undressed, catheter me, then give me my pills before bed. The whole process took a good hour, after which she was exhausted and ready for a long hot bath.

Fast-forward to the hard part, which began the next morning, when it was time to face a new day. Armies have broken camp quicker. Maija would start with my bowel program, catheter me, bathe me, brush my hair, and get me dressed, which is a lot harder than getting me undressed. Then she had to slide me back into that chair.

Not an easy task, and twice as hard as getting me out of it. First she had to muscle my chair next to the bed by hand—and my wheelchair is a 295-pound stubborn mule in the hands of anyone but me. Once that was in position, Maija had to sit me upright. She swung my legs over the edge of the bed. Then she literally climbed onto the bed and slipped her hands under my armpits to hoist me up.

Okay. I'm sitting with my legs hanging over the edge of the bed. Maija must now somehow get her feet back on the floor, working around the chair, without letting me tip over. Because that's what my body wants to do. Tip over. I am a slave to the forces of gravity. It's like trying to balance a quarter on edge on a table, only this quarter weighed 155 pounds.

"Don't move," she said. I think it was a joke. She let go of me for an instant, hoping I'd stay balanced, and hopped off the bed. But the whole dynamics of the air mattress changed when she jumped off, and I felt myself starting to topple backward.

"Timberrr!" I said on my way down.

"Very funny," she said.

She went through the whole thing again, jumping on the bed, propping me up, jumping back down. Again, I tipped over. It wasn't so funny the second time. Frustration was beginning to set in. On the third try we finally got it. Maija had lost about two pounds in sweat.

She still had to slide the board under me—all the while keeping one hand on my shoulder to keep me upright—no easy thing when working with rumpled bedsheets and baggy pants. And in the process of doing that, she discovered the chair wasn't quite close enough to the spot where I was now sitting.

"Aaarrgh!"

"Let's rest for a minute," I said.

There was nothing to do but lay me back down and start over, repositioning the chair. That happened three times the first morning before the chair and I were properly aligned.

Now the final hurdle. Maija had to slide me back across the board, uphill this time, since the bed was four or five inches lower than the wheelchair. (Later we figured out to put pillows between the box spring and the mattress to even up the height difference.)

She did it, making small slides. Start to finish, the whole process took close to two hours.

I was now ready to go. Maija, mentally and physically spent, was ready for a nap. But she showered and got herself dressed, then helped me get into the van. By the time we were starting our day, it was already close to noon.

Still, Maija had proved she could get me up alone. It's something my mother would never attempt. Nor should she, being even smaller than Maija. As time has gone on, Maija's gotten better and better at the procedure, which, like anything else, has a system to it that improves with practice. It's always taxing, but she manages. We both manage. It's just one more part of my life that requires extra time and planning.

One of the things we did that weekend was visit Duxbury Beach, which had recently been made handicapped accessible. I was able to drive the wheelchair out on a long boardwalk and watch the people lying in the sand, watch the kids swimming. It would have been nice to leave the boardwalk, but of course the wheelchair would have gotten bogged down, and I'd never have gotten it out. So we watched. I couldn't help remembering how great it used to feel to have the hot sand beneath my feet, then how the icy shock of the cold water took your breath away when you plunged into the ocean. Then afterward, the feeling of lying back on your towel, the heat rising through the sand to warm your chest, the hot sun drying off your back. Like other victims of paralysis, I'm always thinking about the feelings I miss. It's something I'll never get used to.

Maija, watching the sunbathers and swimmers while standing beside me, resting her arm on the back of my chair, was probably thinking along those same lines: How nice it would have been to join them. But it was one of those regrets that went unspoken.

That afternoon we went to the mall to see a movie. We couldn't go 20 feet without people stopping or doing a double take.

"That's Travis Roy," I'd hear them say. Some would point. They wouldn't think anything about it.

Quite a few people stopped to say, "You're inspirational." Or "Keep fighting. Good luck." Or "It's an honor to meet you." Extremely nice things. But it also made me feel awkward. It still bothered me that I'd become a celebrity for breaking my neck. Why is that special? I'm not sure I'll ever stop wrestling with that. Some days it's fine, even great. Other times it just gets frustrating. You'd like to be anonymous. Movie stars and athletes can wear dark glasses and put on heavy coats. But with my blond hair and in my wheelchair, I'm as conspicuous as a billboard. This is Travis Roy, step right this way. I can't go undercover.

That night Maija and I talked a little about it. It had sort of ruined my mood, and I began wondering where we could go just to be left alone and not have anyone know me. Not Maine. Not Massachusetts, that was certain. It got me thinking, though, and before long I came up with a place. And a plan to take Maija there.

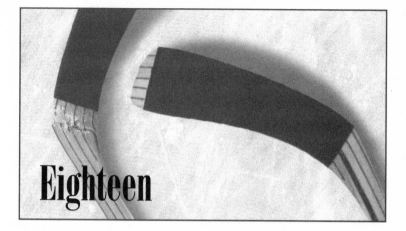

Eighteen

Every summer, while driving to Vermont with my family, we used to pass the Mount Washington Inn in Bretton Woods, New Hampshire. We'd never stopped there, but from the road it had always seemed a little unreal to me, like a place from another time. Almost like a palace. Somehow it popped into my head that the Mount Washington Inn would be the perfect spot for Maija and me to go to be alone.

My parents had only been there one time—on their honeymoon. They hadn't stayed there. They couldn't afford it on their budget. So they'd just looked around and admired it before driving on. Every time we went past that elegant old inn my parents told us that story, usually adding that someday they planned to return there to really stay. Someday. So when I told them of my plan to take Maija there, I could tell they were a little envious, but also very excited for me.

I called the hotel to see if I could afford it, and was given a rate of $250 a night, breakfast and dinner inclusive. Then I asked how handicapped accessible it was. Were the pathways paved? Would I be able to get down to the pool? Could I reserve one of the handicapped rooms? They answered yes to all of my questions, and asked for a credit card to confirm the reservation.

Last name Roy. First name Travis. The reservations clerk paused, then said, "Oh, Travis, how are you doing? I've been following your story." It was kind of ironic, since the whole reason I was going there was to get away from being recognized by people. But he couldn't have been nicer, and told me to let him know if I needed anything special. He also let me trade my inclusive breakfast for lunch, since I'm not ordinarily up by breakfast. I was all pumped up by the time I got off the phone.

I didn't tell Maija where we were going, only that it was someplace special. I told her to bring something nice to wear for dinner, since coat and tie were required in the evening in the dining room, plus a swimsuit and some casual clothes. I knew she'd love the place. She's fascinated by old, historical buildings. The inn offered horseback riding, which she used to do a lot of when she was younger. There was a stream running through the property, and gardens, and a breathtaking view of Mount Washington and the White Mountains.

Our reservation was from Sunday to Wednesday. Maija came up to Yarmouth on Saturday night, and we started out in the van on Sunday about noon on a perfect summer day. I knew the route by heart from all the years of going to Vermont, and I wouldn't even let Maija look at the map. I just directed her: Take a left here. Take a right there. It was a scenic drive. I was as excited as I'd been about anything since the accident, and it felt great to get that pumped up about something again.

I can't imagine what she must have been thinking. We were going through all these towns in the middle of nowhere, passing cows and auto body shops. Maija is a pretty refined girl. Not New York refined. And not stuffy. But not the type to change a carburetor, either. She knew Boston, and she knew Portland. But these back roads and small rural towns were foreign turf to her. I delighted in teasing her along the way. "I think I remember this road," I said doubtfully. "I hope we're going the right way."

Unless I was hunting for a fender to a '68 Rambler, or a litter of beagles, it looked like we were totally lost. Every so often Maija would say, "Travis, you've got to be kidding me. Where are we going?"

Finally we arrived at North Conway, a big retail outlet town about a half hour away from the Mount Washington Inn. Maija's sigh of relief was almost audible. "If worse comes to worst, we can always come back here and go shopping," I said.

"We're not stopping here?"

Check-in at the hotel wasn't until 3 P.M., so I told her we could if she liked. She liked. We bought a sweater and a bag of candy, and had a quick bite to eat. Maija would have been perfectly happy if we'd stayed right there for the next three days. I think she was afraid the next stop was the Moosehead Lodge and Trailer Park—ALL-U-CAN-EAT SUNDAY NITE BUFFET.

We continued on Route 302, and soon were driving through the White Mountains, following a little stream. I told her we were getting close . . . we're almost there . . . I think it's ahead on the right. She was interested. This was looking better.

Suddenly we came upon a huge clearing, and set far back in the mountains was the Mount Washington Inn, a huge white hotel like a castle. The buildings all had red roofs, which were set off by the bluest sky that either of us had ever seen. It looked like a scene from a fairy tale.

"Travis, what is that?"

"Turn here."

We drove across a bridge, and up the winding hill that led to the hotel. When we got there, Maija's mouth dropped open. I'd been waiting for that reaction ever since I'd thought of the idea, and it made me laugh out loud to finally see it. "This is where we're staying?" she asked, incredulous. "This is the place?"

She was in awe that such a structure should have been built in the middle of nowhere. Even I was surprised how beautiful it was, because I'd only seen it from the road. A wide, wooden veranda surrounded the inn, which was encompassed by lovely gardens bursting with color. "We're here," I said. She grabbed my shoulders and kissed me.

We had barely stopped the van when the bellboys were all over us. "We've been expecting you, Mr. Roy," one said. There was a small outside lift for wheelchairs, instead of a ramp, and one of them directed me to it. When we entered the hotel, we were again blown away by its grandeur. The lobby was high-ceilinged, immense, and classically decorated with elegant, threadbare carpets and antique furniture. The weight of my wheelchair made the polished wooden floorboards creak as I rolled across them. Maija's eyes didn't know where to settle. They were darting from one architectural detail to the next.

Our room was on the second floor. The lift, true to the atmosphere of the place, was run by a uniformed elevator operator. Our room, too, was furnished with antiques, and the floorboards were old and slightly buckled. It had a big bay window that provided a spectacular view, and for the first 15 minutes I parked in front of it and just took it all in. I could see the pool, the golf course, the tennis courts, the riding trails, the gardens. I could see the brook winding behind the hotel, and the railroad train that took sightseers up Mount Washington. The whole thing was perfect, like a picture postcard.

Maija unpacked for us, then we returned downstairs to check everything out. The covered veranda, which extended three-fourths of the way around the hotel, was a quarter mile long. We walked around that, pausing every so often to take in a new vista. Chairs and benches had been judiciously placed for people to sit and take in the views. Uniformed waiters carrying drinks on trays walked briskly by. The other guests were all neatly dressed and appeared to be honeymooners, older couples celebrating anniversaries, or gentrified regulars returning as part of an annual rite.

The pace was slow, the atmosphere very relaxed. On the lower level there was an ice cream parlor, which Maija and I stopped off at, and an indoor pool that reminded me of something out of *The Great Gatsby*. It was long and narrow, with hand-carved tiles around the edges of the pool that looked like they'd been there since the 1920s. The outdoor pool was like that, too. Everything about the hotel had that worn-in look that made it even more charming and elegant.

We ordered soft drinks on the veranda. We got an amusing reaction from the waiter, who was about our age, when he was filling out the ticket. "Name?" he asked.

"Travis Roy."

You could see a lightbulb go on in his head. His eyes came up from the charge slip, and they lit up with recognition. "No way!" he gushed. It was such a cute and natural reaction—especially considering the setting—the best reaction I'd had from a stranger since my accident had made me a celebrity. It made both Maija and me laugh out loud. We talked a few minutes, and it turned out he, too, was a hockey player.

We went up to get ready for dinner, and Maija wrestled me into my coat and tie. All the guests eat in the formal dining room, and you are assigned a specific table with a specific waiter. I was hoping to get our young hockey player, but he was nowhere to be seen. Our waiter was an older gentleman, quite proper, very professional. The menu of the day offered a number of options, and for an appetizer I ordered the "Venetian" sausage.

The waiter wrote it down, but he must have given me a funny look, because after he'd gone, Maija started giggling.

"What's so funny?" I asked defensively. I could tell she was laughing at me.

"Do you know what you've just ordered?"

"Some kind of Italian sausage. Venetian, right? Venice style."

She giggled again. "Not Venetian, Trav. Venison. Deer meat."

"Oh," I said.

"Bambi."

"I get the picture." She knew I didn't care for hunting.

"Venetian sausage . . ." she repeated with a laugh.

"Well thanks for telling me. Why don't they just call it deer meat? I didn't know."

"Would you have ordered it if it had said deer meat? No. They don't call veal 'baby cow,' either. They don't call tripe 'stomach lining.' Yuck."

"That'll do."

"I just don't know how you can eat a deer."

She made me feel so guilty about it that I couldn't. I just asked her to sort of push the pieces around on my plate. Maija kept laughing every time she looked at me the rest of the meal. She thought the whole thing was a riot.

The next three days we didn't do a thing, really, which happens to be one of our favorite ways to pass the time. Doing nothing but enjoy each other's company. Maija had no real interest in going riding. So we just talked and ate and walked and sat by the pool. The other guests were all polite and relaxed, quite friendly, and a lot of them offered to take pictures of us with Maija's camera. The few who did recognize me dealt with it the way I liked it: They'd say hello and then would leave us alone. That was perfect.

My one appointment during our stay was a photograph session with the concierge. Our first day he'd shown me a wall of photographs of all the famous people who had stayed at the inn— senators and congressmen and old actors and actresses. Dozens of them, most of whom I didn't know. But I remember that Cam Neely, the former Boston Bruins star, was among them. The concierge asked if I'd pose for him, too. My first reaction was, Give me a break. I don't belong on that wall. But I told him, "Sure." I was thinking that maybe someday when I was married and had kids, I could show them the picture and try to convince them I was someone important.

We set up a time for the following day, and as it approached,

Maija and I were sitting by the pool, eating blueberry ice cream with sprinkles. That was our favorite activity. Maija was holding the cone for me and giving me bites, and for a joke I took a blueberry and, with the back of my hand, stuffed it partway up my nose. Maija hates that kind of stuff, but sometimes I can't help myself. I love to see her reaction.

"Maija, look," I said.

She did. She saw the blueberry and turned away in disgust. "I don't need to see this, Travis. But thank you for sharing."

"You're welcome," I said, chuckling.

She looked at me, frowning, then something caught her eye over my shoulder. "Travis, look who's coming. The concierge. He's got his camera to take your picture."

"Very funny."

She was grinning in a manner that made me nervous. I turned my head and, with a quick flash of panic, saw she was telling the truth. "Take the blueberry out of my nose."

She sat back smugly. "I don't think so."

"Maija!"

"You got it in there, smarty. You get it out."

I was trying, but I couldn't dislodge it with the back of my hand. Blowing proved fruitless, too. I could hear the concierge's footsteps approaching. "Please, Maija. I'm not kidding."

"Uh-uh," she said, smiling at my predicament.

What was the man going to say? "Um, Mr. Roy, for the portrait, what do you think? Blueberry in the nostril or not?" Or, being a gentleman, would he simply ignore it, take the picture, and hang it on the wall next to Cam Neely and all the other celebrities? So that forty years from now my grandchildren could say, "Yep, there's Grandpappy Travis at age twenty-one, with his trademark blueberry up the nose."

Maija leaned forward. "Promise me you won't ever do it again?"

"Swear to God. Hurry."

"And you won't ever open your mouth again to show me your chewed food?"

She was driving a hard bargain. "Yes, yes. Anything!"

The concierge was a few feet away when Maija finally plucked the blueberry out of my nose deftly with her napkin. Unfortunately, she smeared blueberry juice across the tip of it while doing so, so I have a purple nose in the picture. It could have been worse, though. No question about it.

I t was so nice to be able to spend time together, alone, without schedules to keep or places to go. Maija and I talked about the year that had just passed, and discussed how each of us was doing. We decided we were doing really well. We felt closer now than we'd been before the accident. We were each proud of the other for the way we had handled the last 10 months, proud of how strong our relationship had become as a result. Probably stronger than a lot of marriages.

We'd been through so much, cried together so often, talked about our feelings until it seemed like we couldn't *stop* talking about our feelings. We'd told each other everything that was going on inside us. I remember once asking her to play with my hair as we were talking. To put a lock in her finger and curl it around and around. "I really miss being touched," I said. "I miss it so much. You don't know how it feels."

She looked at me and said, "Yes I do." She paused to make me listen hard to what she was saying. "How many people hug *me*? How many people play with *my* hair?" Maija and I used to just hug each other for no reason at all. "I miss it, too," she said.

We talked frequently about school, whether or not I should return to BU in the fall. Maija was really big on school, and had brought up the prospect of my returning in the fall of 1996 back when I was still in the BU hospital. My original thinking was, No way I'll be able to get back by then. Better to take a year off, do as

much therapy as possible, and fill in the time by taking advantage
of the speaking engagements I was being offered, writing a book,
maybe helping turn that into a movie. It sounded like enough to
keep me busy for a year while I tried to figure out a new life.

Maija was against me taking another year off before going
back. Her thinking was that I was already 21. Another year off,
and I'd be a freshman at 22 and would have outgrown college before I'd even started it. I would feel a real separation between me
and my classmates. She was worried that if I didn't go back right
away, when I still knew some people on the hockey team, I'd
probably never go back.

I asked her, What would be so bad about that? What good
were academic letters behind my name going to do me? I'd been
dealt this hand. My life had been turned upside down. I wanted
to get on with that life. Why should I waste my time doing things
I wasn't interested in, learning things that I wouldn't ever apply to
my life? Academics had always been a struggle for me. I wanted to
get on with the things that interested me. Everyday life was struggle enough.

Most of my friends agreed with me. At Tobi's wedding, Maija
had been in an argument with a group of them that had upset her.
They'd said, Why should Travis go back to school? He can get a
job easily. Mike Milbury, the general manager of the Islanders,
had mentioned the possibility of my scouting players and teams
for him by studying film. Education, they said, was overrated, and
the only point of going to college was to be qualified to land a job.
If I could land a job anyway, why bother?

And Maija would argue, persuasively, that college would help
make me a well-rounded person, that the problem-solving skills
I'd learn there were more important than the problems themselves. It wasn't just *what* I was learning, but how I was doing it.
How would I get to class when the sidewalks were choked with
snow? How would I take notes without being able to pick up a

pen? How would I cram for a psychology test? How would I meet other classmates?

It was a place I'd learn to interact with kids my own age, not as an athlete, but as a young man in a wheelchair. It was important for me to be spending time with my peers. And if being a quadriplegic added considerably to the difficulties of going to college—as it would—I had four years to figure out ways to surmount them. *That* process would be something I could apply to the obstacles I'd continue to encounter the rest of my life.

Maija even talked about transferring to BU to help me, and also to get a fresh start on her own college career. She'd missed out on her freshman year almost as much as I had. Maija had spent a total of three weekends at Holy Cross the entire year. But as much as I loved the idea of having her near me at BU, I knew it wouldn't be healthy in the long run for our relationship. We were young. We still needed to be experiencing things on our own rather than always experiencing them together.

My parents were split on the idea of my returning to college that fall. My mother was generally in favor of the idea, provided that BU could handle my special needs. My father leaned toward me taking a year off to concentrate on therapy, because that first year was when things were really going to happen, *if* they were going to happen. But the more we talked about it during those three days at the inn, the more I came around to Maija's way of thinking. This was my one chance for a seminormal college experience. I didn't have to dedicate my year to either education or therapy. I could do both, if I reenrolled and just took a couple of courses.

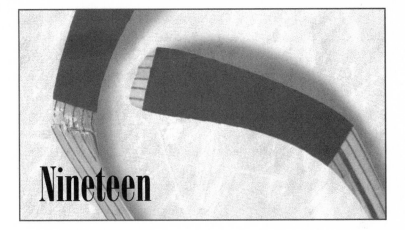

Nineteen

In late August I had another attack of the severe chills that had sent me to the hospital in Vermont. We were home in Yarmouth this time, and the symptoms were identical: shivering, 103° fever, sharp pain in my left side. My teeth were chattering and I was white as a ghost.

It was about ten at night, and I asked my parents to take me to the hospital. I remember my father saying, "Trav, all they'll do is give you some Valium, and it'll knock you out for twenty-four hours." He told me to try to relax and go to sleep, and we'd see how things felt in the morning.

I was in too much pain to relax and go to sleep. I tried to reason with them as politely as I could, and it bugged the crap out of me that neither one would listen. "Try to imagine lying on blocks of ice," I said. "That's what it feels like, only worse. I feel pain in my whole body, and I'm not supposed to feel anything."

My mother was sympathetic, telling me I'd be safe right there at home. For half an hour I kept pleading with them with all the intensity I could muster. "I wish I could make you understand what I'm feeling." I finally lost my patience and became angry.

"Goddammit, listen to me! Who cares if they give me Valium that knocks me out for twenty-four hours? It's only a fifteen-minute drive. I've never cried wolf. I'm not a crybaby. I need to go to the hospital! I'd rather be dead than sitting here going through this. Do you hear me? I'd rather die."

That got their attention. I'd never said anything about wanting to die before. I'd never even thought it. When I was about 10 or 11, I'd been so afraid of dying that I'd actually gone to a few sessions with a child psychologist. Just hearing about a funeral would get me upset. We never really got to the bottom of it. It wasn't my own death, particularly, that frightened me. I didn't want my parents to die. It might have had something to do with a car accident my father had been in a year or two earlier, when he was hit by a drunk driver and, after nearly bleeding to death, had to spend 10 days in the hospital. I had started thinking about death all the time. This went on for a year or so.

I couldn't understand the concept of dying, and it terrified me. I'd go to bed, and my mind couldn't get off the subject. It wouldn't let it go. I started having anxiety attacks. I became afraid of the dark. One time we were sitting in a dimly lit restaurant in Scottsdale, Arizona, waiting to order, and I suddenly got scared and wanted the lights turned up. The restaurant was too dark, too closed in. It felt like a tomb. I ran out into the street, and Dad followed me. When he found me I was crying and shaking, and I didn't know why except I was scared. He hugged me, and it took him quite a while to settle me down enough to go back inside. Nana Roy was with us that night, and she told me that she, too, was claustrophobic and afraid of dying. "You call me anytime it happens," she told me. "We'll talk."

Which is why, I think, I scared my parents when I suddenly said I'd rather be dead than feeling the way I did. My mother called Dr. Haile and told him I was speaking irrationally, even deliriously. Dr. Haile said that being irrational was a symptom, and that something was obviously wrong. He told them to bring me to the hospital right away.

This time I underwent a battery of blood tests and urine cultures, and they finally figured out I had a severe kidney infection. I was immediately given a massive dosage of antibiotics, but I was pretty sick. I spent seven nights in the hospital before it cleared up.

That was a good example of dysreflexia at work. My body had been trying to tell us something for over a month, and finally somebody listened. My parents, I think, learned a lesson.

Packing to go back to Boston University was a strange experience. Mom and Dad had cleared out my dorm room the previous fall, after my accident, storing everything in boxes, and those boxes hadn't been touched since. Sorting through them was painful and sad. My course notebooks were all still there, and it was eerie to see my notes in my own handwriting—handwriting I'd never be able to duplicate. It is such a personal thing to have taken from you. It seemed like I'd been taking those notes yesterday, that I'd been a typical freshman worrying about dressing for that first hockey game, worrying about my grades, running to and from classes, fit and brimming with hope and fun. Maija had sent me a number of letters my first few weeks at BU, and I reread a bunch of them. They seemed like letters from another lifetime, letters from a young girl I had loved way back when. We'd been through so much since then. How much I'd have given to go back.

I said good-bye to Effie, and a few days before fall registration, my parents drove me down to BU, where I would begin freshman year again. It was early September, a beautiful time in New England. The sun's angle sheds a different light on things than at other times of the year. Colors are brighter somehow, more defined. It's a time of year I always associate with going back to school, and I was happy to be going back then. But scared, too. Nervous about the prospect of life on my own. I wanted to have some time to get acclimated to my new routine before the other students came back, too. To get used to getting my wheelchair into and out of the dormitory elevator with my joystick, which I'd started to use full time. I didn't want to be running people over.

All along I'd been telling myself that this was something I had to try, but if it didn't go well, I wasn't committed to anything. I could always come home. But I knew that once I got there, I'd stick it out no matter what. That's the way I am.

I had so much to figure out, so many logistical questions. How would I carry my books to classes? How would I open them, and turn the pages? How would I take notes? Study for exams? Take exams? I had a voice-activated computer to help me write papers, but what about tests and quizzes? How was I going to do them?

I was particularly nervous about meeting my new care attendants and nurses, at least one of whom would be with me 24 hours a day. An agency was providing them, and they'd work in three eight-hour shifts: 7 A.M. to 3 P.M.; 3 P.M. to 11 P.M.; and 11 P.M. to 7 A.M. It's a very weird thing to meet someone for the first time, and then ten minutes later have them doing some very personal things to you. Cathetering you. Giving you suppositories, and all the rest. It's something I doubt I'll ever get used to.

Because Massachusetts law says that only registered nurses are permitted to deal with bodily fluids, I needed an RN to attend me during the night shift, so I could be catheterized before bed. In the morning, before leaving, the nurse would then administer to my bowel and bladder program. Another RN would come in for half an hour in the middle of the day. Insurance wouldn't cover it if I taught a care attendant to do these procedures, even though they're relatively simple and have been mastered by my entire family and Maija. The problem with having to employ a registered nurse is the expense: An RN charges about $35 an hour, versus about $12 an hour for a care attendant. So my bills for

24-hour care at school came to $507 a day. The $100,000 annually allotted me by my insurance would be gone in 198 days.

And I had the best insurance coverage around. What happens to the average person with a spinal-cord injury who doesn't have a great insurance policy? Who doesn't have the benefit of the Travis Roy Fund to draw from when the insurance money runs out? I can tell you, the uncovered expenses get passed down to the families. That's why some of these laws governing home health care and insurance should be changed.

My new room—a suite, actually—happened to be in the same dormitory, Shelton Hall, that I'd lived in the prior fall. It was on the second floor, a minor inconvenience in that my wheelchair only fit into one of the two elevators that serviced Shelton. The room had a study, a handicapped-accessible bathroom, and a bedroom for me, plus a separate bedroom and bathroom for my care attendants. I couldn't have asked for anything more. Well, maybe a better view. The window above my desk overlooked the roof of an adjoining building, and in the distance I could just make out the trees that grew beside the Charles River.

The university had provided me with an elevated desk, which I could slide my wheelchair beneath; a special bed; and a Hoyer lift to get me into and out of the shower. The lock on the door was electronic, opened and closed by a remote control that I kept strapped to the arm of my chair.

My parents stayed in the area four days. This wasn't your typical drop-the-kid-off-at-college-and-bolt scenario that we'd been through the year before. They carried all my stuff in, made sure they met all the care attendants and that the aides knew what was expected of them, and accompanied me on a trial run to my classes.

That first semester I was taking only two courses, both of which I'd started the year before. One was an English composition class that taught writing, grammar, and sentence structure. The second was an introduction to psychology, a field I've always been interested in. I like listening to people and their problems. I'm also interested in sports psychology and, because I love being around kids, child psychology. I had a positive experience with the child psychologist I saw when I became afraid of the dark and of dying. After a couple of visits, my phobia went away as mysteriously as it had appeared. Just talking about it seemed to help. I thought I might want to either major or minor in psychology.

Boston University is a city school. My English class, which met at 10 A.M. Monday, Wednesday, and Friday, was about three blocks from my dorm in the College of Arts and Science building. It took me about 10 minutes to get there, rolling along the city sidewalks. I entered the building through the basement entrance, which has a power door, and then took an elevator to the third floor. My psychology class began at noon, the same three days of the week, which gave me an hour to get from one class to the other. The challenge was crossing Commonwealth Avenue, a busy, four-lane road that's intersected by train tracks—an intimidating route for a wheelchair. Terrifying, in fact. I've figured out I'm all right when I cross Comm. Ave. with other students. But by myself, I worry. Drivers aren't necessarily looking for something low like a wheelchair. Even after the light changes to green, I have to watch out for cars making right turns on red. I'm always trying to look into the drivers' eyes to make sure they see me before I proceed.

When it came time for my parents to go back to Yarmouth, I could see it was difficult for them to leave me. It was especially difficult for my mother. But Tobi and Keith were only a few blocks away, eight minutes by wheelchair, and we all knew it was time for me to get on with my life, and for my parents to return to something of the life they'd known. I assured them I'd be fine and tried my best to believe it.

It was hard, though. From the very first night it was harder than I had imagined, hard in ways I hadn't foreseen. My care attendant from 3 to 11 P.M. was named Gloria. She was a black

Costa Rican woman in her midfifties. We went down for dinner at the dormitory cafeteria that first night, after my parents had left. It's not a big room, and with kids returning to campus for the fall semester, almost all the dining tables were full. The only two places I could find were way back in the corner of the room, where Gloria and I were cut off from the other students. I had to explain everything to her—where to go and get the trays and drinks and silverware, what I wanted to eat—and we had some trouble understanding each other. I felt pretty weird, stuck off by myself with an older woman cutting up my food, helping me eat. All the other students could just plunk themselves down and start a conversation. How was your summer? What classes are you taking? Where are you from? But no one plunked themselves next to us. I'm sure we were an intimidating duo for the other freshmen to consider, so they left us very much to ourselves. I became extremely self-conscious and embarrassed by the end of the meal.

I already knew I didn't have the confidence I had before my accident. And now I found I couldn't just pull up beside people I didn't know and start a conversation. I used to be good at that. I always enjoyed making new friends. I was at three different high schools in four years, so I was always in the position of having to make friends. It was no big deal. I just did it. But now it was a big deal.

And the more time that went by, the bigger a deal it became. Put off by that initial experience in the cafeteria, I started eating more and more of my dinners in my room, where I wouldn't have to deal with the embarrassment of having Gloria feed me in front of the other students. I had no one to hold my hand, to kick me in the butt when necessary, to help bring me back into the mainstream of college life. That's what Matt Perrin or Angus Leary or Ian Conway or Chad Drew would have done if they'd been around. That's what Maija would have done if she'd been a fellow student at BU.

As it was, though, it was all up to me, and for the first time in my life, I didn't give it my best effort. I disappointed myself. I began eating dinners alone in my room five nights a week. I knew it was bad, that I was taking the easy way out. But I couldn't help it. It was one less awkward moment in a day that was already very difficult.

I had a lot to handle. I felt proud of myself for living away from my family, for doing my school work, for beginning to establish an independent life. But I let half of that life—my social life—slip away and go untended. I found myself alone in a big school in a big city, but that happens to a lot of freshmen. My sister had wanted to transfer out of Syracuse her freshman year. The difference was I wasn't doing anything about it. I saw that I was at a disadvantage—being in a wheelchair, being a well-known name and face—so maybe I felt a little sorry for myself, and retreated inside a shell. It was as if my paralysis had spread from my arms and legs to parts of my personality. It had affected my socialization skills. My people skills. I found I couldn't reach out to strangers. Or if I reached out halfway and was ignored, I withdrew behind an ever-thickening emotional wall.

In the mornings and at lunch, things were better. My care attendant for the 7-A.M.-to-3-P.M. shift was Christy, a 19-year-old girl who fit right in when we went down to the cafeteria for lunch. She was also the attendant who accompanied me to my classes. Christy would sit next to me and turn the pages of my textbooks so I could follow the lectures. In English class she took notes for me. In psychology, the teacher's assistant handed me the notes after each class, so Christy could take a break. But once a week there was a multiple-choice test, and Christy and I would go into the hall, where I'd dictate the answers to her. If a test required much writing, I'd go back to my room and do it on my voice-activated computer.

Academically, it was a challenge, especially at the beginning. My psychology teacher, Mrs. Malley, happened to be a paraplegic. She's been in a wheelchair something like 25 years. I'd sit near her in the front of the class, and we'd talk a little bit about the cold weather that was coming, how the ice and snow was going to be a trial. But Mrs. Malley didn't treat me any differently than she treated the rest of the students, and to reinforce that she gave me a D on my first two exams. I had to learn new study habits. I had liked to use notecards before, to make outlines of every chapter in the textbook. But I found that too time-consuming now. So I couldn't cram at the last minute the way I used to. I had to learn to manage my time better, so I wouldn't fall behind.

When Christy and I went from one class to another, the working people we passed on the street—construction workers and policemen and groundskeepers for the university—all seemed to know who I was and always took the time to yell hello. "Hey Travis, keep it up."

"Looking good, Travis. How's it going today?"

But it was different with the students. Very few said more than hi, with a brisk nod of acknowledgment before moving past, looking down at their shoes. I'm sure most of them knew who I was, too. I'd catch them looking at me, and I'd smile to let them know I was in there, and I was human. That I wasn't some freak in a chair. But few of them approached me or tried to talk to me in any meaningful way.

I'm sure they had lots of questions, but they never asked them. What can you move, Travis? What can you feel? It was very rare that someone would even come up and ask me how I was doing. Sometimes they'd hold the door open for me, but even then they wouldn't say anything. They chose to go on with their lives as if I wasn't there. I suppose they were intimidated by the wheelchair, or my disability, or even my celebrity. That it was easier for them not to get involved with my problems, since they no doubt had plenty of their own. But no one had prepared me for their indifference. I hadn't expected them to be so difficult to approach, and it was odd and discouraging to me.

I always left myself fifteen minutes to get to English class, a trip that should only have taken ten, door to door. But I was frequently late because the elevator in the College of Arts and Science building would be filled. I'd enter through the basement, Christy would push the elevator button, but when the lift arrived it was usually filled with able-bodied students who'd ridden it down from the first floor. It was amazing to me, because the building was only five stories high, and it had a perfectly good set of stairs. Very, very seldom would anyone get off to make room for me. I'd have to wait for the elevator to come back again. When it did it was often still full. Sometimes I'd have to wait for another two or three elevators before there was room, by which time I'd be late for class.

I felt like an invisible man. Even in the dorm, where I'd see lots of the same faces every day, few of the students would speak to me unless I spoke to them first. They'd stand in the corner of the elevator silently staring at space, hoping I wouldn't make contact. I could feel it. Even when they did speak, answering my questions about where they were from, or what their names were, the conversations felt awkward. Not normal. The students just didn't know what to say to me. I didn't know why. All I wanted was for them to understand I was a person like them—same age, same needs, same sense of humor—who happened to live in a wheelchair.

It was so hard for me to initiate contact. I wasn't able just to drop by someone's room unless I had something specific to say or do. My very presence was an inconvenience—furniture had to be moved to make room for me. I couldn't even knock unless my aide came along. There were five girls who lived in the room next to mine, three of whom I'd been acquainted with before my injury. They were hockey fans. I hadn't known them well, but well enough to go down to their room and ask for English help. Back then we were all in the same boat. Everyone was new and trying to make friends, and I was an easy person to be around, an easy person to relate to. I made a whole bunch of acquaintances right off the bat. But they weren't lasting friendships like I'd made at Tabor. There hadn't been time for that.

Now I wasn't such an easy person to be around. I wasn't such an easy person to relate to. I went down to the girls' room a few times on one pretext or another. But just a few. Theirs was the only other room I visited in my first three months at BU. I'd stay and listen to them gossip and try to follow along. But I didn't know many of the people they were talking about. They were sophomores now, and all their friendships had already been established. I was trying to catch up, and I knew I never would.

It was very rare for someone to come visit me. My social life was, to say the least, slow. A couple of the girls from next door dropped by a few times, but that was it. That was the hardest thing about returning to college: finding myself unable to interact with the other students because of my disability.

I tried to take steps to break down some of the barriers. To try to fit in. To not look so strange to the other students. I took pains to dress well. I had my hair brushed before going out. I got rid of the sip-and-puff device on my wheelchair, a big off-putting contraption with a hose running back to the motor. I used as discreet a wrist brace as was possible and fed myself when eating at the cafeteria. I didn't wear a chest strap on my wheelchair, like most quadriplegics, because it made me look like I was strapped into an electric chair. I took my headrest off the chair when I went out, so it looked more like a regular wheelchair, and not like some huge 450-pound tank. I kept the medical supplies I needed tucked in drawers, out of sight, in case someone happened to visit. I didn't want my room to seem like a hospital. So many little things, just to try to look normal, not handicapped. But it didn't work.

I talked to Maija about it a lot. We got together every weekend, either at BU or somewhere else. I did a lot of traveling that fall. I still talked to her every day by phone, and she knew I was having a difficult time making new friends. How lonely I was, eating alone in my room every night. We tried to think of different approaches, of different things I could do. But there weren't many. The fundamental problem was that I didn't know who I was anymore. I didn't know how to relate to myself as a person. I wasn't an athlete anymore. I certainly wasn't a great scholar. What was I? What was my target audience for potential buddies? My care attendants and nurses? My therapists, who were all young professionals? The hockey team? Coach Parker and the other coaches? None of those were really peers. I didn't know whom to approach for friendship, whom I would best get along with, what we would have in common.

Without hockey, my self-confidence was gone. Maybe I should have been just as confident because now people told me I was admirable and inspirational. But I didn't want to be looked at as those things. I wanted to be looked at as a good kid with strong morals who was fun to be around. But my classmates weren't seeing me as the person I was, as the person I still believe I am. They couldn't see much past this wheelchair.

Invisible. That's how I began to relate to myself.

It wasn't all their fault. I know that. Much of the fault lay with me. Before the accident, I'd felt like I could do anything, could tackle any problem. But now so little of what I'd been good at was relevant to my day-to-day life. I was starting over in so many areas. It's a hard thing, learning to make friends in an entirely new way—not as the humble jock, the well-rounded hockey star, but as the quadriplegic celebrity desperately searching for ways to relate. Everything I needed to succeed was still inside me, I was sure of that, but it was like there was this big brick wall my personality was hidden behind. I needed to break down that wall and show everyone who I was. I'd broken down one wall by proving I could return to school and do the work. But the other wall still remained, the one between me and my classmates, and breaking that down required a faith and confidence I no longer could summon. The longer I waited, the thicker that wall became. I knew if I didn't do something soon, it would get to the point where I'd be locked in, and the wall would be unbreakable. My classmates would never know me. Or they'd know me as they knew me now, as a reclusive loner eating meals by himself in his room.

I had a grasp of what was going on, but I wasn't changing it. That's what really surprised me. The old Travis Roy had never been like that. He'd always gone after things. He'd never been passive and just let things come to him.

I believed—I still believe, because much of this hasn't changed—that I would eventually start turning things around, that I'd find some sort of step to start building from. It's like Maija had said when we first talked about my going to college: If things were difficult, I had four years to figure out how to overcome them.

Which is one of the reasons I knew I had to try getting involved in hockey. I had to try. It was too much a part of me just to abandon without risking losing a sense of who I was. No. Who I *am*.

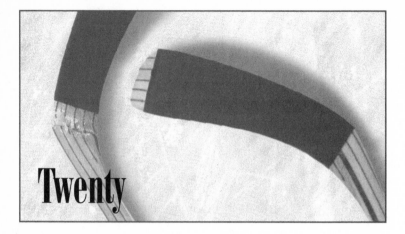

Twenty

Right from the start I'd told Coach Parker I didn't know how involved I was going to get in the program when I came back. We'd take it day to day. I had no real clue if, being unable to play, I could ever enjoy the sport again.

Early in the fall, the coach took me down to Walter Brown Arena for the first time since my accident. I knew it was going to be difficult. To be honest, I thought it might be the last time I'd ever return.

To get in we had to go through the Zamboni entrance on the lower level, which is the same place I'd exited the building on a stretcher 11 months before. We circled around beneath the stands, then the coach started out toward the players' bench. Before we'd made it to the end of the runway, I was crying. This was where my dream had come true, and also where it had ended. So I was filled with mixed emotions. Coach Parker gave me a hug and brushed the tears off my face.

A red carpet lay across the ice for some sort of ceremony that was being held that night, and I was able to roll my wheelchair onto the carpet. The corner where the accident had happened was right in front of us, and Coach Parker said, "You know, Trav, if you run that chair into the boards the exact same way as you did last year, maybe the reverse will happen."

I laughed. I thought about it, too. I retraced the one shift of my college career in my mind. The face-off. The race toward the puck in the corner. The missed check, and quick blackout. "You know, Coach, I must have been doing something wrong if it took me eleven seconds to go from center ice to that corner," I said.

"You didn't take the most direct path, Trav."

"I hope not. I used to think I was fast."

He took me into the locker room. They hadn't had nameplates over the lockers the night that I'd been injured. But now they did, and my name was on a plaque over my stall. Travis Roy. It was emotional for me to look at that. My equipment was hanging on the hooks as if beckoning me. *Get up, Trav. Get out of there.* It all came back. That's where I'd been sitting when I pulled my laces tight on my skates for the last time. That's the exact hook where I hung up my clothes. That's where I watched Drury stretch.

The coach was at my side, wiping my tears away as fast as they fell, saying all the right things at the right times. I don't know how he does it. No one teaches you that stuff. He's awesome. That's all you can say.

I always feel better after I cry. When I'd settled down, I started thinking about how I might get involved again, because I knew beyond a shadow of doubt that I didn't want to go out that door and have it shut behind me for the last time. I wanted to continue being a Terrier under Coach Parker one way or another. If it meant studying film, I'd study film. If it meant cheering at practices, I'd cheer. I knew at times it would be tough, but I wanted to be a part of it again for as long as I could.

I began going down to the arena about four days a week, three times for practices, and once to see a game. I went to a few road games, too. But not usually. The home games were easier for me to get around in, and they were enough.

Practices were more or less social times for me. Coach Parker had listed me in the team program as an assistant coach, but I wasn't exactly coaching. I'd hang out in the locker room so the players could get to know me and feel comfortable with me. I didn't want to be a distraction during games. It was entertaining, watching them practice. I found I could still be amazed by the sport. By its speed and by its beauty. It gave me something to do in the afternoons, after my classes and therapy sessions.

Game nights, I'd arrive two hours before the opening face-off. Bobby Hansen, who was a year behind me at Tabor and was now a freshman hockey player at BU, usually drove me in my van. We'd head directly to the locker room, and I'd spend the next hour and a half or so watching the players stretch out and dress. I loved that time before a game, listening to the locker-room banter and the jokes to ease the tension. Watching the routines and little superstitions. Listening to Coach Parker's pregame talks. They're so simple, but there's a quiet intensity to his words that gets everyone's attention. He has complete control over the team. The players not only like him, they have no doubt that when he gives them the game plan, it's all they have to listen to. His speeches are simple and direct. "Loose and fast out there tonight," he will say. "Hit first, puck second. Stay poised." And I'd think, That's it? But he also does a lot of one-on-one stuff. He's doing more with your head than you think he's doing.

The players would tap me on the hand on their way out to the ice. Then I'd take an elevator to the mezzanine level and would watch the play from a handicapped-access area behind our goal.

I was surprised how enjoyable it was. The games seemed to go by in half an hour. The time just flew. Before every game, Coach Parker would hand out sheets that diagrammed the other team's power-play and forechecking systems, and my job was to watch for changes in the systems, to look for adjustments the other team was making as the game progressed. Sometimes they were easier to spot from an elevated position.

But even with the sheets, I couldn't tell what the other team was doing. My dad often sat with me, and he couldn't figure out the systems, either. Like me, he's never looked at the game from a tactical point of view. He never coached at a level where tactics were used. When he played, hockey games were a skills contest. The better teams, skills-wise, nearly always won. It didn't have anything to do with which was the better-coached team.

That's changed. Look at the New Jersey Devils of 1995 who won the Stanley Cup, sweeping the Detroit Red Wings in the finals. Or the Florida Panthers reaching the finals in 1996. They weren't as skilled as Philadelphia or Pittsburgh, but their tactics were better. More effective. Maybe they were also better motivated. That's another strength of Coach Parker's. And he does a great job of skills development—making his players better players along the way. He's more than a coach. He's a teacher.

The only side of the game I'd known before my accident was the physical side: how to actually play the game. The strategy and tactics were brand new to me. I was always able to perform the plays the coach drew up, but I never knew why I was doing them. I never saw the whole picture the way I was trying to do now. Coach Parker had me studying film, but it was hard to watch the flow of the game on film, because you couldn't see the whole play developing. I could pick up on an individual's skills by watching film, and tell you everything about that one player. But I couldn't tell you anything about all five. And watching from the stands, I couldn't pick out what was going right and what was going wrong with the strategy as a whole. Not yet, anyway. I found it almost impossible.

My thoughts, invariably, would get caught up in the game itself, and I'd forget to look for systems. I'd get totally absorbed in the action, and would think about what I'd have done in a certain situation. A good passing play, a good goal, a good hit—all made me excited. All I cared about was that we win. The numbness I'd first felt when watching hockey from my wheelchair had long passed.

There was only one thing that bothered me, that snapped me back from my enjoyment of the game. The most dangerous play in hockey is to hit someone from behind along the boards, and when I saw that happen, regardless of whether it was one of our players who did it or an opponent, I'd get upset. I couldn't believe how stupid it was—a cardinal sin. Those were the only times I became agitated when watching the game, the only times I'd think about what could happen, and what had happened to me. Once in a while, when someone went down in the corner where my accident took place, I'd silently acknowledge the location with a quick thought: That's where my career ended. It would just pop into my head. I didn't dwell on it. There was no emotional breakdown that followed.

Between periods, I'd head back to the locker room. Sometimes on the way to the elevator a young boy would intercept me and ask for an autograph. I'm not quick at it, but I don't mind. I'd have to ask him to put his pen in my mouth, and I'd print *Travis Roy, 24,* on whatever he wanted me to sign. He'd have to hold the paper or program in front of my face. It surprises people, I know, that I'm unable to hold a pen in my hand, or write my name. But then life is full of surprises.

I liked hearing what the coach had to say between periods. He's always making the team play better. He never needed my input about systems. Any problems we were having he'd already have spotted long before I had. And even if the team had demolished the opposition in the first period, Coach Parker would invariably make five or six adjustments to improve things. Only once all season can I recall him saying, "You're doing great; keep doing what you're doing."

More likely, it was, "Look, this isn't working," and in two seconds he'd draw up some adjustments on the board, sliding a wing down on the breakout, or moving the defensemen wider on the power play. He always knew the perfect thing to do. If the game was tied after two, he'd always say, "Win the third, win the game."

He seldom threw any tantrums, but the guys liked to tell a story about one time he did. It was during the University of New Hampshire game last year, when we'd played a lousy period and had fallen behind. Coach Parker came into the room, and he was all wound up. He started to light into the entire team, cursing and storming around the room. He could be scary when he was mad. Halfway across, he slipped and fell on his ass.

Thud. There was total silence. The whole room quivered on the edge of laughter, but the guys were terrified what the coach's reaction might be if they started to giggle. They were biting their hands, staring at the floor, unwilling to catch anyone's eye. Coach Parker got up, red-faced, equal parts fury and embarrassment. He was fully aware of how ridiculous he'd looked. "Okay, you've got two minutes to get it out of your system," he said, walking out. "I'll be back."

They let it out then, relieved howls of laughter. When the coach returned, everyone was focused and ready for business. He'd turned an embarrassing moment into a tension breaker, and the team went on to win the game.

I knew that if I were going to feel a part of this team, I had to spend time with the players away from the locker room, too. We had to see each other in places besides the rink. So one Saturday night after a game I went with some of the guys to T's Pub, which is a place on Commonwealth Avenue where the players traditionally hang out. I've never been much of a drinker, and I wasn't about to start now. But I thought it was important to make an effort to socialize on that level.

There was a four- or five-inch lip in front of the pub that a couple of the players had to lift me over. Right away I saw that this experience was going to be tough. The bar was jammed, which was a problem for my big, bulky wheelchair. Some of the players wanted to dance, and I wasn't going to dance. The rest of us found a table, but my chair was too tall to fit under it. So I was kind of sticking out, too far away to be heard above the loud music. I couldn't hear the conversations going on across the table, either. So I just ended up sitting there and watching everything go on around me. It was like a dream, but not a pleasant dream. I didn't enjoy it at all. I was there maybe an hour and a half, but I wasn't involved. Nothing was normal. I had to drink my beer through a straw, and the straw fell back into the bottle and I couldn't get it out. Not that I cared. I wasn't upset or pissed off. It was just one more incident, and one more place where things weren't natural, and I've started to get used to things not being natural.

When I got back to my room, I called Maija, and she was happy to hear I'd made the effort to go out. She keeps getting after me to socialize more. I didn't really tell her how it went, though. I mentioned that it was awkward, and that a loud, crowded bar wasn't the best place for me to interact with people. But I didn't want to worry her. It was no biggy. It was my problem, and I'd figure out a way to deal with it.

In early October Ed Carpenter, BU's sports information director, called to tell me that another young college hockey player had suffered an injury similar to mine. His name was Erik Drygas, and he played for the University of Alaska, Fairbanks. The injury had occurred in one of the first practices of the year. The University of Alaska coach had called Jack Parker, and Coach Parker passed the young man's number on to Ed Carpenter and my parents. Erik had said he wanted to talk to me.

As soon as I heard about it, I literally felt sick inside that another family would have to go through what we had. It put me out of sorts for two or three days. I talked to Dad, who'd already talked to Erik's parents, and asked what level injury Erik had sustained. He was a C5, the same as my friend from Shepherd, Steve

Sheline. Dad said that Erik was a defenseman, six feet two and 220 pounds. It's very difficult to be that big and in a wheelchair. It would be tough on his parents to roll him around and get him dressed.

I gave Erik a call that afternoon. He was still in the intensive care unit, and I talked to his father first to get my facts straight. I asked him what Erik could feel and move, and he told me that Erik could move his arms already, but not his fingers. He wasn't sedated, and he wasn't on a ventilator.

I wanted to make sure he really wanted to talk to me; that this wasn't something being forced on him. His father assured me that he wanted to talk. He switched me onto Erik's speakerphone, which was a little awkward, since his teammates and coaches were with him. I started out by asking him how he was doing. You know he's not doing well, but I couldn't think how else to begin a conversation like that.

I told him that this was a hard thing to do, and that I'd just start talking, and if he had any questions, to feel free to interrupt and ask. If it wasn't helping, if it was making things worse, to feel free to tell me that, too. I told him I remembered all too clearly the other quadriplegics who'd talked to me early on, before I was ready to listen, all cheerful and positive about how this wasn't so bad, about how life would be better than I thought. I told him how it really hadn't helped me at all. You had to work through all this at your own pace.

I told him a little about my own experience, how I didn't know what was going on for the first four months, how I couldn't talk. I told him how weird it had been not to feel any pain, how you're lying in bed and quite comfortable, because you can't feel enough to know if you're uncomfortable. I told him to be honest with his parents and himself, and not to hide things and keep them inside.

At that point Erik interrupted me to ask what my level of injury was, what I could move. I told him. I said I'd love to have what he had, to be able to move both my arms; I told him I knew that sounded stupid to him, but he'd understand down the road what it meant as far as his capabilities went. Then I paused and said, "How are we doing, Erik? Is this helping or not?"

"Yeah. It is."

I told him a little bit about how much I was able to travel. How I was traveling more than I ever had before my accident. I gave him my phone number and told him to please, please call with any questions, night or day, if he just wanted an ear to talk to. Not to worry about bothering me. And I expressed how great a place Shepherd had been for me, so at least he could start thinking about it.

In the end, though, Erik decided to go to the Craig Center in Colorado, another facility that specialized in spinal-cord injuries. It was closer to his home, and the Craig Center also has a fine reputation. I hope his battle goes well.

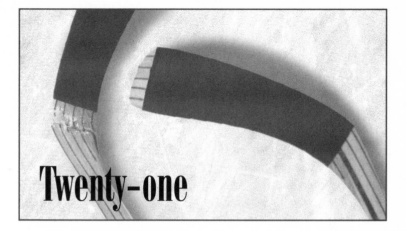

Twenty-one

Around that time I flew down to Washington, D.C., at the invitation of Senator William Cohen of Maine. He'd asked me to be one of five speakers to address a joint session of the Senate Appropriations Committee and the Committee on Aging, which he chaired, on behalf of the National Institutes of Health, which was seeking a 6.9 percent increase in research funding. I'd have seven minutes to make a presentation.

I have confidence when talking about spinal-cord research, so I wasn't particularly nervous. To be truthful, though, I didn't understand how big a deal it would be. Arthur Ullian, one of the nation's leading advocates for paralysis victims, worked with me on what to say. He was responsible for Senator Cohen's having issued the invitation. Arthur is a quadriplegic who's dedicated his life to finding a cure for paralysis, and he's been trying to bring all the various factions and organizations that raise money for spinal-cord research under one umbrella.

The problem, as Arthur sees it, is that paralysis victims have yet to find a common, cohesive voice. The two biggest factions in the broad spectrum are the American Paralysis Association (APA) and the Paralyzed Veterans of America (PVA), but neither one has attracted the sort of national attention that, say, Christopher Reeve has been able to do all by himself. If these groups were consolidated into one organization dedicated to finding a cure for neurological disorders, like the American Cancer Society is dedicated to fighting cancer and the March of Dimes is dedicated to fighting cerebral palsy, the ability to raise funds for spinal-cord research would increase dramatically.

Fifteen years ago, if you were paralyzed, you were pretty much told that was it. The medical community wasn't even doing research to try to cure it. The assumption was that the central nervous system was incapable of regenerating itself, and that once it was damaged, the 800,000 long nerve fibers, or axons, that travel through the spinal cord had to be individually reattached to their exact partners before signals from the brain could get through, an impossible task.

Scientists know now that isn't the case. They know that in certain conditions, nerves do regenerate themselves after having been damaged or destroyed. The regeneration of nerves is the key to curing not just spinal-cord injuries, but also degenerative nerve diseases like multiple sclerosis, Alzheimer's, Parkinson's, and Lou Gehrig's disease. It's the same neurological puzzle, only in those diseases the nerves gradually degenerate, whereas in the case of a spinal-cord injury, the damage happens all at once.

Researchers in Sweden had the biggest breakthrough ever in the summer of 1996, when scientists at the Karolinska Institute in Stockholm succeeded in severing the spinal cords of rats and then helping them regain movement in their hind legs. They did it by building a bridge over the injured area of the spinal cord by grafting nerves to it from another part of the rat's body. Some of those nerves successfully reconnected. The rats didn't get up and run away, but they were able to move their hind legs a little and support their own weight.

What made the Swedish announcement so exciting was that it

was the first time in history that scientists had proved that spinal-cord nerves could regenerate. *Proved* it. That had always been the hope, but it was theoretical. No one had known for a fact if it were true. Now they did. Scientists now believe there will be a cure for paralysis. It's only a question of when.

I've seen X rays of my spinal cord, and where it's healthy, above and below my injury, it looks dark. At the spot of the injury, there's just a white, dense impassable knot of scar tissue. One way to cure my paralysis, in theory, is to remove that knot of scar tissue surgically, severing the cord completely, then to build a bridge around it with nerves from another part of my body—my chest, say, or my foot—reconnecting the undamaged parts of my spinal cord. A nerve graft. If it were to take, if the nerves regenerated, I might someday walk again.

I expect that to happen. I know it will happen in my lifetime, but for it to happen sooner rather than later, more money is needed for research. One of the things Arthur Ullian told me was that the federal government allocates only $40 million a year for nerve regeneration research: 1/36th of the $1.431 billion it spends on AIDS research, 1/57th of the $2.281 billion it spends on cancer research, and 1/35th of the $1.379 billion it spends on heart and lung research. Obviously they're all worthy causes, but nerve regeneration, which is not a myth, and which could have such huge implications in curing other neurological disorders besides paralysis—MS, Alzheimer's, Parkinson's, Lou Gehrig's disease, even the aftereffects of strokes—is little more than an afterthought in the current scheme of things.

I get frustrated with the shortsighted nature of our government. If the federal government dedicated itself to the cause of discovering how to regenerate nerves the way it did to putting a man on the moon or building an atomic bomb, if the best scientific minds in this country were given complete financial backing, it would happen. And it would be money well spent, since right now, according to Arthur Ullian, some $3.5 billion a year of Medicaid and Medicare payments go to paralysis victims, who live an average of 31 years after suffering their injuries. When this country is dedicated to a cause, it finds a way, and I honestly can't think of a more dramatic difference the scientific community could make toward saving and improving the lives of American citizens than by discovering how to regenerate nerves.

My appearance before Senator Cohen's committee was on a Thursday, and Dad and I flew down to Washington on Wednesday night. We checked into our hotel, and Dad told me, "We have to go over what you're going to say. Let me see your speech."

I started throwing out some ideas that Arthur and I had discussed, and Dad looked at me in mock horror. "Travis, you still haven't written any of this down?"

"I'm only speaking for seven minutes."

He was amused. He has more confidence in me than anyone in the world. If my mother had been there, she'd have gone through the roof. But my dad did at least suggest I make an outline.

He wrote down what I told him. I saved it, and you can probably fill in the blanks.

A—Travis Roy
    —From Maine, C4 quad
    —How it happened
    —Back at B.U.
B—I want
    —Hug girlfriend
    —Children
C—Neurological disorders
    —Not just spinal cord injuries
    —Parkinson's; Alzheimer's; M.S.

D—Past Challenges and Solutions
    —A-bombs; Manhattan project
    —Space Age, man on moon
    —Desert Storm, Smart bombs
E—Conclusion
    —Scientists/Doctors/Researchers>>Next heroes
    —Technology—we have
    —$$$-Financial Resources>>>to find cures for neuro-
    logical disorders

I rehearsed it in my hotel room three times, then went to bed.

In the morning I had an interview with the *Today* show and *USA Today* before my appearance, so everything was a little rushed. When they brought me into the committee room, the other four panelists and the attending senators were already there. It was a very serious, intimidating setting. TV cameras were set up on the side of the huge room, broadcasting the hearing live over C-SPAN. The Senate emblem was on the wall. There were about 100 spectators in the gallery, my father included, and 20 to 25 staff members were seated behind the senators on the committee.

Senator Mark Hatfield of Oregon was the chairman of the Appropriations Committee, and he was sitting behind a big formal U-shaped table with the five other senators: Senator Cohen and Senator Connie Mack and I forget who else. The other panelists and I were in the middle of the U. General Norman Schwarzkopf was on my right. I was more intimidated by him than anyone else. He's an enormous man, a real physical presence. I talked to him briefly, but otherwise kept my mouth shut.

General Schwarzkopf was the first one to give a presentation. He opened a thick leather folder, which carried the official U.S. Army seal and had his name embossed in gold on the leather. Out came something like 25 neatly typed pages, in huge print, triple spaced. I'm holding this single handwritten piece of paper with an outline on it, and thinking, Oh, no. I felt like the little drummer boy surrounded by these great wise men bringing myrrh, frankincense, and gold. Me and my drum. General Schwarzkopf was speaking on behalf of prostate cancer research, and I kept sneaking glances at the page numbers, wondering, How long is this thing?

Rod Carew, the baseball Hall-of-Famer, was next. He'd lost a daughter to leukemia, and talked movingly about that. He'd brought a video with him, and also had his speech all typed out. Next was a lady who spoke on behalf of Parkinson's disease research. At least she didn't have a typed speech, which made me feel better. Then they called on me.

I was quite calm, to be honest. I followed the outline, as planned, and it went smoothly, I think. Mine was more personal than the other presentations. I was by far the youngest person there, and the way I put it to them was basically: I have my whole life ahead of me, and you guys have the chance to cure me. It's all a matter of time and money. If you spend the money now, it will take a lot less time.

When I finished, Senator Cohen gave me a thumbs-up and a wink. After the final presentation, from a student who wanted to enter the field of medical research but was fearful there would be no grant money to support her, all the senators spoke a few words about their impressions of the hearing. It had been quite an emotional series of speeches, and it was something like 45 seconds before Senator Connie Mack could even talk. Another senator said it was the best hearing he'd ever attended, and Senator Hatfield agreed. He sent me a note later that I've saved: *Your courageous and heartfelt testimony made this forum one of the most memorable and important events in my tenure as committee chairman.*

Afterward General Schwarzkopf went out a separate way to avoid questions from the news media about the recent bombing that President Clinton had ordered against Iraq, so I didn't get his autograph. But before he left he told me he was involved in the Miami Project in Florida, a well-known facility that works with victims of spinal-cord injuries, and that the fertility program down there had given birth to eleven babies. He said that when the time came, I should get in touch with them.

My dad told me afterward I did a great job. When he says something like that, he doesn't just say it. I could see the pride all over his face. Pride, in our family, is an emotion, and his emotions are easy to read.

Most important, when the time came, the Appropriations Committee did, in fact, give the National Institutes of Health the 6.9 percent increase in research funding that they'd sought.

Research funding is only half the battle. The other area where money is needed is funding quality-of-life improvements for victims of spinal-cord injuries. Which is one of the reasons my family helped me start the Travis Roy Foundation.

We wanted to give something back. I was lucky. Because of the Travis Roy Fund, because of all those angels who pitched in after my injury, I'll be able to live a pretty comfortable life. Not extravagant, by any means. But not wanting. I have a wheelchair so I can get around. I have a van with a motorized lift so friends can drive me places. I have a special bed so I won't get bedsores. I have a speakerphone so I can telephone by myself; a Hoyer lift that lets me get in and out of the shower; an environmental control unit for turning electrical appliances off and on; a voice-activated computer for writing papers. It's all expensive, but I've seen firsthand what this stuff can do: Basically it enables you to take on life again.

So we set up the Travis Roy Foundation to raise money for other wheelchair victims who've not been so fortunate. I hear these stories that upset me so much. There's a quadriplegic man who lives in an apartment on the second floor that isn't handicapped accessible. The only way he can leave his house is when his friends come and carry him down the stairs. Maybe this happens once every three days; maybe it happens once a week. There's another man who can't afford to have care attendants come in every day. His wife left him after his accident. So he spends entire nights sleeping in his chair, or entire days lying alone in bed. I'll do anything to find a cure, don't get me wrong, but I have a hard time hearing about people who have to live like that. It's impossible to help all of them, which makes it all the more frustrating. I have a hard time coming to terms with the fact that I've been given all this support while others have not. And why? Because I broke my neck in my first collegiate hockey game, a game that was televised, and they broke their necks some other way.

Believe it or not, Christopher Reeve has been criticized some in the quadriplegic community for raising all this money solely in an effort to find a cure. Everything he brings in goes to research. Meanwhile there are a lot of people in wheelchairs who just want to get out of the house, or out of their nursing home, and they don't have the means to do so. I don't think the criticism of Reeve is warranted. Everyone in a wheelchair would like to see a cure, and most would rather suffer through years of tough times to know they might one day walk again. That's the big picture.

But the Travis Roy Foundation is looking at the small picture, too. Let's face it—the money I can raise is like a single vote in a presidential election. It really doesn't matter in the big picture. It's a raindrop compared to what's now being spent on research, and what will be needed in the future, not even a fraction of 1 percent. So the foundation money that we raise through golf tournaments and the sale of Travis Roy Foundation caps, and auctions, and whatever else we'll come up with, will go both to research and to individual, case-by-case quality-of-life issues. People can write in and ask for grant money to buy specific big-ticket items, a wheelchair, say, or an elevator. That way I can see money raised in my name making a tangible difference in somebody's life, helping individual spinal-cord victims who are less fortunate than I am.

Twenty-two

Academically, my first semester back at college was a qualified success. I passed both my courses: B in English, C– in psychology. I can do better, and as time goes by, I will. But just proving to myself that I could do the work in those two gave me the confidence to sign up for a full load of four courses the second semester, a step I made without consulting my parents, who thought I'd be better off taking three. I signed up for Introduction to Communications, Social Psychology, an earth science course called Beaches and Shores, and Oral Presentation. I have an idea I'll probably end up in the school of communication. That seems to be where my strengths now lie.

The Terriers Christmas party, delayed until after the break, was held at Coach Parker's house in Melrose on January 9. His house is seven or eight steps up from the street, a climb that included two landings, so it was quite a production to get me in. Five guys from the team carried me, and we took the batteries out of my chair to make it as light as possible. Even so it was tricky, because the stairs were narrow, and there were bushes growing on either side. But we made it, and once inside, we just left the batteries out. They put me down in the center of the room so the party could go on around me. But it was difficult, because I wasn't able to mingle.

It's a tradition that the players exchange gag gifts, with the names drawn randomly out of a hat. I happened to have drawn Coach Parker, and I gave him a neck brace, because if you're going to coach in Walter Brown Arena, it seems like you'd better have one handy at all times. Tommy Noble, one of our goalies, who's a little vain about his appearance, was given a copy of *GQ* magazine and a can of hair spray. All-East defenseman Jon Coleman, who is injury prone, got a PlaySkool doctor's kit.

Most of the gifts were inside jokes, the kind that even the coaches wouldn't understand. I didn't understand most of them, either, and no one took the trouble to explain them to me. During the party, I wasn't able to have a meaningful conversation with any of the guys. They were kind of off talking among themselves. I couldn't yell across the room to them. As always, the players were glad to see me, and treated me the way I like to be treated—like one of the guys—but after the generic questions about grades, Maija, family, maybe a little hockey, there wasn't much more to discuss. We really didn't seem to have that much in common. I talked awhile to a new player from Finland, Tommi Degerman, who'd just joined the team for the second semester. He didn't know what any of the gag gifts were about either. He was playing with Chris Drury and Mike Sylvia, my old linemates, and I joked that he'd better not get too used to it, because I was coming back.

Coach Parker came over and asked if I'd had enough to eat. His daughters, Jaqueline and Allison, had been sitting with me most of the party, feeding me dinner. I told him I was fine. At the end of the night my father returned to get me in the van, and a bunch of the guys carried me back down. The coach asked if I'd had a good time. I wasn't going to lie to him, but I told him I was glad I'd come. He can read me pretty well, and he could see that things weren't going that great. That as hard as I was trying to fit in with the other players, it wasn't working. They'd jelled and bonded as a group, and I wasn't a part of it. The guys didn't know me much better than they did the first week of the season.

Dad drove me home, and the entire ride back to the dorm, I was on the edge of tears. I held them back, though. I really didn't want to get into it then.

We played Northeastern two nights later, and the team played a solid game and won, 5–4. Afterwards I went down to the locker room, still thinking about the Christmas party, and I listened to the coach give his postgame talk to the team. No one had much to say to me as I sat there. Maybe I was just noticing it more. I don't know. I went to leave, and Dad and Coach Parker were talking in the hall. I was kind of upset, so I went past without saying anything. To be honest I was wondering when it was ever going to end. I felt like I'd been given a punishment, and it was time for the punishment to be over.

"Don't you want to talk to us anymore?" Coach Parker asked after I'd passed.

I kept going. I wasn't doing that great. He followed me out the runway until we were sitting near the rink. The ice looked so beautiful, fresh and cleanly resurfaced.

"How are things going?" he asked.

"Not terrific."

"How did things go at the Christmas party?"

I told him it was tough, that I felt separated from the team. "I want so much to be part of it," I said. My eyes started to well up.

"Trav, just let it out," he said.

I did. I burst into tears, sobbing in a way I hadn't in a long time. I told him how much I wanted to get out on that ice, that looked so perfect, like it was just waiting for me. I actually tried to lunge out of my chair. I told him if I could be allowed out of the chair just to skate and play hockey, I could accept that. I could live with that. If only I could skate. The rest of it wasn't that important.

He shed a few tears with me, too. Coach Parker was doing everything he could to keep me involved, but it still sucked. I told him that the more I watched the Terriers play, the more I realized what a big part of this team I would have been. Coach knew. The team didn't have a lot of depth, and I'd have played on the power play. I'd have done penalty killing. I'd have played with Chris Drury, who at the time was leading the nation in scoring. Things would have worked out like I'd always hoped.

It was a good talk. Coach Parker mostly listened, which is what he does best. I told him how my father didn't really like to talk about things that hurt him. He never, ever talked about his own father, for instance, who died a number of years ago. My grandfather had been a teacher and antiques dealer, and my father loved him a great deal. I know he thought about him a lot, but he never talked about him. And he didn't talk to me about my not being able to play hockey, which was on both of our minds all the time. What was the point? It just brought both of us pain. It was time to let go and get on with our lives. But like my mom, sometimes I need to talk about things.

Coach Parker told me he had to go meet with the Boston reporters about the game. He asked if I was okay, and I told him to go ahead. I was better now. I wanted to stay right where I was and just look out at the ice that was so inviting. I hadn't cried like that for a long time, and the tears were still wet on my cheeks.

My dad came up behind me. He wiped my face and hugged my head, so I could smell and feel his chest. He was crying, too. It hurt him that I wasn't playing hockey anymore. I knew that. He didn't have to talk about it for me to know it. But it hurt him more to see me torn all to pieces inside.

"I miss the game, Dad."

He was nodding, wiping his own face now. "I miss watching you play the game, son," he said.

Twenty-three

The 1996–97 BU hockey team finally came together as a unit in late February, after being shellacked in a weekend series up in Maine, 3–0 and 7–2. In retrospect, those two humbling losses were the best thing that could have happened to us. The guys really pulled together afterwards, focusing on defense, and managed to win seven straight games to qualify for the Final Four of the NCAA hockey tournament in late March. It took an overtime goal by Chris Drury against the University of Denver in the Eastern Regionals to get us there, but the team had come to expect that sort of heroics from my one-time linemate. Drury finished the season with 38 goals in 41 games and was runner-up for the Hobey Baker Award, which goes to the NCAA player of the year.

It was the fourth straight year that Boston University had gone to hockey's Final Four. The tournament was being held at the Bradley Center in Milwaukee, and I flew out Wednesday night with Jack O'Brien and my dad. No one expected BU to win. We had drawn the University of Michigan in the semifinal game on Thursday, March 27, and the Wolverines were the defending national champions. They entered the game with a 35–3–4 record and had been the top-ranked team in the country all season long. The year before, the Wolverines had crushed BU, 4–0, in the semifinals of the NCAAs. They outshot us by a margin of 15 to 1 in the first 10 minutes and never let up, holding our high-powered offense to just 18 shots on goal. This year's Michigan team was supposed to be even better.

I got to the Bradley Center about an hour and a half before game time, and watched a little of the other semifinal: North Dakota against Colorado College. North Dakota won rather easily, 6–2, but I wasn't overly impressed with them. They'd beaten and tied BU during the season, but I thought now we looked like a better hockey team.

Afterwards I went down to the North Dakota locker room to try and meet Mitch Vig. He was the North Dakota defenseman I'd tried to check 18 months earlier, when I'd tripped and broken my neck. I'd never met Mitch, but his mother had written to my mother, and I wanted him to know I was doing okay. I wanted to make sure he didn't feel guilty about what had happened. It was a lousy thing for him to go through, too. He seemed like a real nice kid, and after a few minutes of conversation, we said good-bye and wished each other luck.

Over in the BU locker room the guys were pretty loose, kicking a soccer ball around the hall, which was their usual way to warm up before a game. I was glad to see them relaxed. I'd been worried we'd go out there too tight. Coach Parker came into the room before warm-ups, and even though I should have known better, I thought he might make some big speech about how important the game was. But he didn't. Everyone knew the stakes. All but the freshmen had been in that situation before. Coach just told them, "Fast and loose," as he often did, and, "It's great to be an underdog." It seemed great. The guys were really confident.

Peter Donatelli, a sophomore, was saying, "This is a fight, guys," while other players were reminding each other that Michi-

gan had jumped on them early last year. "Start off with some big
hits, big bumps," someone said. The last college hockey team to
repeat as national champions was the BU team that won in 1971
and again in 1972. So that was another little incentive for us to
knock off Michigan.

The game plan, basically, was to let our offense come from our
defense. Counterattack. Our biggest asset all season had been defense, and we were going to forecheck conservatively and make
sure Michigan, which had the top offensive team in the nation,
didn't get any odd-man rushes. It required discipline and patience.

Right from the start the Terriers set the tone by rocking the
Michigan players every time they touched the puck. I was sitting
with Dad across from the BU bench, and bodies were flying all
over the rink. It was great. Even when the Wolverines took a 1–0
lead, I felt good about the way things were going. Falling behind,
which we'd done in four straight games, only made our guys work
harder. We just kept banging and banging, until by the end of the
period the Michigan players were thinking twice before they
touched the puck. We were completely controlling the play, even
while killing penalties, and the vaunted Wolverine offense managed only six shots on goal.

Between periods Coach Parker made a couple of minor adjustments to help us break out of our defensive zone, moving the
wings up higher along the boards and changing the angle at which
the center skated across. He told the guys to keep hitting and to
stay poised.

Our patience paid off in the second period, as Greg Quebec,
Chris Heron, and Tommi Degerman put together three unan-
swered goals. That turned out to be enough, as my former roommate, goalie Michel Larocque, didn't allow Michigan to score
again until the final minute of the game. The final was BU 3,
Michigan 2. We'd beaten the best team in the country.

When I came down to the locker room after the game, guys

were shouting to each other, "We're going to the finals!" It was the most psyched I'd seen them all year. But they weren't going crazy. It wasn't as if they'd stolen the game or anything like that. We'd deserved to win, and the guys knew it. It's tough to be number one all year, and Michigan hadn't played as well that night as their record indicated they should.

"Michel, you played awesome," I told Larocque, putting my hand up so he could bang fists with me.

"I didn't have to do anything," he said. He'd only faced 18 shots all game, the lowest total Michigan had put on net all season. "I wanted more shots."

I went to the practice on Friday, and the guys were still really loose and confident. But not overly so. I didn't sense a letdown after the Michigan win. It was a light workout, which was appropriate for that stage of the season. They went over a few things strategically. Afterwards Coach Parker invited me, my dad, and Coach O'Brien to join him and Mike Eruzione for dinner. We didn't talk about the national championship game at all. Eruzione's a great storyteller, and so is Coach Parker, and between the two of them and my dad, it was a fun meal with a lot of old hockey stories.

The team had a 9 P.M. meeting at the hotel, which I went to. Coach Parker showed the guys a video of the North Dakota–Colorado College game. He went over the North Dakota power play, pointing out that it was similar to Maine's. The Fighting Sioux liked to keep three guys low, so they would outnumber you in front of the net. To counteract that, Coach Parker made an adjustment in our penalty killing, moving one of our wings down to cover the post on the weak side. Then he went over the North Dakota forechecking scheme, which wasn't very aggressive. They liked to sag back, keeping two forwards up high, near the blue line, which meant our wings had to start the breakout from lower in the zone.

Because the game was going to be televised live on ESPN, it

was a noon start, early for a hockey game. I was obviously aware of the irony of us facing North Dakota, of all teams, for the national championship. I remembered so clearly that night a year and a half ago, when the same two teams took the ice, and they raised the championship banner in Walter Brown Arena. It had all come full circle, in a way, except that for me it was now a different lifetime. I didn't see our facing North Dakota as a sign that victory was in store for BU, that a win over the Fighting Sioux in the finals was inevitable, retribution of a sort for all I'd been through. My dad kind of looked at it that way. He told me later he was sure BU would win, and that the victory would be bittersweet. He saw a divine hand pulling the strings, a conspiracy of the hockey gods at work.

I didn't, though. I believed BU would win, for sure, but I wasn't thinking about it the same way my father was. I didn't see it as a match that was somehow meant to be. These were two of the best hockey programs in the nation meeting for the national championship. BU had won the title four times; North Dakota had won it five times. It wasn't that surprising that they should be playing for it again. What was surprising, for me, was that I was watching it instead of playing.

It was weird for me to sit in the locker room while my teammates dressed and taped their sticks before the game. It's really happening, I thought. You aren't dreaming. Your teammates are getting ready to go out and play for the national championship, a game you've always dreamed of playing in, and you are paralyzed in a wheelchair, watching and awake.

I still have to remind myself of that because, even after all this time, I can't believe I'm a quadriplegic. I bet it's like that forever. It'll always be a crazy thing to me. I'm comfortable in my wheelchair. It even feels like home. I'm used to what I look like in it, how I feel in it, what the world looks like from this perspective. It's how my life works right now, and I'm thankful to have it. But it won't ever feel right, or natural. Not tomorrow. Not in twenty years. It'll never feel normal, because when I look around, everyone else is walking. If everyone else were in a wheelchair, it would be different. Then maybe I wouldn't feel like the odd man out.

The team seemed just as relaxed and confident in the locker room as they'd been two days earlier before the Michigan game. I didn't sense any loss of focus. And once the puck was dropped, things started very well. We took a 2–0 lead in the first period, scoring a couple of nice goals by Donatelli and Drury. Sitting with my father, I was thinking, BU is going to win. There was very little hitting, which bothered me, but North Dakota wasn't doing much hitting either. Michel was playing very well in goal, as he had throughout the play-offs, and at one point, when he cleared the puck right to a North Dakota defenseman and was forced to make another save, I had to smile. Michel wants more shots again tonight, I thought.

I went down to the locker room after the first period feeling pretty good about things, but as soon as the guys came in they started saying things like, "We need to relax. We've got to stop yelling at each other!"

Oh-oh, I thought. What was going on here? We had a two-goal lead, things were going fine, now what was this? Coach Parker came in and told the guys, "That's the worst period you guys have played in a long time. You're lucky to be leading two–zero. You're not playing the hockey you've been playing the last month and a half."

He made a couple of adjustments, but I could sense that things hadn't settled down enough by the end of the intermission. You'd have thought North Dakota was ahead. The guys weren't really ready to go out and start fresh.

And, sure enough, the second period was all North Dakota. They got a goal on a long screen shot about seven minutes into the session, and then Chris Kelleher and Chris Drury—roommates and two of our best players—each made a turnover that sent a North Dakota player in on a clean breakaway. Both players scored, and suddenly we trailed, 3–2. My dad and I looked at each other, and right then I knew it wasn't meant to be. Drury and Kelleher, one a first-team all-America, the other a second-team all-America, were the last two people you'd have thought would give the puck away. North Dakota scored five times in all, including a backbreaker that gave them a two-goal lead with just six seconds left in the period. I'd already left my place and was waiting by the elevator when I heard the roar. It was the worst 20 minutes we'd played all year.

Coach Parker came into the dressing room right away and was obviously upset. "We've got to settle down, guys. Why aren't we following the game plan? No one's doing what they're supposed to be doing."

The guys had simply stopped playing as a team. Everyone, I suppose, was trying to do too much. Coach Parker walked out of the room, and it was pretty quiet after he left. "Let's get some hitting going," I said to no one in particular. A couple of the guys talked about taking the body first, and then the puck. That's fundamental BU hockey, and for some reason it hadn't been happening out there. When Coach Parker came back in with about five minutes left in the intermission, he was relaxed again, obviously trying to get the team to relax, too. "Win the third, win the game," he said. "Play the systems we're supposed to play."

The third period went better, but we'd dug ourselves too deep a hole against a good defensive team. There weren't many scoring chances on either side in the final session. After pulling Michel for a sixth attacker, we scored to get within 5–4 in the final 36 seconds. But North Dakota added an open net goal to clinch it, and won the national championship, 6–4.

They held the awards ceremony on the ice after the game. I went down to the locker room, which I had to myself for about ten minutes while the guys received their runner-up trophies. I later heard that Coach Parker and the team were asking for me, wanting me to join them on the ice, which I'd done after our wins at the Beanpot and the Hockey East tournament, but I really didn't want to see my picture flashed all over the country on ESPN. I could imagine the story line. I could imagine which photograph sports editors around the country would choose to run. So, as much as I wanted to congratulate the North Dakota team and be with my teammates, I stayed where I was. I didn't want to face the interviews and all the rest of it. I sat in the locker room by myself, and once again I found myself thinking, It really happened, Travis. It's not a dream.

When the guys finally came in, I was glad to see they really weren't that upset. No one had expected that team to get as far as they had, and, for the seniors—Billy Pierce, Shawn Bates, Shane Johnson, Matt Wright, Shawn Ferullo, Jon Coleman—they were leaving behind an amazing set of accomplishments. They'd won four Beanpots, had made it to the Final Four all four years, had gone to the national championship game twice, and had won the title once. It was a heck of a record, and they were justifiably proud.

Coach Parker came in then and told the team he had something to say, and he wanted to get it out right now. This was the most fun he'd ever had coaching a group of guys. To see how the team had come together, had cleared hurdles, had managed to get around trouble spots and gone so far with so few players, with so little depth, was something he'd always remember. It's why he coaches, he said.

The team had reserved a room at a restaurant for a team dinner and celebration at five o'clock. To be honest, I wasn't sure if I wanted to join them there or not. I remembered how awkward I'd felt at the Christmas party. But I'd spent more time with them the past three days than I had all year, so I figured I might as well see it through. I went into the room a little tentatively, but as soon as I came through the door, Shawn Bates, seated at the bar, shouted across the room, "Trav, I got a beer for you right here."

It made me feel so good. "I'd love nothing better than a beer,"

I told him. Even though I'm not much of a beer drinker, it was true.

I took my place at the bar with the rest of the guys, and we talked about what everyone was planning to do that spring. No one moped or was depressed. Hockey season's a long, long haul, and everyone was happy it was over and looking forward to some time off. When it came time to eat, I asked Dan Ronan, my former roommate, if he'd mind feeding me. "Not at all, Trav," he said.

It really makes me feel good when someone helps me in a way that seems natural, no big deal. We sat down at the table, and Coach Parker brought me a plate of food. Dan cut it up and fed it to me. It was the first time one of my teammates had done that. We all kept talking. It was such a relief. That's all I'd wanted to be able to do all along. Just to sit and eat a meal with the guys. It seemed so natural, finally. It was the ending of the hockey season, but for me, it felt like a beginning. I'd made a little, tiny step forward. It was a start.

I went to bed early that night. My dad got me ready, then flipped off the light, and went back down to talk to some of the other parents in the hotel bar.

I lay in my bed thinking. A lot had been going on in my life away from the hockey team, too. My family was just beginning to come to grips with some things they hadn't really faced before, like how much my injury had affected each of them. I wasn't the only one who'd been going through hell. To some extent my parents, Tobi, and Maija had spent so much time worrying about me that they'd sort of lost track of themselves.

At least that's how Tobi was feeling. She'd recently decided to see a therapist. Way, way back, in the first weeks after my accident, doctors at BU Hospital had told each member of the family it would be a good idea to talk to a psychologist, someone who could help them deal with the stress my accident had unavoidably added to their lives. None of them had followed that advice. I think my own experience with psychologists may have put them off the whole idea of therapy. I talked to one doctor at Boston University Hospital, and another one at Shepherd, and I never felt comfortable with either man. I sort of believed I should be able to cope with everything on my own. I got that trait from my dad, and I think it's a trait shared by a lot of people in Maine. I knew what I had to do. Even in the area of my social life, which for a long time I've recognized is a real concern, I knew what I had to do. I just had to kick myself and start doing it.

But Tobi had been feeling a little like she didn't know who she was anymore. Was she a sister? A daughter? A wife? A nurse? Ever since my accident she'd felt she'd lost control of her life, and she didn't like the direction things were going.

So she made an appointment with a woman whom she'd been referred to, and after her first session, she called to tell me how good it had been. She called my parents, too. Tobi recalled how she had just started talking. And in the process of talking, she was able to answer most of her questions herself. The therapist had told her not to expect any answers, if that was what she was there for, because there weren't any clear-cut answers to the situation my family found itself in. Not answers we really wanted to hear, anyway. I was paralyzed. There wasn't going to be a happy ending to plug into that—not without a medical breakthrough, which, at best, was several years away. I wasn't ever going to suit up again and play college hockey and fulfill my most precious dreams, and the dreams my family had for me. Nothing the therapist said or did was going to be able to alter that.

But what really struck home was when the woman asked Tobi, "Have you grieved yet?"

Tobi hadn't. No one in my family had. The therapist explained there were several stages of grieving one had to go through after a great loss, but outside of the first few moments of sorrow the night of my accident, my family had kicked right into survival mode. No self-pity. No denial. No rage. My father had held his press conference, telling everyone we were all right, and would be all right. That we'd get through this. Then we all set about stoically facing one day at a time, trying to shield ourselves and each other from this deep and abiding pain.

No time had been set aside to grieve for what had been lost.

Tobi had been so excited at the prospect of finally being able to see me play hockey, at the prospect of getting to know me again as a brother—not as a "little brother," but as an equal. Then, after eleven seconds, through no fault of anyone's, that had been taken away from her. It wasn't just me who had suffered. She'd lost something dear, too. But she'd been so busy caring for me, distracting me from the realities of my situation, trying to keep me from thinking about the limitations of my condition, that she hadn't had a chance to acknowledge her own loss. She hadn't had a chance to mourn those times we *should have* spent together in Boston, doing the things we'd have been able to do if I'd been healthy: Rollerblading along the Charles, going to Red Sox games, spontaneously getting together and having fun.

Tobi had been so busy being strong, so busy pretending not to be all broken up inside, that she hadn't allowed herself to really feel anything since the first three or four days after the accident. She'd discovered that if you said things were fine often enough, if you told people that Travis was back in college, working with the hockey team, and life was getting back to normal, pretty soon you started to believe it. Even if deep down you knew something important was amiss, that you were out of balance in some essential way. Suppress pain in one part of your life, and pretty soon you're suppressing all your feelings.

That's what was happening in my family. We'd all been so focused on taking things one day at a time, one week at a time, patching up holes as they appeared, that my parents and sister and even, to a certain extent, Maija hadn't taken the time to grieve for the old Travis who was now gone. I'd grieved all along. I had no choice. I faced my situation every day, and knew the difference between the old Travis and the new one. They hadn't properly grieved for how my accident had affected *their* lives, *their* dreams, *their* futures, *their* relationships. They hadn't really dealt with all that sadness, or if they did, they'd just touched the surface of it.

Then once I was back in school, it was easy to pretend that everything was more or less back to normal. How are things? their friends would ask. And my parents, like Tobi, got into the habit of painting as rosy a picture as they could. Because who wants to hear that things suck? And pretty soon they, too, started to believe it. They hadn't quite realized what was going on with me at school, that I wasn't sitting around thinking happy thoughts most of the time, that I was having trouble making new friends, that I was lonely and frustrated and being around the hockey team wasn't going that terrifically, either. They hadn't realized it because I'd never told them.

No question about it, I'm the biggest piece of this puzzle. I take up three-quarters of the puzzle. Because for my parents to understand the situation, for us to really come together as a family, I need to tell them what's going on inside my head. Good and bad. Maija knows what's going on inside my head. Most of it, anyway. She's the one person I've expressed all this stuff to—my fears, my frustrations, my sadness. And I now realize I've been putting too much on her shoulders. It's too much for her. It'll sink her under its weight, and our relationship will sink with it. I've got to start spreading the load.

I hesitated to tell them things because I didn't want my family worrying about me. I felt I'd put Mom and Dad through enough, frankly, and I wanted to deal with all this stuff myself. Tobi's the same way. Keith told me that, recently. My sister and I both tend to keep everything inside us and not discuss things. We accept things and deal with them, the same as my father. And that's worked fine our entire lives. But not this time. We're just in over our heads with this one.

And the thing is, I need to know what my parents are thinking, too. It's tough, because it's not just a can of worms we're opening here. It's more like an entire country full of worms. It's huge. But until you get the pain out, you can't move beyond it. It doesn't help to bury your emotions. It doesn't help to hide the anger and sadness and sorrow. You can only keep so much inside you before you become emotionally paralyzed, too.

So I've decided we're all going to be a little more honest with each other. And we're already making progress, I think. Now when people ask my father how things are going, Dad can be pretty blunt. Things stink right now, he might say. My mother hates to hear those words come out of his mouth, but it happens to be pretty close to the truth, and if people can't deal with it, they shouldn't ask. We're all beginning to realize we have to reconnect with ourselves emotionally as individuals, reconnect with our true feelings, before we can reconnect as a family. Structurally, we've reconnected. I'm back at school. My parents are back working. Tobi's married and working. But we haven't really reconnected emotionally. And it's important that we do. They keep me going, these loved ones. I love and admire them more than I'm able to express.

So all of that is good. I have a feeling of excitement when I look ahead now that I haven't had since the day of my accident. This spring I'm going to transfer into the school of communications. Public relations is what I'm thinking of right now as a major, with a minor in psychology. I already know so much about TV interviews and so many people in the newspaper and magazine business that I might as well try to pursue it. Ed Carpenter, the sports information director of Boston University, has certainly been a tremendous role model to watch. They don't come any better than him—as a person or as an SID. I've had internship offers from both the Los Angeles Kings and the Pittsburgh Penguins.

I'm starting to think about my future a lot. Sometimes I'll say to Maija that I can't wait to play hockey again, or go swimming, because I believe researchers will one day find a cure for paralysis. Soon. I see myself on my own two feet again in ten years. It kind of surprises Maija when I say that, because she's content with the way things are today. She's accepted that this is the way things will be for a while, and if it's forever, that's fine, too. For my sake, she'd like me to be able to walk and swim and skate. But she's not counting the days until it happens. So it always catches her a little off guard when I bring it up.

I see myself around hockey somehow, perhaps at the professional level. I'm still trying to figure out how I can relate to the game again the way I related to it as a player. I'm trying to discover what might excite me the way Coach Parker gets excited. You should have seen his face when the Terriers beat Michigan. Or when, after we beat Boston College to win the Beanpot tournament, he leaped over the boards and hugged me as the guys put the trophy on my lap. It made the whole experience for me. I wonder if I'll ever be able to find a role in the game that gives me that sort of thrill.

I've thought about coaching, but for me, the real problem would be accessibility. There's no room for my wheelchair behind the players' bench, and I'd probably have trouble getting into a lot of locker rooms. I'd have to wear a helmet and face mask when I was on the ice, since I couldn't duck any high-flying wayward pucks. I suppose I could be an assistant and wear a headset and be the "eye in the sky" sitting in the stands. But what I'd really like to do is work with the players on their skills.

I wonder, though, how effective a coach I'd be explaining things without being able to demonstrate them. Some skills, like skating, I'm sure I could teach. I'd tell the players to work on their balance. To stay low to the ice. To keep their heads up. To get full extension from their legs. I could talk my players through all that, and tell them when they were doing something wrong.

But I worry about teaching stickhandling and puckhandling

skills. How would I describe certain moves, like rolling your wrist when you shoot the puck? Or drawing a face-off? Using your feet to dig out the puck? It would be so much easier just to show them. But I'm getting more verbal since my injury. I'm getting better at explaining things I want done.

I feel ready to take control of my life again. I'm tired of sitting in the backseat. Matt Perrin will be coming to live with me this summer. What a great friend he's been to me. It will be just the two of us living in the camp I bought on Goodsell Point. Last summer I was able to use some of the money in the Travis Roy Fund to buy one of the five original Goodsell homesteads on Malletts Bay, the only one that had been sold out of the family. Now I own it. It's a small camp: one-story, two bedrooms, one bathroom, an open living room and kitchen. Very modest and simple, but with a great view of Lake Champlain and the Adirondack Mountains. And the best part is I'll be independent from my family but will still be able to see them when they come to Vermont.

Matt and I will be going there in mid-June, and he'll do a lot of my care. I'll still have nurses come in the morning to do my bowel and bladder program. But Matt will cook, brush my teeth, bathe and dress me, stretch my joints, drive me around, and do everything else I need. He's thinking seriously about becoming an occupational therapist.

There's even a chance Matt will transfer to BU's Sargent College of Occupational Therapy. If he does, I've already decided that we shouldn't room together. It would be better for both of us if Matt remained independent and did his own thing. That way he'd make his own college friends, and I'd make mine. But it would be great to have someone at school who knew me and could relate to me outside of the hockey team. Who would be there to help me break down the wall that enclosed me my freshman year.

I'm disappointed in myself because, socially, I didn't give it my best effort last year. I tried reaching out to other students a couple of times in the dormitory cafeteria, and once when I went with the hockey team to T's Pub after a game. But when it didn't work, I gave up. I came out, swung once at the wall, and when it didn't fall down I just went back to my room. I have to go back and swing again. And again. I have to start chipping away at the wall. I'm going to take some lumps, but I have to go back out there and knock it down.

As for Maija and me, we're continuing to grow, which is scary, but also good. And necessary. Maija's going to Spain with two girlfriends for July and August. She's a Spanish major, and she'll be taking some courses there. It's something she's always dreamed of doing, and even though I'll miss her and would love to go to Spain with her, it will be good for both of us to spend a couple of months apart. I really mean that.

We've been so close the last 18 months. We've probably lived the equivalent in intensity of ten years of a normal relationship. We've learned so much about one another, but maybe not as much as we need to about ourselves. We have to realize that I'm 21, and she's 20. If we're going to be happy in the long run, we need to have experiences away from each other, too. We're still developing our personalities. We need to find out who we really are.

Still, Maija and I talk about our futures all the time. She wants to go back to Tabor to teach for a few years after getting out of Holy Cross. It's harder for me to project into the future because my life now is so uncertain.

I do like to think about having a family. That's what I look forward to most now: having my own children. It used to be hockey. I want to be a great father. I worry about not being able to hold my kids. When they're small, I won't be able to be alone with them, or baby-sit them. It makes me sad, but I'm sure I'll find alternatives that will be just as good.

But I don't count on anything anymore. In the hospital, quite a few nights I cried and cried, thinking about how I always had this dream of playing hockey. Ever since I was a boy, that was what I was going to do with my life. And it got taken away from me so quickly. That dream just got tossed out, overnight. And my dream now is to have a family, and I worry that it, too, will be taken away from me so quickly, that it will be tossed out overnight.

What I worry about most of all is that it's not in my hands. Not entirely. With hockey, if I hadn't made it in the pros, that would have only had to do with me and my abilities. But my dream of having a family involves a husband and a wife. I can only control 50 percent. The prospect of having Maija in my life makes me happy, but there are no guarantees. Neither of us can tell the other that we'll be there till the end. Not now, and maybe not ever.

The way I look at it, I've passed my first year as a quadriplegic. I've learned an entirely new way of living, and have gone through the first round of lessons. But I haven't graduated yet, and now I'm excited to tackle year two. The competitive side of my nature is growing in me again. I feel it so clearly. I'm pissed off, pardon the language. But that's exactly the way I feel, and it's a feeling that has a direct correlation to sports. I realize the mistakes I've made, and I want to get back out there and correct them. It's not going to be easy. There are going to be good days and bad days. I realized that before, but there's something very different this time. I got knocked down last year, and it's taken a long time, but I'm ready to get back up.

I've learned—at least I think I've learned—what it will take to get my confidence and spirit back to where it was 18 months ago. I need to extend myself toward my classmates next year, rather than waiting for them to extend themselves to me. It's going to be very difficult. I'm not the kid wearing number 24 who's in the photograph beside the door of the BU locker room, standing at the red line, waiting for the first and only face-off of his college hockey career. That kid was ready to take on the world. He hadn't yet discovered that the world can be a pretty formidable opponent.

That's where I want to get back to. I'm not there yet. But I know that kid. He's alive inside me, and I feel him trying to break out.

—Travis Matthew Roy
April 3, 1997

The Travis Roy Foundation was created at the request of myself and my family. The primary focus of the Foundation is the rehabilitation of spinal-cord injuries, and research and education programs relating to those injuries.

My family and I tremendously appreciate the outpouring of support and kindness that has been shown to us by the professional and amateur athletic community and the general public at large.

We hope that through the Travis Roy Foundation, this generosity and support will be able to help others who have suffered spinal-cord injuries and perhaps even prevent possible future injuries.

If you are interested in making a donation or learning more about the foundation, please visit the Web site at Travisroyfoundation.org.

Afterword

It's been eight years since I finished writing *Eleven Seconds*. Looking back, I realize that was the hardest time of my life. While my paralysis hasn't improved since then—I still have no sensation from my shoulders down and only limited mobility in my right arm—mentally and spiritually, things are a lot better for me. I'm secure about who I am and optimistic about my life, neither of which was true when I first finished the book.

During my first year of physical therapy, Christopher Reeve and I both shared a dream that we'd be out of our wheelchairs in five years. Well, those five years came and went pretty fast, and a cure still hasn't been found. Now I'm thinking ten, probably fifteen, more years is a more realistic goal for finding a cure for chronic spinal cord injuries like mine. To me, a cure means being independent. I know I won't ever be jumping up and down or be playing hockey again, but living independently, being able to take care of myself—that's my dream. And I'm still very hopeful it will happen someday.

I was in Vermont when I heard the news about Christopher Reeve's death. I listen to talk radio at night when I go to bed, and I'd forgotten to hit the snooze button. When I woke up the first thing I heard was, "Superman has died."

My first thought was, He's finally free. He's no longer trapped in that body. But a short time later, I heard his wife, Dana, interviewed on *The Oprah Winfrey Show*. She said a lot of people had had that same reaction: His death was a blessing. They'd told her as much. But she didn't feel that way at all. More importantly,

Christopher hadn't felt that way either. From their point of view, he still had a lot of living to do. Being on a ventilator, being as restricted as he was, it's amazing what he was able to accomplish. But right till the end, he wanted to keep doing more. And when we finally find a cure, he'll be the first person I thank in my prayers. He carried the torch for all of us when we most needed it. He made a lot of people believe a cure was possible.

There were only three or four spinal cord research studies going on when my accident happened. Now there's closer to a thousand. Researchers have made great progress rehabilitating the spinal cords in mice. They're still a long way from doing it with humans, but everything is in place for a cure to be found. A lot of money is being devoted to a cure and the possibilities afforded by stem cell research—the next frontier—are huge. Work still has to be done determining where our government stands on this critical area of research; a couple times a year I go up to the statehouse to testify before Massachusetts legislators on stem cell research and funding. Fortunately, it isn't just in the United States where these studies are being done. All over the world, and in China especially, they're working to find the answers. In the medical community, the question no longer is whether we can find a cure, but *when*.

In the meantime I'm focused on living my life productively. I want to enjoy my life, as opposed to spending all day every day waiting for a cure. I still do range-of-motion exercises with a physical therapist, but not as often as I should. I probably do them three or four times a month instead of three or four times a week. My body's slowly changing, which can be a little depressing. My fingers are starting to curl. Calcium deposits have been building up in my left hip, which leads to a general sense of pain coming from that part of my body. It's called heterotrophic ossification. I still have my muscle spasms, and because they're not symmetrical spasms, one leg has become slightly longer than the other. The good news is my spine is still straight.

But if I were to work with a physical therapist as often as I should, to ensure my body is in optimal condition when the so-called cure comes, it would almost be a full-time job. That's the problem. How much therapy do I really need? No one knows. So I'm more focused on my quality of life. That's what's most important to me now. I want to have time to do the things I really want to do. There'll be plenty of warning when they're getting close to a cure. That's the way I look at it. And when they're getting close, that's when I'll step up the physical therapy.

In the meantime, life goes on. I was able to graduate from Boston University with a degree in communications in only four years, which almost no one believed I could do. The first semester after my accident I took only two courses, but once I realized it would take me eight years to graduate at that rate, I decided to risk the workload of four classes a semester. By adding a couple of summer courses I was able to catch up with my class. It took a lot of effort, but the feeling of pride and accomplishment it gave me made it worth it. Best of all, after that first, awkward year in my wheelchair—the year I wrote the book—I made huge strides both socially and psychologically.

I started with small changes. When I returned for my sophomore year, I decided when I got on an elevator or passed students on campus in my wheelchair, I'd look them in the eye, smile, and say, "Hello." It forced people to acknowledge me. That was a big step for me. When I'd first arrived on the BU campus with a hockey scholarship, I was automatically a "big man on campus." Confident and outgoing, I made friends quickly. There was always a continuous stream of people coming in and going out of my dorm room. Being outgoing was easy for me.

The second time around was a different story. Confident and outgoing, I wasn't. I no longer knew who I was and I certainly didn't know how to relate to my peers. I hated going down to the cafeteria for dinner with my home health aid. But sophomore year that changed. I started leaving my dorm room open and people started to pop their heads in to say hello. I made friends with some girls on my floor and they'd meet me in the dining hall and help me with anything I needed. It felt a lot more natural than going down and being fed by my home health aid, an older woman whose English wasn't very good. Rather than bring my home health aid to class to take my notes, I'd find students who'd share their notes with me. I learned my fellow classmates had wanted to help me all along. They just needed me to tell them what needed to be done. I finally began interacting with my peers and having a social life. If I have any advice for my fellow spinal-cord-injured survivors, it is that if things don't go well the first time, or the second time, don't give up. Eventually you'll find a way that makes nearly all things possible.

You've got to know yourself, really understand yourself, in order to be successful. It took me awhile to figure out the differences between Travis Roy, the kid who walked into BU with his hockey sticks and a scholarship, and Travis Roy, the kid who rolled in with his medical supplies. As time passed, I discovered the pre-accident Travis Roy wasn't really so very different from the paralyzed Travis Roy. The values that had made me successful before my accident were the same values that would enable me to be successful afterward. Our values are what make us who we are. They're what differentiate us from everyone else.

I talk about these things during the motivational speeches that I now give. I do thirty or so engagements a year, which I really enjoy. I like speaking to kids because, even though I'm getting older, I still feel I can relate to them better than most adults can. I'm also starting to branch out and speak at medical and corporate settings.

My message really hasn't changed from the "Ten Rules of Life" speech I gave back at Tabor Academy. I still think the number one priority in life should be your family and friends. I still believe in a strong work ethic. And I've learned that a positive attitude will take you further in life than any other skill you can have. Opportunity and optimism go hand in hand. That's what the Shepherd Center in Atlanta was all about. That's what turned my life around. Other rehabilitation centers help victims of spinal cord injuries get back into their homes. Shepherd helped me get back into my life.

So I'm optimistic, which is important because being a quadriplegic isn't something that gets easier. After a while it's a different kind of normal, but it's never normal. I still have to take twenty pills a day. I still have twenty-four hour care, which fortunately my insurance pays for. That's not at all typical for victims of spinal cord injuries. My story is a best-case scenario of how to treat someone with paralysis.

When I dream, I'm still never in my wheelchair, but they're not real happy dreams. There's always something wrong, something troubling me, something related to my paralysis with which I have to cope. I rarely dream anymore that I'm playing hockey, but when I do, those are the best dreams. That's when I'm happiest. That's when I feel most excited and most alive.

My days aren't busy, but they're full. I spend two or three hours a day on the phone or doing e-mail. In addition to the motivational speaking, I spend a lot of time working with the Travis Roy Foundation, which has been a great organization. It gives out grants for research and for specialized equipment, like motorized wheelchairs and voice-activated computers. It's unbelievable how good the voice-activated software is now compared to eight years ago, when I first started using it. The foundation doesn't raise a ton of money, but we continue to have people step forward by hosting fundraising events, some of which are quite unusual as well as fun. We have a whiffleball tournament in Jericho, Vermont, hosted by Pat O'Connor, that's played in an exact miniature replica of Fenway Park. Last year that event raised nearly $20,000. We have benefited from a snowmobile ride near Moosehead Lake, Maine, hosted by NASCAR driver Ricky Craven, just before the Daytona 500. We have a golf tournament in Orange,

Connecticut, and in past years have had golf outings in Cape Cod and Rochester, New York. We've had art auctions. If we lose one fundraiser, we always seem to pick up another. Most of the hosts have read *Eleven Seconds.* They step forward out of the blue to start new fundraisers. It's inspiring to be part of these events.

My family and friends have remained the biggest and best part of my life. My parents are living in what they call the golden years, both working at jobs they love. My mother's retiring after finishing her ninth year as principal of Deering High School, where she's worked for twenty-seven years. Dad, meanwhile, is having the time of his life working as regional director of the Grand National Busch North series, a division of NASCAR. He wouldn't trade that position for any other job in the world. He used to sneak in the back gates to watch the races, and now he's got an official pass so that he can go wherever and whenever he wants at NASCAR events. He and I have always enjoyed motor sports, and for some reason we have a better time bonding over motor sports than hockey. He still loves watching hockey. We both do. He got out of the hockey arena business, which was never the same for him after my accident.

My sister Tobi and Keith are still happily married, living in Pittsford, New York, with three small kids, Olivia, Grady, and Sophie. It's great to see them doing so well. We always go to their home in upstate New York for Christmas. At Thanksgiving, the family comes to my condominium in Boston's Back Bay. Tobi, Keith, and Keith's parents get hotel rooms and my parents and the grandkids stay with me. Everyone pitches in. Mom does the turkey. We make homemade sticky buns. Tobi and Keith's three kids, who range in age from five to one-and-a-half years old, climb all over me and sit on my footrest while I ride them around spinning circles in my wheelchair. This is the only way they've ever known me, and, no question, Uncle Travis's wheelchair is pretty cool.

As for Maija, in the spring of '97 we broke up. That was just after I'd finished writing my book. I guess I knew we'd eventually go our separate ways, but I'm happy to say we remain friends. She's married now and teaches Spanish on the North Shore. We see each other once or twice a year and talk on the phone occasionally. I did date a girl after Maija. Not for long, but it was good to know I could do it. At this point I'm not really looking for someone to get involved with. If it happens, I'll take it though. I do know that life is more exciting when you have someone to share with. My personal life is complicated by my twenty-four hour care, and I'm still not sure how to deal with the awkwardness of that. There's not a lot of opportunity for me to meet single women anyway. I'm thirty now. I've always said I wanted kids, and in the back of my mind I continue to ask myself, How old is too old to get married and start a family? But I know I still have plenty of time for that.

I'm finally at a point where my life is stable. I love the excitement of living in the city. I own a terrific two-bedroom apartment on Commonwealth Avenue, on the seventh floor facing due south, so it gets sun all day long. It overlooks Back Bay and off to the right you can see Fenway Park. When the Red Sox won the World Series last fall, I was able to watch the Duck Boat parade out of my back window, as they headed up Boylston Street. It was a lot of fun. I've lived here for the last four years and I still feel the same excitement I did when I first moved in. It affords me a lot of independence. I love rolling around by myself in my wheelchair and can meet people in places as far as two miles away. I can get to the Boston Aquarium by myself, or to BU's new Jack Parker Rink, which is a much more enjoyable experience than seeing a game at the old Walter Brown Arena. I probably go to eight or ten games a year. Sometimes, when the weather's nice, I just take my wheelchair across the walking bridge over Storrow Drive and roll down to the Charles River, where I can watch the joggers and walkers and sailboats. That's when I feel most alive.

In the summer I go to Vermont, where I spend two or three

months at our family cottages on Lake Champlain. My cottage is next to my parents'—that's where they're going to retire. Weather permitting, I go out and check my vegetable garden every day. Or I can go to the beach and watch the waves rolling on the lake. Or I can play with my nieces and nephew. Those are things I really look forward to. For the first couple of years after my accident, I didn't look forward to anything. Now I do. That's what life is all about, I've discovered: having things to look forward to.

My parents are also planning to spend time in Florida and I'll visit them there sometimes. But I don't see myself moving south on a permanent basis. As inconvenient as it can be for someone in a wheelchair, I still love winters. I love sitting at my window and watching the snow fall. I enjoy the change of seasons. That, too, is something that I look forward to in life.

I've kept in touch with some of my roommates from my freshman year. Dan Ronin. Michel LaRocque. I was in Michel's wedding in Philadelphia and that meant a lot to me. I remain close to Jack Parker. We go on regular outings to restaurants and sometimes go to movies together. He's still very competitive, still passionate about coaching, and he believes the new Jack Parker rink will make recruiting easier. The president of Boston University and I dropped the ceremonial first puck the night they played their opening game there. It was a wonderful night and a great honor for me to be involved in the festivities. It's very special to be a part of the BU hockey family. Coach Parker looks after his players long after they have played their last game for him.

During my junior year, Coach Parker and I went out to dinner. During the course of the night, he told me he was considering retiring my number and wanted to know my thoughts. I honestly didn't know what to say and the conversation didn't go much further. Boston University hockey had never retired a number and I was very aware of the magnitude of the gesture.

Over the next couple months I had many thoughts cross my mind regarding the retirement of my jersey. I eventually said to him, "Coach, I don't care what you do, but I'd like my name associated with the program somewhere. I don't care if it's the Travis Roy skate sharpener or whatever. Because in years to come, when someone looks in BU's record book, there will be no mention of me."

That's how we left it. The following summer Coach arranged a dinner with the largest gathering of past BU players ever. It was then that he announced that he was retiring my number. I sat at a table with all of the past players that wore the number 24, including three previous captains and an Olympian. I felt so proud and honored and humbled.

On October 30, 1999, at the first game of the season, Jack Parker and my family and I stood on the ice and raised my number 24 banner to the ceiling. So many great names have gone through that program, and to be the only one whose sweater is hanging from the rafters . . . I don't take that lightly. To tell you the truth, it puts pressure on me to live up to such an honor.

In the past year or so I've also started to explore my faith. I've never been much of a churchgoer, but one of the things I've always wanted to do in my lifetime was to read the Bible. One of my nurses introduced me to The New Student Bible, which is more readable than the King James version. I keep it on my desk and read it often, turning the pages with my mouthstick. I've had fun exploring it on my own. At this point I don't necessarily believe all the stories in it, but I'm open to learning more. I've heard from so many people who've told me they prayed for me after my accident. I always thought they were praying I'd get better and would walk again. I figured, therefore, their prayers weren't answered. Now I'm beginning to think those people were asking for something different from God. They were asking that things would somehow come out all right for me in a larger sense. I used to think of prayers being black and white: Heal this. Cure that. Now I'm not so sure. I think maybe those prayers were answered more than I realized. And I take a great deal of comfort in that. I feel I'm getting to the point where I'm ready to surrender to God's will, like everything's going to be all right. That thought gives me the strength to continue to try to do my best and, whether there's a cure for my injury or not, to move my life forward in a positive direction.

As I do, I'm aware of certain milestones that mark the passage of time. I'm on my second wheelchair and it probably won't be long until I get my third. When I do receive it, that will be another milestone reminding me how long I've been at this. My beloved dog, Effie, was put down in February 2005. She was sixteen and had a good long life. But that, too, was a significant time marker, because I'd always hoped I'd be able to get down out of this chair and play with her before she died. It didn't happen. The ultimate time marker for me is to get out of my wheelchair while my parents are still alive. From the day of my accident, my dad has always said there was no doubt in his mind he'd live to see me out of this chair. That's what I'm shooting for now.

Still, when I think about my life, I feel lucky. No, I can't do the physical things I used to be able to do, but I can laugh and cry and enjoy the people around me. I've found these are the most important things in life. I continue to be carried forward by the love and pride I share with the people around me. I can still set goals and find ways to achieve them. I've learned that when life takes an unexpected turn, we have to hang on to the goals that are still realistic and reassess those that are not. Our value system shouldn't change. It's the values that lay the foundation for setting a new course.

I've no doubt we all have an inner spirit that makes us capable of doing things we never imagined. Setting new goals, finding new passions—these are the things that prevent us from becoming stagnant. They can lead us to accomplishments of which we only once dreamed.

—Boston
April 13, 2005